The Cinema of James Wan

ALSO OF INTEREST AND FROM MCFARLAND

Murder Movie Makers: Directors Dissect Their Killer Flicks,
by Matthew Edwards (2020)

*The Rwandan Genocide on Film: Critical Essays and
Interviews,* edited by Matthew Edwards (2018)

Twisted Visions: Interviews with Cult Horror Filmmakers,
by Matthew Edwards (2017)

*Klaus Kinski, Beast of Cinema: Critical Essays and
Fellow Filmmaker Interviews,* edited by
Matthew Edwards (2016)

The Atomic Bomb in Japanese Cinema: Critical Essays,
edited by Matthew Edwards (2015)

*Film Out of Bounds: Essays and Interviews on Non-Mainstream
Cinema Worldwide,* edited by Matthew Edwards (2007)

The Cinema of James Wan
Critical Essays

Edited by
FERNANDO GABRIEL PAGNONI BERNS
and MATTHEW EDWARDS

McFarland & Company, Inc., Publishers
Jefferson, North Carolina

This book has undergone peer review.

ISBN (print) 978-1-4766-8335-5
ISBN (ebook) 978-1-4766-4332-8

LIBRARY OF CONGRESS AND BRITISH LIBRARY
CATALOGUING DATA ARE AVAILABLE

Library of Congress Control Number 2021057461

© 2022 Fernando Gabriel Pagnoni Berns
and Matthew Edwards. All rights reserved

No part of this book may be reproduced or transmitted in any form or by any means, electronic or mechanical, including photocopying or recording, or by any information storage and retrieval system, without permission in writing from the publisher.

Front cover photograph by Christian Mueller (Shutterstock)

Printed in the United States of America

*McFarland & Company, Inc., Publishers
Box 611, Jefferson, North Carolina 28640
www.mcfarlandpub.com*

Table of Contents

Acknowledgments — vii

Introduction: James Wan, Auteur
    FERNANDO GABRIEL PAGNONI BERNS *and* MATTHEW EDWARDS — 1

Migratory Anxieties and Diasporic Communities

Insidious Identity Politics: The Horror of Home
    REBECCA WYNNE-WALSH — 17

Aquaman as Meta-Utopia: A Nozickian Reading
    ADAM LOVASZ — 33

Occupy and Replace: A Migratory Reading of Possession in *The Conjuring 2* and *Annabelle: Creation*
    SHASTRI AKELLA — 53

Aquaman and American White Supremacy
    LUIS A. GRANDE BRANGER — 71

A Gendered Cinema of Violence and Horror

Make Technology Suffer: The Hypermasculine in *Death Sentence*, *Furious 7* and *MacGyver*
    FERNANDO GABRIEL PAGNONI BERNS — 93

State of Exception in *Saw* and *Death Sentence*: Choose Your Type of Antihero
    EMILIANO AGUILAR — 109

The Absent/Omnipresent Female Voice in *Dead Silence*
    FERNANDO GABRIEL PAGNONI BERNS — 127

Wan and the Classical (New) Horror Film

James Wan's Dead Space: *The Conjuring* Films, Siegfried
Kracauer and the Revenge of Physical Reality
    Joshua Schulze   143

Chromatic Hauntings: The Uncanny Color Design of James
Wan's Horror Films
    Cody Parish   155

Suburban Gothic and Cosmic Horror in *Insidious*
    Elisabete Cristina Simões Lopes   173

"Do you want to play hide and clap?" The Jump Scares
of James Wan's Supernatural Horror Films
    Brandon R. Grafius   193

About the Contributors   209
Index   211

Acknowledgments

This book was made possible thanks to my family, Irma, Fabiana and Nestor. Also, by the friends who always push me forward. I would like to thank all the contributors for all their hard work on the essays in this collection. Finally, my thanks to McFarland for publishing this project.
—Fernando Gabriel Pagnoni Berns

This book would not have been possible without the help of both my family and friends and the contributors who participated. Thank you also to my Mum and Dad and my brothers Paul, Mark and Daniel for their support during the production of this book and with my writing. Thank you to Doug and Rosemary and also to Mimi the cat and my nieces Lily, Poppy, Naomi and Eliza and to Mandy and Kate. Thank you also to Patrick Prescott for his support in my writing endeavors and for continuing to support and spread the word about my books. I would like to extend my thanks to the editorial staff at McFarland for agreeing to publish this collection and for their help in realizing the project.

Last, but not least, a huge thank you to my wife Johanna for her love and support during the writing of this book. Without her, it would not have happened.
—Matthew Edwards

Introduction

James Wan, Auteur

Fernando Gabriel Pagnoni Berns *and* Matthew Edwards

"James Wan has started filming his next horror movie...."
The above line frequently crops up in many horror magazines and online websites, promising new horrors coming from the mind of one of the most original American directors. It seems that audiences and fans alike—worldwide—are always expecting James Wan to return to "his roots" with a new horror film.[1] Like other directors who started their careers working on horror films (Sam Raimi or David Cronemberg, for example), Wan seems to have departed from his "rightful" place after a series of Hollywood blockbusters and as in the case of these other directors, Wan is always hinting at the possibility of making a new horror film. Since exploding onto the horror scene with *Saw* (2004), Wan has fast become one of the hottest tickets in American horror cinema with fans. This is indicative of Wan's significant status in the horror community and for genre cinema over the last few decades.

James Wan (born February 26, 1977) is the director of some of the most successful and influential films of the new millennium, his blockbusters have generated entire filmic universes, two of which are more active than ever. The Malaysian-born Australian director is a master of the horror genre and his films have started a number of popular franchises including *Saw* (eight films) and *The Conjuring* (seven films). Some images from his films—a creepy puppet riding a bicycle, a deep voice saying, "I want to play a game," a pair of hands coming out from a closet clapping in the middle of a sunny morning and a red-faced demon (or "the man with the fire in his face")—have become iconic within mainstream culture. He is also responsible for (re)introducing Ed and Lorraine Warren, the two famous American paranormal investigators and authors associated with prominent cases of the supernatural (the Perron family, the Enfield poltergeist, Amityville, Snedeker house, Smurl family) to audiences of the world. He even made "Annabelle" a name to fear.

Furthermore, Wan is renowned as an excellent producer through the company he founded in 2014, Atomic Monster Productions, which signed a development deal with Chinese company Starlight Culture Entertainment Group in 2016 to co-finance horror films. Among the films he financed as a producer or, executive producer, are box office hits including *Annabelle* (John Leonetti, 2014), *Lights Out* (David Sandberg, 2016) and *The Nun* (Corin Hardy, 2018). For television, he produced the new iteration of *MacGyver* (CBS, 2016) and the much-maligned *Swamp Thing* (DC Universe). On top of this, Wan is known for being financially efficient, as his origins in indie cinema have taught him how to proficiently handle small (or enormous) budgets. He is also the writer of the highly successful *Saw III* (Darren Lynn Bousman, 2006), *The Nun*, *Annabelle Comes Home* (Gary Dauberman, 2019), *The Conjuring: The Devil Made Me Do It* (Michael Chaves, 2021) and *The Crooked Man*.

What is more important, Wan is considered, rightly so, an *auteur*. In his "Paratexts and the Commercial Promotion of Film Authorship: James Wan and *Saw*,"[2] Tyson Wils argues that Wan should be considered such, together with classic and contemporary directors such as Alfred Hitchcock, John Ford, Steven Spielberg or James Cameron. In other words, Wan is a creator whose work is infused with a very particular corpus of themes and aesthetics.

The *politique des auteurs*—the auteur theory—was developed by the loosely knit group of critics who wrote for the French magazine *Cahiers du Cinéma*. It sprang from the conviction that "the American cinema was worth studying in depth, that masterpieces were made not only by a small upper crust of directors, the cultured gilt on the commercial gingerbread, but by a whole range of authors, whose work had previously been dismissed and consigned to oblivion."[3] The business of introducing a variant of the *politique des auteurs* into American film criticism is associated with an individual critic, Andrew Sarris and his "Notes on the Auteur Theory" (1962).[4] This framework provided a critical tool that allowed critics to take popular cinema seriously and evaluate movies as personal works that voice the internal visions of the directors. It stated that many directors, rather than simply putting screenplay into images, *created*. Rather than being products of a studio, some films were highly personal. The auteur theory was first applied to directors such as Hitchcock and Ford to find, within their works, logical patterns of repetition, both in terms of aesthetics and in narratives and themes. In brief, the auteur leaves, in each of his or her films, signposts that lead to a very personal universe. As Wils argues, a school of British auteur-structuralists, including Peter Wollen and Geoffrey Nowell-Smith, continued auteur theory with a shift: rather than treating the author as an expressive individual, whose intentions can be extracted from a film or group of films, the author was understood "as a textual system or an underlying, unconscious structure." Even if the director tried to create something completely new, obsessions and themes reappear recurrently under the films' textures.

The latter is especially fitting in a director as Wan, creator of complete filmic universes. Before his success in the mainstream film industry, Wan made his first feature-length film, *Stygian* (2000), which won "Best Guerrilla Film" at the Melbourne Underground Film Festival (MUFF) in 2000. In the film, a young couple, Jamie (Ryan Gibson) and Melinda (Lorna Petiffer), find themselves trapped in another world known as Exile. Thought the film, Jamie must seek out Melinda in this weird world. It is easy to observe that the film acted as a blueprint for Wan's critically acclaimed *Insidious* (2010), a story formulated around the horrors of astral projection. *Stygian* was also the first time in which Wan worked with Australian screenwriter, actor, producer, and director Leigh Whannell, as the latter interpreted a creepy clown.

Prior to 2003, Wan and Leigh Whannell had begun writing a script for a horror film, citing inspiration from their dreams (dreams as inspiration is very telling since Wan also cited as an influence in his work the cinema of horror Italian master Dario Argento, who famously stated that many of his stories came from his dreams[5]). Upon completing the script, Whannell and Wan selected an excerpt from their script and filmed it as a way of pitching their film to studios. Whannell and Wan shot the film with a low budget (with Whannell starring in the film as well). The result was the short *Saw* (retrospectively also referred to as *Saw 0.5*) in 2003, a little film which ignited their successful path to Hollywood. The short was expanded a year later into a feature film, the popular and controversial *Saw* (2004), and the "torture porn" label was born amid a sea of blood and viscera.

Torture porn is a distinctly American genre that presents torture and dismemberment in as explicit a way as possible. Reviled by critics and audiences unaccustomed to such visceral violence being played out on screen in all its uncensored glory, torture porn was a reaction, albeit oblique, to the climate of its time. The Iraq war had just started and the terrorist acts of September 11, 2001, were still fresh in the minds of audiences.[6] Aaron Michael Kerner explains:

> the box-office success of the first *Saw* film—an amazing feat for first-time filmmakers—speaks to the resonance of the film. Although coming from Australia, the first *Saw* film, and the subsequent franchise, tapped a nerve in the American market (and abroad). Whannell speculates that *Saw* (and other films like it)

satisfied a desire for a more visceral type of horror film. And, if only obliquely, the films approached the political environment in 2004.[7]

The first flirting with the politics of auteur took place when Wan was declared member of the unofficial "Splat Pack,"[8] a term coined by film historian Alan Jones for the modern wave of directors making brutal, gory horror films. The other "Splat Pack" members at the time were Alexandre Aja, Darren Lynn Bousman, Greg McLean, Eli Roth and Rob Zombie. However, watching and analyzing *Saw* from the advantage of temporal distance, it is easy to note how little blood and torture the film actually contains. Kerner argues that the film better fits within the thriller genre than within the frame of what Beth A. Kattelman labels the "carnographic culture"[9] of post–September 11 cinema. "While the sequels increasingly relied on the spectacle of the individual traps and the grisly exhibition of bodies being ripped apart, the first film is truly more akin to psychological thrillers such as Jonathan Demme's 1991 film *The Silence of the Lambs* and David Fincher's 1995 film *Se7en*."[10]

"The *Saw* franchise of films," editors James Aston and John Wallis explain, was one of the largest-grossing horror franchises of all time. "Over the course of seven films (2003–2010), the series has grossed more than '$872 million at the box office and more than $30 million on DVD.'" Further, "it has also spawned two video games (*Saw*, 2009; *Saw: Flesh and Blood*, 2010), an amusement ride (Saw: The Ride at Thorpe Park Theme Park, Lincolnshire, UK), several mazes, and a comic book (*Saw: Rebirth*, 2005)."[11] James Aston and John Wallis' *To See the* Saw *Movies: Essays on Torture Porn and Post–9/11 Horror* (2013) was created to investigate the philosophical, ideological, sociological and even theological issues running through this successful series, thus validating the franchise and the sub-genre as valuable.

After the success of *Saw*, Wan endured two back-to-back setbacks. Both *Dead Silence* and *Death Sentence*, made in the same year (2007), were critically ignored and box-office flops. Retrospectively, however, the films were important steps in his career. Rather than a gore-fest, *Dead Silence* presented the first clues as to where Wan's interest really resided: old-school horror. Wan consistently claimed that a major motivation to make supernatural horror films was to alter the reputation he had gained from being associated with the *Saw* franchise, thus leaving the "splat-pack" label behind.[12] Far from being the critical and financial success of his last film, *Dead Silence* starts to point to Wan as a dignified successor of producer Val Lewton and director Jacques Tourneau's kind of "creepy," atmospheric haunting cinema that leaves more to the imagination than what is shown on the screen. Like Tourneau, famous for his works *Cat People* (1942) and

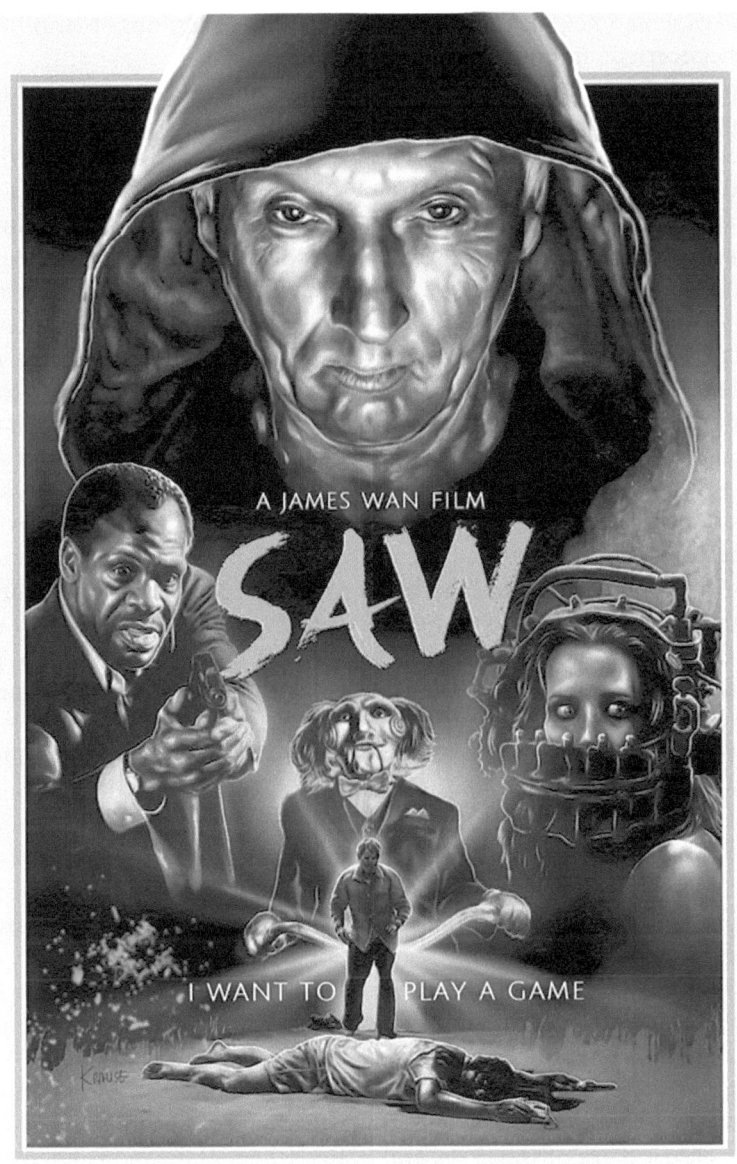

Poster for James Wan's infamous debut film *Saw* (Lions Gate Films). *Saw*, and its subsequent franchise, would come to define the controversial "torture porn" subgenre of horror cinema.

6   Introduction

I Walked with a Zombie (1943), Wan "makes the conditions of visibility an overt concern of his films."[13]

Death Sentenc was the director's tribute to the 1970s violent thriller (especially the vigilante film so popular at the late 1970s and first half of the 1980s). The first Wan film that neither he nor his partner Leigh Whannell did not script themselves, the movie presents the first "signs" of a particular, very personal creative universe. In the scene where John Goodman's character is killed, graffiti in the background can be seen showing the Jigsaw doll from *Saw*. Stygian Street, a place in the film, also makes reference to Wan's first film. Slowly, Wan begins to present himself as an auteur, a director with a very personal, intricate and subjective inner universe. Furthermore, *Death Sentence* was Wan's first venture into realms foreign to the horror genre. A short comedy, *Doggie Heaven*, revolving around a man who dies and goes to the heaven of dogs, came next in 2008. The film, lasting only 10 minutes and starring Leigh Whannell, united Wan with actress Lin Shaye for the first time, triggering a rich relationship that would develop further in Wan's horror films.

After years of setback, there was a (huge) comeback. Wan returned to smaller budgets (both *Dead Silence* and *Death Sentence* cost $20 million each) and global success with *Insidious*, a low-budget film that garnered much critical acclaim. The film, telling the story of a family haunted by spectral demoniac beings, began its American theatrical release in the first weekend of April 2011 and was Wan's first big hit after *Saw*. *Insidious* established the taste that Wan has for creepy, restrained atmospheric horror films that leave all the terrors to the powers of imagination. Elise Rainier (Lin Shaye) pointing to horrible, darker things only she can see established the tone not only for Wan's other films, but also triggered countless imitations in a very brief span of time. Thanks to Wan, Hollywood recuperated the aesthetics of classical old-school horror.

In 2013, Wan directed two films: *Insidious: Chapter 2* (a title that reveals his intention in creating a whole universe rather than just a sequel) and *The Conjuring*, the film that definitively established him as a "Master of Horror." Much more than a box-office hit, *The Conjuring* created a complete, coherent universe akin to that created by the Universal Studios in the classical era of the 1930s and 1940s, when all his monsters cohabited together. Rather than a string of sequels, *The Conjuring* was followed by a series of films led by the uncanny creatures that appeared as secondary menaces in the previous films—*Annabelle*, *The Nun*, the upcoming *The Crooked Man*—all taking place in the same universe and with a strong interconnection between.

Two more critical and financial successes were waiting for him, further solidifying his reputation of a man of many genres: *Furious 7* (2015), the seventh film in the successful *Fast & Furious* franchise, is the second highest-grossing motion picture released by Universal Pictures in the history of the studio. The film signified a strong shift in Wan's career, as the genre (adventure) and its particularities (part of a franchise not created by Wan) marked the director's interests in expanding his storytelling interests. *Furious 7* was the first film in the franchise to reach $1 billion at the box-office and surpassed James Cameron's *Avatar* (2009) as the fastest movie to do so. Furthermore, it was a critical success.

Wan's final film to that point was his personal take on the superhero cycle: *Aquaman* (2018). Again, Wan smashed records and the box office, creating the most successful film of the DC Universe. It was the first DCEU (DC Extended Universe) movie to cross $1 billion worldwide. Taking a minor character from the DC pantheon, Wan found more freedom than other directors to transforms the blond, white-skinned hero into a new creature. Still, horror seems to be lurking close to Wan's heart. *Aquaman* was described by the director as a "monster horror movie."[14] Wan cited the sea monster film *Creature from the Black Lagoon* (Jack Arnold, 1954)[15] and H.P. Lovecraft[16] as influences on the portrayal of the Trench monsters for this movie.

Even when considered a man of many genres, Wan is mostly associated with horror. Currently, Hollywood has discarded the classical "jump-scare" to embrace the subtler "Wan jump-scare," a complex mix of old-school technique with awareness of the mechanisms of cinematographic horror. Crafting a good scare is important for the director: "We think craft is important, and the irony has always been that horror may be disregarded by critics, but often they are the best-made movies you're going to find in terms of craft. You can't scare people if they see the seams."[17] Studying Wan's work, it becomes pertinently clear that the director displays an understanding of how classic horror films are constructed and how they execute their jump scares. Wan adopts the approach that less is more, leaving the viewer to fill in the gaps, or taking familiar household objects and subverting our perception of them as a way of violating our senses. In both the *Insidious* series and *The Conjuring* franchise, the relationship between Wan and classic horror cinema can be discerned by Wan's skill at conjuring sudden pangs of horror derived from less obvious sources, turning what can be deemed normal practices or objects into artifacts with the capacity of possessing a sinister, uncanny or twisted edge.

Likewise, Wan understands that through the playful manipulation of our senses he can increase the feelings of horror and the uncanny in his movies. Time after time, Wan transports objects that, on the surface, pose little significance into something that imbues terror into the viewer. After watching Tobe Hooper's *Poltergeist* (1982), how many people felt comfortable keeping a clown doll in their room? Likewise, Wan uses the familiar, including childhood, as a means of driving conflicting emotions from his viewers. When we should be seeing objects that bring pleasure, practicality or, at least, a sense of familiarity, instead they are rendered in a manner that conveys the exact opposite: the non-familiar, producing a disconcerting, eerie effect. Consider *Insidious: Chapter 2*, where Wan goes for the jugular in his use of harmless toys as a means of subverting familiar objects against the viewer. Simple tin-can telephones become a conduit for contacting the dead; rocking horses eerily move in unison as if touched by an invisible hand; and perhaps the most unnerving, especially for viewers with a newly born child, when a mother hears strange voices emanating from a baby monitor. Wan's ability, like that of Hopper, to bore into our psyche and disturb, through the distortion of household/familiar objects can be argued as a superior way to elicit scares and get under the spectators' skin. Whereas the *Saw* franchise reveled in its explicit violent content as a means of repulsing, unsettling and shocking its audience, Wan's approach to the horror genre has since evolved to scaring his audience instead of bludgeoning them with excessive gore.

The linkage with Hooper's *Poltergeist* is fitting, as one of Wan's trademarks is his complex mixing of previous texts, literature and aesthetics into novel filmic textures. In this sense, scholarship has found different forms of intertextuality in the director's cinema. Author David Christopher sharply notes how Wan evokes the slasher cycle of the 1980s, concretely, the trope of the "negligent parent" who is always absent when it comes to defending the family, as seen in *Dead Silence*, *Death Sentence*, *Insidious* and *The Conjuring* franchise. Christopher also notes how reminiscent of the *Nightmare on Elm Street* franchise the oneiric realm from *Insidious* really is. That dream-like landscape named the Further is "a spectacular dream-world, similar to that of the Elm Street films, in which all manner of supernatural entities maintain residence, a labyrinth of Josh's nostalgic unconscious."[18] Julio Ángel Olivares Merino finds echoes of other films and directors, varying from *The Innocents* (Jack Clayton, 1961), *The Haunting* (Robert Wise, 1963) and *The Exorcist* (William Friedkin, 1973) as well as the previously mentioned *Poltergeist* and *A Nightmare on Elm Street* (Wes Craven, 1984). Olivares Merino also mentions Dario Argento and weird fiction writer Thomas Ligotti as influences on Wan's oeuvre.[19]

Besides the come back of classical forms of cinema, Wan presents another authorial preoccupation, albeit less explicit that his love for pastiche: gender and race. Indeed, all of the director's films are framed by concerns related to gender and/or race, the latter, especially visible in *Aquaman*. As Maja Pandzic notes, female "madness" is the driving force behind many of Wan's horror films. Thus, the supernatural is conflated with patriarchal oppression: "the home for the heroines is not the place of safety and stability, but a haunting ground gradually driving them insane. The home is after all the location where their potential identities have been buried to preserve the patriarchal system."[20] Certainly, the home, rather than a shelter, becomes a site for dread and horror through the politics of domesticity and spatiality. As argued, "hiding beneath a patchwork made of images of domesticity and violent and morbid outbursts, complex issues such as domestic abuse, abandonment, male and female spatial coding, etc. slowly emerge and additionally play upon the viewer's fears and anxieties."[21] As we make clear in this collection, Wan's cinema is informed by a politics of gender, an authorial decision of working and playing with the conventions of gender, macho narratives and the female monstrousness.

The auteur label is justified and Wan's signature style runs through his

James Wan directing on set (IMDb).

films on both a stylistic level as well as socio-level, all of which are covered in the essays found in this collection. More so, Wan asks fundamental questions about race, identity, nationalism, suburbia and these tensions permeate both his horror cinema and big budgeted fare such as *Aquaman*. Following the trajectory of Wan's career, and the themes embedded in his films closely, it is possible to see that Wan is more than a schlock horror director but an auteur with his own distinct voice and visual style.

This collection is intended to make up for the lack of scholarship on one of the most creative and successful new directors of the new millennium. As such, this volume ranges from Wan's earlier films to his peak, directing Hollywood blockbusters like *Aquaman*. In this collection, scholars from all parts of the world have united to express their love, interest and respect for Wan's cinema. Yet, a facet frequently missed in Wan's cinema is his loyalty to cast and crew, both of whom have played a significant role in his success. Like auteur Abel Ferrara, director of *Driller Killer* (1979), *Ms. 45* (1981), *King of New York* (1990) and *Bad Lieutenant* (1992), Wan is ferociously loyal and surrounds himself with key crew members and cast whom he can rely on to help fulfill his dark visions. Wan has turned to actor/writer Leigh Whannell on many of his projects, while Patrick Wilson, Joseph Bishara, Lin Shaye, Judith Roberts and Ty Simpkins frequently pop up in Wan's films. Likewise, John R. Leonetti has often been the choice of Wan to lens his films, which have included *Dead Silence*, *Death Sentence*, *Insidious 1, 2* and *Insidious: The Dark Realm* (2020) and *The Conjuring*. Promoting from within is a sign that Wan trusts the crew around him. Case in point is Wan's newest feature to date, *Malignant* (2020), where Wan has named Michael Burgess as his cinematographer. Prior to this, Burgess worked as a camera operator on *The Conjuring 2* and *Aquaman*, before being assigned cinematography duties on a number of Wan produced features, *The Curse of La Llorona* (2019) and *Annabelle Comes Home* (2019). Faith in his crew, and those who know Wan and his methodology, have also been instrumental in shaping and helping Wan fulfill his creative visions. The participation of these recurring collaborators cannot be understated and have equally played a fundamental role in Wan's success.

The Collection

The first section, "Migratory Anxieties and Diasporic Communities" deals with Wan's engagement with issues of transnationality, a topic that has passed mostly unnoticed for many scholars. Rebecca Wynne-Walsh opens the section with her essay on identity politics as depicted in the film *Insidious*. According to the author, Wan's cinema can be read as an allegorical platform for the exploration of transnational and diasporic cultural identities. Wan's films may be interpreted as reflections of contemporary identity politics and issues engendered by diasporic communities as lines of cultural specificity, which are increasingly blurred in this transnational world order. As such, Wynne-Walsh positions Wan's own transnationality in association with socio-cultural identity tensions within his horror cinema. In the second essay, Adam Lovasz reads Wan's blockbuster *Aquaman* as part of the narratives of utopia, following Robert Nozick's *Anarchy, State, and Utopia* (1974), a text that establishes the foundations of a political theory that seeks to legitimize the existence of a minimal state. For Lovasz, *Aquaman* and the society the story presents can be described using Nozick's ideas on cohabitations and tensions within a common country as a main framework. Next, Shastri Akella explores the topic of transnationality through the lens of migratory reading. For Akella, the trope of evil possession is a metaphor for shared social anxieties present during the temporal axes of both *The Conjuring 2* and *Annabelle: Creation*. Through a Deleuzian reading of the possession acts, Akella offers a reading of the right-wing fear of the Outsider entering and altering Western spaces. The section closes with Luis A. Grande Branger's essay on *Aquaman*, offering his own take on the superhero film. To him, *Aquaman* can be read as part of the heated discussions on race, immigration, nationalism and white supremacy. The film methaporizes anxieties and fears regarding the position of the extreme right in contemporary America, post–Donald Trump's ascension to presidency.

The next section, "A Gendered Cinema of Violence and Horror" offers readings on how Wan addresses concerns around masculinity, femininity and the individual. Fernando Gabriel Pagnoni Berns studies the gender politics informing three works of James Wan: *Death Sentence*, *Furious 7* and the pilot episode for *MacGyver*. These works share more than their status as thrillers, as the director plays with the ideals of hypermasculinity in relation with the destruction of high-tech technology. As argued by the author, the hypermasculinity of the main male characters is predicated upon the mastery and complete destruction of technology, thus rendering themselves as truly superior to the non-human. Next, Emiliano Aguilar reads Wan's thrillers *Saw* and *Death Sentence* as examples of what Giorgio Agamben has named "state of exception." According to Aguilar, both films engage with men who establish a micro-society where torture and killing is an acceptable path to "betterment." As Agamben argues, rather than being circumstantial, the state of exception as depicted in both films is symptomatic of our current society. In his essay on the Gothic film *Dead Silence*, Fernando Gabriel Pagnoni Berns closes the section, arguing that, even if the female presence seems to be recurrently undermined through the film, a distinctive supernatural female voice is actually the main architect of the story. The ghost of Mary Shaw came back from the grave not to talk for all women (as she kills women) but for herself, enacting a vengeance after being silenced by society. It is this female subjectivity that grounds the film fittingly into Gothic territory.

The last section, "Wan and the Classical (New) Horror Film" involves different readings on James Wan's input on horror cinema, arguably, the genre with which he is most associated. Joshua Schulze constructs his essay around the novel topic of dead space as a form of the "non-human." Following Siegfried Kracauer's *Theory of Film: The Redemption of Physical Reality* (1960), Schulze analyzes both *The Conjuring* and *The Conjuring 2* with the aim of pointing out the ways the films decenter human characters. Schulze examines the presentation of non-human matter and how it manipulates and is manipulated by the passage of time through Wan's use of the long take. Next, Cody Parish investigates the bold use of color in Wan's horror films. For Parish, Wan's choice of a red and black palette in his *mise-en-scène* produces a meaningful affect beyond solely contributing to atmospheric tension, an affect that influences the viewing experience of his horror films. In her essay, Elisabete Cristina Simões Lopes emphasizes the original use Wan makes of suburban settings. Concentrating her efforts on *Insidious*, Lopes studies how cosmic horror introduced itself into domestic space, creating a new form of haunting, as forces that emanate from a parallel realm interact dangerously with the residents of suburbia. Through the essay, Lopes analyzes Wan's suburban Gothic and how it intersects with the works of H.P. Lovecraft and Thomas Ligotti. Closing the section and the collection, Brandon R. Grafius analyzes how James Wan (re)constructs the old trope of the "jump scare." According to the author, Wan is aware of viewers' expectations, a fact the director manipulates in his favor in his horror films, thus creating a creepy universe where audiences are trapped within frames of expectation and surprise.

For the new millennium, Wan has created a form of film horror that relies more on atmosphere than in jump scares—a kind of dread almost extinct on the big screen since the times of director Jacques Tourneur and producer Val Lewton. Wan has imposed a uniquely rich style and vision which does not reject commercial or genre formulas, but in fact, embraces it. Despite his forays into mainstream cinema, having assumed directorial duties on *Furious 7* and *Aquaman*, Wan has shown, with his return to the directorial chair on the *Insidious* franchise with *Insidious: Dark Realm,* that he still cannot shake his horror roots.

Notes

1. https://www.hollywoodreporter.com/heat-vision/james-wan-set-direct-original-horror-movie-1228232.
2. Tyson Wils, "Paratexts and the Commercial Promotion of Film Authorship: James Wan

and *Saw.*" *Senses of Cinema*, N.p., 16 Dec. 2013. http://sensesofcinema.com/2013/issue-69-december-2013/paratexts-and-the-commercial-promotion-of-film-authorship-james-wan-and-saw/.
   3. Peter Wollen, *Signs and Meaning in the Cinema* (Bloomington: Indiana University Press, 1972), 74.
   4. Andrew Sarris, "Notes on the Auteur Theory," in *Film Theory and Criticism*, ed. Leo Braudy and Marshall.
   5. https://www.thetimes.co.uk/article/six-facts-about-cult-horror-favourite-dario-argento-gj00nx2j6tq.
   6. Benjamin Poole, *Saw*. Leighton Buzzard: Auteur, 2012.
   7. Aaron Michael Kerner, *Torture Porn in the Wake of 9/11: Horror, Exploitation, and the Cinema of Sensation* (New York: Rutgers, 2015), 77.
   8. Alan Jones, "Blood Brothers." *Variety* (December 24, 2006).
   9. Beth Kattelman, "Carnographic Culture: America and the Rise of the Torture Porn Film," in *There Be Dragons Out There: Confronting Fear, Horror and Terror*, ed. Shona Hill and Shilinka Smith (Oxford: Inter-Disciplinary Press, 2009).
   10. Kerner, *Torture Porn*, 78.
   11. James Aston and John Wallis, eds. *To See the* Saw *Movies: Essays on Torture Porn and Post-9/11 Horror* (Jefferson, NC: McFarland, 2013), 5.
   12. Wils, "Paratexts."
   13. Chris Fujiwara, *Jacques Tourneur: The Cinema of Nightfall* (Jefferson, NC: McFarland, 2015), 10.
   14. https://movieweb.com/aquaman-movie-james-wan-pitch-horror-monster-movie/.
   15. https://www.cinemablend.com/news/2437019/how-james-wans-horror-background-plays-into-aquaman.
   16. https://comicbook.com/dc/2018/12/19/aquaman-h-p-lovecraft-james-wan-comments-influence/.
   17. https://thefilmfatale.me/post/52734291271/we-think-craft-is-important-and-the-irony-has.
   18. David Christopher, "*Insidious* and the Return of the Negligent Parent: The Elm Street Kids Come of Age," *The Word Hoard Journal* (Issue 3, January 2015), 61–2.
   19. Julio Ángel Olivares Merino, "El sentido de lo abisal en *Insidious*: James Wan y Joseph Bishara: Sintaxis y síntesis del horror," *Brumal. Revista de investigación sobre lo fantástico* (Vol. VI, 2, Autumn 2018).
   20. Maja Pandzic, "Female Madness as the Driving Force Behind the Monstrous in the Insidious Film Series," *Outskirts* (Vol. 35, 2016), 4.
   21. Marko Lukić and Tijana Parezanović, "Challenging the House: Domesticity and the Intrusion of Dark Heterotopias," *Komunikacija I Kultura online* (Godina VII, broj 7, 2016), 35.

Works Cited

Aston, James, and John Wallis. *To See the* Saw *Movies: Essays on Torture Porn and Post-9/11 Horror*. Jefferson, NC: McFarland, 2013.
Christopher, David. "*Insidious* and the Return of the Negligent Parent: The Elm Street Kids Come of Age." *The Word Hoard Journal*, Issue 3 (January 2015): 55–66.
Fujiwara, Chris. *Jacques Tourneur. The Cinema of Nightfall*. Jefferson, NC: McFarland, 2015.
Jones, Alan. "Blood Brothers." *Variety*, December 24, 2006. https://variety.com/2006/film/news/blood-brothers-1117956275/, accessed June 18, 2019.
Kattelman, Beth. "Carnographic Culture: America and the Rise of the Torture Porn Film." In *There Be Dragons Out There: Confronting Fear, Horror and Terror*, edited by Shona Hill and Shilinka Smith, 3–10. Oxford: Inter-Disciplinary Press, 2009.
Kerner, Aaron Michael. *Torture Porn in the Wake of 9/11: Horror, Exploitation, and the Cinema of Sensation*. New York: Rutgers, 2015.
Lukić, Marko, and Tijana Parezanović. "Challenging the House: Domesticity and the Intrusion of Dark Heterotopias." *Komunikacija I Kultura online*, Godina VII, broj 7 (2016).

Olivares Merino, Julio Ángel. "El Sentido De Lo Abisal En *Insidious*: James Wan Y Joseph Bishara. Sintaxis Y Síntesis Del Horror." *Brumal. Revista De Investigación Sobre Lo Fantástico*, Vol. VI, 2 (Autumn 2018): 283–305.

Pandzic, Maja. "Female Madness as the Driving Force Behind the Monstrous in the Insidious Film Series." *Outskirts*, Vol. 35 (2016): 1–20.

Poole, Benjamin. *Saw*. Leighton Buzzard: Auteur, 2012.

Sarris, Andrew. "Notes on the Auteur Theory." In *Film Theory and Criticism*, edited by Leo Braudy and Marshall Cohen, 515–518. New York: Oxford University Press, 1999.

Wils, Tyson. "Paratexts and the Commercial Promotion of Film Authorship: James Wan and *Saw*." *Senses of Cinema*, N.p., December 16, 2013. http://sensesofcinema.com/2013/issue-69-december-2013/paratexts-and-the-commercial-promotion-of-film-authorship-james-wan-and-saw/, accessed July 18, 2020.

Wollen, Peter. *Signs and Meaning in the Cinema*. Bloomington: Indiana University Press, 1972.

Migratory Anxieties and Diasporic Communities

Insidious Identity Politics
The Horror of Home
Rebecca Wynne-Walsh

The contemporary global popularity of horror cinema calls for a critical re-analysis of the genre and emerging auteurs as culturally significant filmmakers and products. We wish to call attention to Michael Wood's statement that "all movies mirror reality in some way or other."[1] In response to this statement, this essay positions the cinema of Malaysian-Australian filmmaker James Wan as an allegorical platform for the exploration of transnational and diasporic cultural identities. Contemporary conceptions of cultural specificity are increasingly destabilized due to the increase in diasporic filmmaking communities and globalized film distribution. In this context, Wan's films can be interpreted as reflections of the identificatory turmoil engendered by the conditions of diaspora and transnationalism. We position Wan as both a diasporic and transnational filmmaker, arguing for the legibility of associated socio-cultural identity tensions within his particular brand of horror. For the purposes of this essay *Insidious* (2010) will serve as a case study of the interpretation of identity politics in Wan's work. It is not suggested here that Wan's intention in this film was to present a direct exploration of transnational and diasporic identity politics. What is offered, however, is a reading of this film that argues for the interpretation of Wan's formal and narrative techniques as reflective of and relevant to expanding contemporary understandings of transnational identity tensions. In the most obvious sense, *Insidious* can be considered a transnational film due to its multinational auteur, production personnel and cast as well as its style, narrative and themes which are aligned in this essay with Hamid Naficy's definition of "accented cinema," a decidedly transnational arena of film theory. Will Higbee and Song Hwee Lim offer a useful definition of Naficy's category which:

> Combines concepts of authorship (the interstitial or exilic filmmakers from outside of the West working on the margins of the European and American film

industries) with genre (a specific category of "cine-writing," iconography and self-narrativization linked through themes of memory, desire, loss, longing and nostalgia).[2]

Higbee and Lim are quoted at length here as this essay employs Naficy's category in similar terms, presenting *Insidious* as a key contemporary example of accented cinema with Wan as an "accented filmmaker" owing to the multi-national nature of his heritage. This essay features an in-depth textual analysis of Wan's film in terms of "accented" identity politics. Wan's status as a multi-national auteur, a diasporic Malaysian-Australian director working within the Hollywood filmmaking industry, situates him in the "interstices of culture and filmmaking practices."[3] The central narrative themes apparent in *Insidious* are further reflective of Wan's status as a diasporic and accented filmmaker, allegorically legible both within and without his diegesis. The key characteristics of accented cinema, as outlined by Naficy, include chronotopes of home, narratives of journey, instances of border crossing, questions of identity, engagement with a traumatic past, and doubling.[4] *Insidious,* as this essay will proceed to detail, directly aligns with these themes as it explores anxieties surrounding the concept of home, the instability of established borders, the instability and power of memory as well as themes of displacement, parentage and return to origin. Regarding the latter, it is intriguing that Wan has noted that "the whole point" of this film "was to go back to my roots."[5] While Wan was speaking in relation to a general return to the structures of classic horror, the terminology used highlights a central theme in diasporic cinema, that essential search for origin, a theme of course equally central in the narrative of *Insidious.*

Wan's manipulation of an established Hollywood genre "writes back" to the cinematic center. This dialogue with traditional horror cinema is introduced in the highly stylized title sequence. Its black and white images of the central "haunted" house and the blood red font of the title text evokes the style of 1970s American horror cinema, for example, *The Omen* (Richard Donner, 1976). This reference to classic horror foregrounds thematic engagement with the past, indicated throughout the film as the camera repeatedly returns to the grandfather clock looming in the hallway, a persistent reminder of the central family's vulnerability to the passing of time. A concern which itself is extra-diegetically connected to the wider concerns of diasporic distance from origin.

Insidious follows parents Renai (Rose Byrne) and Josh Lambert (Patrick Wilson), their sons Dalton (Ty Simpkins) and Foster (Andrew Astor), and infant daughter Cali as they move into a new house. What was their dream home rapidly turns into a nightmare as Dalton suffers a severe fall, in the aftermath of which he enters an inexplicable comatose state. In the absence of a medical solution the couple turns to Elise (Lin Shaye), a

Promotional poster for James Wan's acclaimed horror film *Insidious*. Like *Saw*, the film would launch its own franchise. With a budget of $1.5 million, the film would gross close to $99.5 million at the box-office.

demonologist and professional medium in an effort to save their son. Under Elise's guidance Josh must harness his own ability to travel to the spirit realm where Dalton is trapped in order to save his son. Wan's diegesis thus presents a distinct theme of travel and journeying, themes which Naficy directly aligns with diasporic filmmakers, such as we define Wan. Naficy describes three key "journeys" frequently explored by such filmmakers:

    1. Outward journeys of escape that deal with home-seeking and home founding.
    2. Journeys of quest that explore homelessness and lostness.
    3. Inward journeys of homecoming.[6]

The characters of *Insidious* enact each of these journeys in their respective searches for stability of home, memory, family and identity. It is worth drawing attention here to Avtar Brah's observation that "paradoxically, diasporic journeys are essentially about settling down, about putting roots 'elsewhere.'"[7] Wan's characters are searching for a place to settle down, a place to call home. This search launches a journey of border crossing and return to origin that highlights the multivalent and multi-sited quality of home within the concept of diaspora. Within Wan's diegesis the home site acts as a locus for diasporic themes of origin, memory, travel and borders within the film.

This case-study of Wan's text is presented as an example of contemporary accented cinema created by a diasporic auteur, in three sections entitled "Space," "Self" and Time. "Space" will address the re-presentation of the home both visually and ideologically within the text. This section will also explore themes of borders, travel and journeying as they manifest in the film. "Self" then will focus on the identity politics enacted in the narrative with particular reference to the place of parentage in identity construction. Finally, "Time" will explore the role of temporality and memory in the content and format of Wan's diegesis.

Space

This section will explore Wan's formal and narrative representation of and movement through space. Of course, the family home, or in the case of this film homes, is central to the textual analysis in this section. Themes of borders and journeys will also be explored as well as the role of astral realm the "Further." The highly stylized title sequence which opens the film provides an excellent point of entry into the themes to be explored. Authorial identity is firmly inscribed on the text as the sequence begins and ends with the respective declarations: "A James Wan Film" and "Directed by

James Wan." Throughout the sequence Wan's highly mobile camera moves through the central family home in a series of black and white images. This integrates the themes of journey and travel into the style as well as the narrative.

It is useful here to draw attention to Fred Botting and Justin D. Edwards's essay "Theorizing Globalgothic" (2013) as they address the manner in which specificity of national identity is threatened in the contemporary era of globalization. They argue that narratives of vampires, ghosts and demons, "creatures of collective dread," signal a fixation with the revenant past as a "response to the impacts of globalization" and a "tangible reaction to the distress and anxiety of a globalised system."[8] The work of Botting and Edwards is referenced here as it is relevant to the legibility of Wan's "accented" or transnational concerns as "globalisation engenders a context of un-belonging through the rupture of communities" and the blurring of boundaries between or the dilution of specificity of cultural heritage and identity through multi-generational and multi-national migration.[9] The anxieties stimulated by this "context of un-belonging" can be read in Wan's accented filmmaking techniques and narrative themes, thus solidifying his position as a diasporic auteur operating within a transnational contemporary world order.

To return to the analysis of the title sequence, although it moves through the entire house, it is the interstitial spaces that dominate the *mise-en-scène*. Wan privileges images of hallways, doorframes and staircases so as to undermine any concept of the stability of home. Indeed, in the most basic sense, this film subverts the home space with its opening title card. The text reads "A James Wan Film," superimposed over what at first appears to be a white circle but, upon a 360-degree turning of the shot, is revealed to be a home lighting fixture. *Insidious* as such seeks to redefine the home as an unstable border-site. The repeated image of the staircase is an ideal visual signifier of this theme. The staircase both connects and traverses different levels and planes of the home. The staircase contradicts the supposed stasis of the family home as it is a multi-leveled border site of consistent movement, the staircase also serves as a connection between spaces in the home. The foregrounded interstitiality of the staircase is again highlighted with Wan's focus on windows and doorways. These visual themes reoccur throughout the film but are usefully introduced in the title sequence as it becomes apparent that, hiding in the shadows of these transitional spaces, the viewer witnesses the first glimpses of the demonic entities that are set to terrorize the Lambert family as the film continues. These hiding malevolent figures become increasingly prominent throughout the title sequence which serves to imbue the home space with a sense of claustrophobia and a decidedly disturbing un-homeliness.

The Lambert family home is thus introduced to the audience in Freudian terms of the "uncanny." Freud's exploration of the uncanny addresses key aspects of the Gothic and Horror genres, which Wan works within, such as the unfamiliar within the familiar, and the connection between repetition and inescapable fate. Freud illustrates that the root of the word uncanny lies in the German "*unheimlich*," a term which "etymologically corresponds to unhomely."[10] In establishing the central family home as in fact unwelcoming, un-homely and uncanny, Wan draws attention to narrative uncertainty and anxiety surrounding the concept and stability of home. The title sequence employs black and white exterior and interior images of the central house to achieve a certain "stranging effect." Interior shots also reveal Wan's preoccupation with the excessive filling of space as toys and furniture conspicuously occupy the negative space of the home in a rather Von Sternbergian manner.[11]

The home in this text is both a threatening and an unstable location. As mentioned in relation to Wan's visual focus on the staircase, the director presents the home as a multi-leveled border site of constant movement. This is of course epitomized as the definition of home for the Lambert family is in constant flux; the narrative opens with the family moving into a new home, only to leave this apparently haunted house to return, temporarily, to Josh's childhood home. The Lambert family as such is forced to constantly redefine their definition of home as they repeatedly move from one to another. Beyond this, the houses themselves are presented as sites of internal travel as Dalton and Josh astral project their spiritual bodies from their physical home location to the spiritual realm of "The Further." When Josh first enters the Further, he is in an uncanny version of his own home, a mirror image that both is and is not the space his physical body remains in. Elise's description of the Further as "a world far beyond our own yet it's all around us, a place without time as we know it," highlights the tension Wan's film places on spatial and temporal relations. This tension is one that is highlighted by Naficy as a key feature of accented cinema's focus on borders and interstitiality, and thus a direct indication of Wan's diasporic identity as it is legible in his film texts. The home for the Lambert family then becomes not only a site for the movement between houses but the movement between physical and astral planes of existence, and, as the spirits are granted access to the realm of the living the home becomes a border site between life and death, drawing attention to the permeability of such borders and threatening their fixity. The Lambert home is as such presented as an uncanny site of blurred boundaries highlighting anxieties of displacement which relates once again to Brah's assertion that the "problematics" of "home" and "displacement" as being "integral to the diasporic condition."[12] Such diasporic problematics are visible in Wan's *mise-en-scène* as characters are rendered helpless in the home, tormented by the haunting spirits. Wan's framing visually entraps his characters as they are dwarfed by the borders of the home, indicative of their threatened identities within it. This is suggestive of the trauma of the diasporic existence and the tension between fear of and fascination with the unstable concept of home as definition of personal identity is threatened within and by the home. This becomes obvious at the narrative as well as the visual level as Josh and Dalton's connection to their physical bodies and physical realities is threatened as they travel within the home to the astral plane.

At first, Wan's film seems to follow the traditional horror narrative structure of the "Terrible House," to use Robin Wood's term. Wan's choice of font in the title sequence further draws attention to Wan's self-conscious re-performance of the classic 1970s American horror films; the red font of the title text evokes the obvious stylistic overlap with such classic "Terrible House" texts as *The Amityville Horror* (Stuart Rosenberg, 1979), for example. Renai vocalizes this as she articulates a sense of "sickness" that pervades the home.[13] This sees Wan seemingly present a typical haunted house genre device, however, the film goes on to defy the classic genre traditions it references. Once it is exceedingly apparent and vocalized by Renai that the new home is haunted and un-suited to family living, Josh agrees to his wife's plea to move home. The "homeless" state of the central family is re-iterated in Wan's *mise-en-scène* which is cluttered with moving boxes which store the family's possessions and shared memories—one box for example holds the family's photo albums. Photographs in fact play a crucial role in Wan's diegesis as they not only serve to illustrate family histories but reveal the presence of spirits or demons as they encroach on the human world. This is seen when, for example, still frames from the video footage of Elise's "séance" make visible the demon's presence in the home. Another key example of the importance of photographs in the narrative occurs with the recounting of Josh's childhood interaction with the demonic spirits of the Further. In the wider sense of Wan's style speaking to concepts of diasporic identity, the photographs further serve as a key plot device as they connect past and present as well as connecting family members across generations.

This concept of transtemporal, transgenerational connection and identification through photographs is one further explored by cultural theorist Alison Landsberg in direct relation to cinema. Landsberg's landmark text "Memory, Empathy, and the Politics of Identification" (2009) presents the concept of "prosthetic memories" as are disseminated in film images and the "usefulness" of the ethical and political dimensions of identification through cinema and images as a mode of forging empathy across difference.[14] Such prosthetic memories, as Landsberg defines them, are "not the product of lived experience, but are derived from engagement with a mediated representation."[15] The photo albums in Wan's diegesis act as an interface between the characters and "a historical narrative about the past" as they are physical embodiments of the past in the present and underline a sense of inescapable temporal connectivity.[16] This is particularly relevant in cases of intergenerational memory transmission so central to the formation of diasporic identities and so suppressed in the Lambert family so as to leave the children vulnerable to external malevolent forces. The Lambert children are denied a certain generational memory transmission as Josh refuses to have his photograph taken, thus excluding himself from the family history visible through Renai's otherwise extensive photo albums. In being denied access to these prosthetic, generational photographic memories the Lambert children are detached from their past, their family history. They as such are denied Landsberg's "moment of contact ... through which a person sutures him or herself into a larger historical narrative."[17] The anxieties visible in every aspect of Wan's diegesis speak to a larger diasporic anxiety surrounding the cultural identity dilution and dislocation from point of origin.

The photographs in this text are multivalent as they symbolize both desire and fear surrounding a tangible connection to the past. They also reveal Josh's possession by the demon from his childhood and as such are key markers of identity fluctuation within Wan's text. This is further indicative of the diasporic identificatory crisis associated with traumatic dislocation from origin.

Self

This section centers on the parental characters, Josh and Renai. Josh is played by Patrick Wilson, a casting decision itself worth calling to attention. The casting of Wilson can be considered as a director trademark given the actor's frequent appearance throughout Wan's filmography—he also appears in *The Conjuring* franchise, the sequel to *Insidious* and, most recently, *Aquaman*. Wilson is here positioned as a marker of Wan's diasporic authorial signature within this film and as such, a crucial vessel for the exploration of the film's relation to diasporic identificatory concerns. This section utilizes Wilson's paternal character Josh and his wife Renai in the analysis of issues surrounding the re-presentation and expression of the self in *Insidious*.

Tensions within Josh and Renai's parental roles and relations within this film highlight wider diasporic issues of parentage or heritage within an increasingly globalized world that threatens to de-stabilize cultural specificity as diasporic communities continue to distantiate from point of origin, from home as it were. Despite the couple having the sense to move the family out of their own, apparently, haunted home, they fail to escape the malevolent spirits. It is here that Wan's film defies traditional genre structures as Elise reveals it is not the house, but the child that is haunted. With Dalton's astral body travelling through the Further, his physical body is left an open vessel for malevolent entities. In repeating his father's unresolved traumatic history Dalton's own identity falls victim to disappearing within the Further, losing his self in travelling too far from home. These tensions between personal and parental identity permeate this film, particularly within Josh's return to his mother's home and reliving of his own childhood trauma as his son re-embodies and indeed re-performs, his father's past. This is visually legible when father and son are re-united in the Further and are presented as mirror images, their placement and costuming mimic each other. The son here is literally presented as a projection of his father. The issue of a performative self is prominent in the climactic scenes in which Josh tracks Dalton through the Further to find his son hiding in the "Lipstick faced demon's" (Joseph Bishara)—as he is listed in the film's credits— lair. Wan's *mise-en-scène* at this point in the narrative is again particularly Von Sternbergian as the demon's lair is claustrophobically cluttered with masks and puppets which visually underline the theme of identity performance and re-construction.

The theme of self-expression and the construction of identity comes to the fore once more with the place of music in Wan's text. Firstly, music is central to Renai's identity, she works from home as a composer and is frequently seen singing, writing music or playing her piano. Renai channels her professional and creative ambition through her musical expression. Music is presented as her voice of sorts; she notes that all of her songs are written "for Josh" her husband and one scene intriguingly illustrates the tension between her maternal and her creative role as watching over her children interrupts her work at the piano. As Renai works from home, the house becomes a site of another spatial overlap as it functions both as her personal, or private, and her professional, or public, sphere. This blurring of spatial boundaries indicates the tension between her sense of self as an individual and that as a mother. One of the malevolent spirits' first taunting acts in the physical world is to move around and hide Renai's sheet music from her. Through music, her own form of personal identity, the mother is at first the most susceptible to the presence of the demon in the physical world. Furthermore, before the supernatural status of Dalton's position becomes clear, Renai is the first victim of classic haunted house antics as she is perturbed by the song "Tiptoe Through the Tulips" (Tiny Tim, 1968) persistently playing of its own accord on the family's record player. This song punctuates the film, becoming more and more frequent as Dalton's life is placed in deeper and deeper peril. The song is played almost in its entirety by the Lipstick-faced demon as Josh is finally reunited with Josh in its lair. Wan's camera appears to be almost ejected from a Victorian-esque gramophone before panning through the demon's toy workshop in a series of panicked motions and rapid cuts. It is worth noting that Bishara, the film's composer, plays the role of the Lipstick-faced demon. This makes its presence even more "insidious" in nature as, in a way, the demon's own musical compositions are heard scoring every scene, giving the menacing figure control over the musical re-presentation of the narrative and its characters. This relates to the earlier description of characters visually "enveloped" by the confines of the home. Here, Wan's diegesis is also extra-diegetically enveloped by its antagonist, who within the narrative seeks to consume the home and identities of the central characters.

Time

This final section will address time and memory in the narrative with particular attention paid to the passing on of memory in direct relation to the construction of identity and family dynamics in the text. Josh's profession as a schoolteacher alone positions him in a role defined by the passing on of memory and knowledge to future generations. Pierre Nora asserts that "the quest for memory" is the search for one's history.[18] Wan's style, as it appears in *Insidious*, is presented as indicative of the plurality of memory and identity that characterize Naficy's definition of the accented filmmaker. Wan's multinational heritage is reflected in his multi-national cast and crew and the multi-sited temporal, spatial and identificatory relations in his film. Multiplicity is further apparent in the memories each character holds as, for example, each member of Josh's family remembers his traumatic childhood haunting experiences differently. Nora efficiently discusses the concept of memory as remaining in,

> Permanent evolution, open to the dialectic of remembering and forgetting, unconscious of its successive deformations, vulnerable to manipulation and appropriation, susceptible to being long dormant and periodically revived.[19]

We argue for the direct relevance of Nora's definition to the collective diasporic relationship to shared cultural as well as individual memory and identity. In Wan's work the realms of collective and individual memory often intersect. This is seen in *Insidious* as characters both individually and collectively experience haunting and venture into the Further. Wan's character trajectories, particularly that of Josh, enact Nora's memory state of "permanent evolution," as each character is forced to adapt their understanding of past events for the sake of both their personal and shared survival. Indeed, Josh's suppressed memories of his childhood haunting displays the vulnerability of his own memories to "manipulation and appropriation" which later affects the identity of his son Dalton, who falls victim to the revival of his father's past from which the family had become dislocated. This example from the narrative highlights Wan's style as indicative of his diasporic identity, this element of his diegesis may be interpreted as indicative of the younger generations of a diasporic community whose shared cultural heritage, memory and identity is vulnerable to manipulation and dilution if un-engaged with or, in Nora's terms, allowed to fall dormant. This aspect of Josh's relationship with the past relates to a wider diasporic community in need of conscious remembering of its cultural heritage. J. Roger Kurtz posits that the central "task of postcolonial healing … involves remembering what has been dismembered and re-integrating what has been disintegrated."[20] While this essay in no way seeks to offer a reading of *Insidious* as a post-colonial text, Kurtz' terminology here proves useful within the diasporic framework of approach. What is however sub-textually legible in much of Wan's work is the great importance placed on this "remembering" and "reintegrating" the events of the past into the actions of the present. Josh's profession as a schoolteacher positions him as an authoritative figure in the integration of essential knowledge in the lives of the younger generation. This public role as an educator is one that he cannot escape in his private role as a father, which necessitates his passing on of knowledge to his own children. In blocking out his childhood memories of the Further, he fails to pass an understanding of this space to his children. The suppression of this heritage from his and his children's lives, places Dalton's life in direct peril as father and son alike are left unaware of the family's connection to the dangerous astral realm.

Temporality then, the passing of time is both visible and audible throughout Wan's text. Elise uses a ticking metronome to form a connection of sorts between herself and Josh as they venture into the Further. The persistent ticking sound mirrors what Michael Koresky has called the film's "inexorable forward motion"[21] and lends a sense of inescapability to the film's temporality. Time is interwoven prominently into Wan's *mise-en-scène* as a grandfather clock is centrally placed as a sort of "beating heart" in each house the Lambert family comes to inhabit. The swinging pendulum recalls the ticking motion of Elise's metronome and brings the theme of passing time formally to the fore. Narratively, the characters repeatedly draw attention to their own relationship with the passing of time, something that Josh seems particularly anxious about. Throughout the film Josh is shown to be highly concerned with his own appearance as a reflection of his aging. One scene for example sees him in the bathroom inspecting for and pulling out grey hairs, in another he is applying anti-aging cream to his face before bed. This aspect of Josh's characterization displays a certain fear that time moving on, aging, has a direct effect on his sense of self, the care and pride he then takes in his physical appearance sees him attempting to exert control over the passage of time, to somehow freeze himself in the moment he currently occupies.

The aforementioned prominence of photographs in this text also indicates the anxious nature of Josh's relationship with the past. Josh's mother Lorraine (Barbara Hershey) is surprised when looking through Renai's family album to encounter a relatively recent photograph of Josh, apparently the only one he ever allowed Renai to capture. Josh's discomfort, in fact, his fear of having his photograph taken stems from his suppressed memories of photographs revealing his childhood interactions with demonic spirits. Photographs then, as a frozen moment in time, have the uncanny ability of keeping the past alive in the present. Josh's phobia of being photographed articulates this temporal tension and its effect on Josh's concept of his identity and his history. That the evil spirit manifests in photographs highlights a certain fear of both shared and personal history and loss of the self in the past thus engaging with a diasporic tension between desire to both return to and detach from the past and place of origin. Josh's refusal to be photographed indicates his troubled relationship with the past in both a personal sense and more generally in relation to his unease at the prospect of the unrelenting passing of time. Wan formally draws attention to this unrelenting forward motion of time with his own camera movements and the visual prominence of clocks in the *mise-en-scène*.

Returning to the importance of photographs, particularly Josh's family photographs, we turn here to the work of Marianne Hirsch and the transmission of memory in direct relation both to family and photography. Hirsh references Jan and Aleida Assmann to highlight the family as a crucial unit of memorial transmission.[22] In the same article, Hirsch describes photography in similar terms as a privileged site for such memorial transmission:

> In seeming to open a window to the past and materializing the viewer's relationship to it, they also give a glimpse of its enormity and its power. They can tell us as much about our own needs and desires (as readers and spectators) as they can about the past world they presumably depict.[23]

Photographs in *Insidious* clearly fulfill this role as defined by Hirsch. The hidden childhood images of Josh offer clarity in understanding the turmoil of his past and thus shine a new light of understanding on his son's condition in the present. It is not difficult to discern the relevance of Wan's narrative themes here to tensions in diasporic identity definitions. Hirsch ultimately presents the family unit as a communicative and embodied form of memory transmission, further arguing that photographs offer both "inscriptive" and "archival" memorial practices while incorporating the same "embodied dimension" associated with the family unit.[24] The photograph, as it functions in Wan's work, not only connects past with present but re-engages the latter with the former, resulting in characters being forced to re-address suppressed past issues and fears. Family and photography for Wan are the embodiment of memory as it is both created and re-created in this film offering Hirsch's "affective link" and "living connection" to the past.[25] Hirsch suggests that photographs may solidify a connection to the past driven by the desire to attach meaning and narrative to past events as they "become screens—spaces of projection and approximation and of protection."[26] Hirsch also posits that photography's promise to offer direct access to the event itself and its symbolic power make it a "uniquely powerful medium for the transmission of events that remain unimaginable."[27] We argue that not only does Wan employ family and photography to create affective links between past and present but his film itself embodies anxieties and tensions associated with the diasporic relationship to evolving and generationally transmitted memories as well as crucial identity constructing narratives of history and heritage whether personally constructed or culturally shared.

Wan's narrative is preoccupied with the trajectory of Josh's life, and his family as a site of generational memory transmission as embodied in the re-enactment of his past as it is repeating itself through his son. Dalton, just as Josh did as a child, astral projects himself into the Further, with dangerous, haunting consequences. The son, though detached from his father's history and true identity as a "traveler," is nevertheless drawn toward this familial heritage and apparent pre-destined identity. This raises concerns of personal and shared inheritance of identities but also of communities and responsibilities therefore drawing attention to prevalent diasporic anxieties.

Conclusions

As mentioned earlier, the opening sequence introduces crucial images and themes that resurface throughout the film. Throughout this essay these themes were analyzed within the categories of Space, Self and Time and explored these concepts in relation to Wan's work not only as an auteur but as a prominent diasporic or "accented" filmmaker whose work presents central characteristics of "accented cinema" such as the aforementioned chronotopes of home, narratives of journey, instances of border crossing, questions of identity, engagement with a traumatic past, and doubling.[28] A perfect example of this is witnessed during *Insidious* when a nightmare Josh suffers amid the stress of supporting his ailing son and anxious wife offers an interesting revelation. Wan's opening sequence begins with a highly mobile camera moving through a cluttered child's bedroom while the young boy sleeps deeply that leads the viewer to connect this image with Dalton as enters his comatose state. This assumption is overturned during Josh's nightmare in which he dreams of watching his younger self, fast asleep, the same sleeping child from the opening sequence. This highlights Dalton as both a mirror image and an extension of his father and his familial heritage. This blurring of identificatory boundaries between father and son displays not only an uncanny doubling in Wan's film but the lack of control each character holds over their respective identities. Each character's sense of self is vulnerable to envelopment by respective familial responsibilities, placement in the home sphere, and inescapable histories whether a lived traumatic past as in Josh's case or an intergenerational inherited memory, as is seen with Dalton's re-embodiment of his father's "traveller" identity and the dangers that engenders.

The inter-generational relations in this film relate to the earlier discussed memory studies conducted by Hirsch, who declares,

> To grow up with such overwhelming inherited memories, to be dominated by narratives that preceded one's birth or one's consciousness, is to risk having one's own stories and experiences displaced, even evacuated, by those of a previous generation.[29]

This is a condition of generational transmission and diasporic identity tension that is enacted, even embodied, by Dalton's relationship not only directly with his father but indirectly with his father's hidden heritage. To such memorial transmissions Hirsch ascribes the term, "postmemory" which she defines as:

> The relationship of the second generation to powerful, often traumatic, experiences that preceded their births but that were nevertheless transmitted to them so deeply as to seem to constitute memories in their own right.[30]

This manner of connection to the past is "not actually mediated by recall but by imaginative investment, projection, and creation," for example in photographs and cinema.[31] This statement allows for the reading of Wan's text as site of memorial and identificatory transmission both intra- and extra-diegetically as a film that is narratively preoccupied with the power of the family and the photograph.

As mentioned, it is not argued here that Wan's creative intention in his filmmaking style as exhibited in *Insidious* is meant to overtly suggest a direct reading as texts focused on diasporic identity struggles. It is argued however that Wan's status as a transnational filmmaker allows for his work to be interpreted within Naficy's category of accented cinema. The associated individual and cultural identity politics permeate Wan's work and call for a critical re-examination of the director's particular brand of horror within the context of global tensions surrounding cultural heritage, movement across borders and memorial transmission as these factors shape contemporary conceptions of the community and the self.

Finally, to return to a pivotal moment in *Insidious*, before Josh re-enters the Further under the guidance of Elise, she offers a quote from the ancient Chinese philosopher Laozi. This argument concludes with these words as they encapsulate the tensions between space, selfhood and temporality which have been analyzed throughout this essay and have been positioned as reoccurring themes in Wan's oeuvre as a diasporic, "accented" auteur:

> The universe is deathless; Is deathless because, having no finite self, it stays infinite. A sound man by not advancing himself stays the further ahead of himself, by not confining himself to himself sustains himself outside himself: By never being an end in himself he endlessly becomes himself.

Notes

1. Gianluca Fantoni, "A Very Long Engagement: The Use of Cinematic Texts in Historical Research," in *Film History and Memory*, ed. Jennie M. Carlsten and Fearghal McGarry (New York: Palgrave Macmillan, 2015), 22.
2. Will Higbee and Song Hwee Lim, "Concepts of Transnational Cinema: Towards a Critical Transnationalism in Film Studies," *Transnational Cinemas*, Vol. 1. Issue 1 (2010), 9.
3. Elizabeth Ezra and Terry Rowden, "Global Cinema in the Digital Age," in *Transnational Cinema: The Film Reader*, ed. Elizabeth Ezra and Terry Rowden (New York: Routledge, 2006), 72.
4. Hamid Naficy, *An Accented Cinema* (Princeton, NJ: Princeton University Press, 2001), 33.
5. Michael Koresky, "The Big Chill," *Film Comment*, Volume 47, Issue 2, p. 28.
6. Naficy, *An Accented Cinema*, 33.
7. Avtar Brah, *Cartographies of Diaspora: Contesting Identities* (New York: Routledge, 1996), 182.
8. Fred Botting and Justin D. Edwards, "Theorising Globalgothic," in *Globalgothic*, ed. Glennis Byron (Manchester: Manchester University Press, 2013), 12.
9. Botting and Edwards, "Theorising Globalgothic," 23.
10. Sigmund Freud, *The Uncanny*. Translated by David McLintock (London: Penguin Books, 2003), 124.
11. The film style of director Josef von Sternberg is instantly recognisable for its intricately detailed opulence; that is, what film historian John Baxter refers to as the animation of the "dead Space" that separates the camera from the subject. John Baxter, *The Cinema of Josef Von Sternberg* (London: A. Zwemmer, 1971), 20.
12. Brah, *Cartographies of Diaspora*, 193.
13. Robin Wood, "An Introduction to the American Horror Film," in *Movies and Methods* Vol. II ed. Bill Nichols (Berkeley: University of California Press, 1985), 212.
14. Alison Landsberg, "Memory, Empathy, and the Politics of Identification," *International Journal of Politics, Culture, and Society*, Vol. 22, Issue 2 (2009), 221.

15. Landsberg, "Memory," 222.
16. *Ibid.*
17. Landsberg, "Memory," 223.
18. Pierre Nora, "Between Memory and History: Les lieux de mémoire," *Representations*, Vol. 26, Special Issue: Memory and Counter-Memory (1989), 13.
19. Nora, "Between Memory," 8.
20. J. Roger Kurtz, "Introduction," in *Trauma and Literature*, ed. J. Roger Kurtz (Cambridge: Cambridge University Press, 2018), 14.
21. Koresky, "The Big Chill," 29.
22. Marianne Hirsch, "The Generation of Postmemory," *Poetics Today*, Vol. 29, Issue 1, 110.
23. Hirsch, "The Generation of Postmemory," 117.
24. *Ibid.*
25. Hirsch, "The Generation of Postmemory," 111.
26. Hirsch, "The Generation of Postmemory," 117.
27. Hirsch, "The Generation of Postmemory," 108.
28. Naficy, *An Accented Cinema*, 33.
29. Hirsch, "The Generation of Postmemory," 107.
30. Hirsch, "The Generation of Postmemory," 103.
31. Hirsch, "The Generation of Postmemory," 107.

Works Cited

Baxter, John. *The Cinema of Josef Von Sternberg*. London: A. Zwemmer, 1971.
Botting, Fred, and Edwards, Justin D. "Theorising Globalgothic." In *Globalgothic*, edited by Glennis Byron, 11–24. Manchester: Manchester University Press, 2013.
Brah, Avtar. *Cartographies of Diaspora: Contesting Identities*. New York: Routledge, 1996.
Ezra, Elizabeth, and Rowden, Terry. "Global Cinema in the Digital Age." In *Transnational Cinema: The Film Reader*, edited by Elizabeth Ezra and Terry Rowden, 71–73. New York: Routledge, 2006.
Fantoni, Gianluca. "A Very Long Engagement: The Use of Cinematic Texts in Historical Research." In *Film History and Memory*, edited by Jennie M. Carlsten and Fearghal McGarry, 18–31. New York: Palgrave Macmillan, 2015.
Freud, Sigmund. *The Uncanny*, translated by David McLintock. London: Penguin Books, 2003.
Higbee, Will, and Lim, Song Hwee. "Concepts of Transnational Cinema: Towards a Critical Transnationalism in Film Studies." *Transnational Cinemas*. Volume 1. Issue 1 (2010): 7–21.
Hirsch, Marianne. "The Generation of Postmemory." *Poetics Today*. Volume 29. Issue 1 (2008): 103–128.
Koresky, Michael, "The Big Chill." *Film Comment*. Volume 47. Issue 2 (2011): 18–20.
Kurtz, J. Roger. "Introduction." In *Trauma and Literature*, edited by J. Roger Kurtz, 1–19. Cambridge: Cambridge University Press, 2018.
Landsberg, Alison. "Memory, Empathy, and the Politics of Identification." *International Journal of Politics, Culture, and Society*. Volume 22. Issue 2 (2009): 221–229.
Naficy, Hamid. *An Accented Cinema*. Princeton, NJ: Princeton University Press, 2001.
Nora, Pierre. "Between Memory and History: Les lieux de mémoire." *Representations*. Volume 26. Special Issue: Memory and Counter-Memory (1989): 7–24.
Wood, Robin. "An Introduction to the American Horror Film." In *Movies and Methods Volume II*, edited by Bill Nichols, 195–220. Berkeley: University of California Press, 1985.

Aquaman as Meta-Utopia
A Nozickian Reading
Adam Lovasz

Introduction

In his landmark 1974 book, *Anarchy, State, and Utopia*, Robert Nozick lays down the foundations of a political theory that seeks to legitimize the existence of a minimal state. As opposed to anarchists, Nozick maintains that the presence of a state is not only beneficial to individual rights, but actually is unavoidable. Sooner or later, something very much like a government based on universal taxation is bound to come into existence. It will be the result of a spontaneous process of evolution. Individuals shall voluntarily assent to being subject to protection levies, in exchange for a universal guarantee of their security. However, somewhat more controversially, Nozick also maintains that a minimal state is the sole form of government that does not violate the rights of the individual. Anything larger than small government will result in compulsion. Hence, the state is a necessary evil which must be tolerated, albeit without any government there can be no rights whatsoever either. This position sounds like a doctrinaire position without very much room for leeway. Furthermore, it seems to lack many of the more positive aspects of some other political ideologies. During the course of the first two parts of *Anarchy, State, and Utopia*, we as readers do not receive much illumination as to what a libertarian society would actually look like in practice. Nozick provides information regarding the limitations of a minimal state, yet little else. Why would the citizens of a libertarian society want to sacrifice themselves in case of conflict? What values would they be fighting for in the case of, say, a war of self-defense fought against other, less tolerant societies or, say, expansionist empires? It is in order to explain this that Nozick worked out Part Three of his influential book, entitled "Utopia."

For Nozick, as distinct from many other utopians, a libertarian utopia would be a society tolerant of difference. It would be nothing more than a neutral global framework, which would give room for as many varieties of social life as possible. Even societies and cultures opposed to libertarian ideals, such as communistic or highly conservative communities, would be included within the "meta-utopian" framework, provided they desisted from forcing their ideals upon other communities. While there are many unanswered questions regarding the Nozickean meta-utopia, this essay argues that it does nonetheless meet the criteria for constituting an "inspiring" political ideal. Without seeking to impute libertarian motivations to James Wan, we utilize his 2018 film *Aquaman* as an interesting fictional equivalent of a meta-utopia representative of Nozick's ideals. In my interpretation, Aquaman himself constitutes a metahuman embodiment of a meta-utopian framework that allows not only several kinds of human political communities to coexist, but also permits a multitude of non-human modes of being to flourish without being violated and destroyed by outside interference. A Nozickean libertarianism would be a mode of politics which recognizes that, in spite of our inhabiting one Earth, we nevertheless live in several different worlds, many of which are all but incommensurable. An agonistic politics would be one that is inclusive of even radical forms of heterogeneity.

Meta-Utopia as a Utopia of Utopias

At this juncture, we must commence in medias res, right in the middle of things. We are in the aftermath of Nozick's proof of the legitimacy of the minimal state. Against the anarchists, Nozick has shown that a minimal state is not only necessary, but even inevitable: it is bound to arise as the result of a process of evolutionary selection amongst several competing "protection agencies." Its legitimacy is twofold, for not only is a minimal state superior to the absence of government, it is also the sole legitimate form of government imaginable. As Nozick maintains, "no state more extensive than the minimal state can be justified."[1] The question Nozick asks is, "Would anyone man barricades under its banner?"[2] The answer is far from certain. If the realization of all ideals is impossible, the "minimal state" cannot be a global, one-size-fits-all solution. The ideals, preferences and choices of different individuals differ in fundamental, culturally coded ways. No single community can exist which caters to every preference. Paradoxically, a libertarian utopia must be a tolerant framework for as wide a variety of societies, even worlds, as possible. We do not inhabit the same world. Individuals, if they may be said to be free, must be given the choice to emigrate wherever they see fit. As Nozick emphasizes, "if they [emigrants] choose to leave your world and live in another, your world is without them. You may choose to abandon your imagined world, now without its emigrants. This process goes on; worlds are created, people leave them, create new worlds, and so on."[3] Migration is creative of new worlds, new ways of coexisting—or not. Nozick's own idea of "utopia" inseparably connects with the notion of stability. A utopian society is one that nobody would even dream of leaving. We must therefore differentiate between a utopian society—a community characterized by stability, defined as the absolute absence of individuals willing to leave—and a meta-utopian global framework. Nobody is willing to exit a "stable association."[4] In order to qualify as "utopian," this stability must stem from the individuals wills of those living within the said community. What counts as the "best" society cannot be determined apart from individual preferences. As Ralf M. Bader comments on Nozick's utopia, "the betterness ordering" governing the comparison of societies with each other "is determined by the criteria of bestness and these criteria vary from individual to individual."[5] There is no objective measure according to which anybody can determine which community is better.

Realistically, counting with human nature and the power of utopian impulses, Nozick holds that some human preferences will be all but impossible to achieve. Certain expectations transcend the realm of the possible, yet this too must be integrated into a meta-utopian framework. As he notes with refreshing sincerity, "I do not laugh at the content of our wishes that go not only beyond the actual and what we take to be feasible in the future, but even beyond the possible."[6] There is something noble in the utopian impulse: the greatness of the human spirit lies in the aspiration to go beyond the limitations of the human condition. Nozick recognizes that if it is to amount to something more than a daydream, libertarianism must become inspiring, an ideal worth making sacrifices for. That being said, not all possible worlds are desirable ones.[7] We must therefore limit the range of possible societies, precisely so as to uphold the rights of the individual to choose amongst various social forms. Strangely, for Nozick, utopia lacks any specific content. It is not a model of what an ideal society must look like. Rather, it is a dynamic process, always open to further experimentation, refinement and reform. No form of community will be good for everybody. A libertarian utopia is an empty category that can be filled with an infinity of social forms. It means nothing in itself, apart from the ability of human individuals to choose from among radically divergent societies thrown up by the lottery of history:

> The conclusion to draw is that there will not be one kind of community existing and one kind of life led in utopia. Utopia will consist of utopias, of many

different and divergent communities in which people lead different kinds of lives under different institutions. Some kinds of communities will wax and wane. People will leave some for others or spend their whole lives in one. Utopia is a framework for utopias, a place where people are at liberty to join together voluntarily to pursue and attempt to realize their own vision of the good life in the ideal community but where no one can impose his own utopian vision upon others.[8]

Global libertarianism would consist in the untrammeled ability of persons to choose those communities most suited to their own preferences. Under the libertarian framework, persons are permitted to live among those similar to themselves if this is their own voluntary choice. Diversity would hence pertain to the framework as such, containing as it does pockets of both cultural homogeneity and heterogeneity. Ideally of course, the libertarian social system would nonetheless presumably emerge victorious, for, if libertarianism is truly the most ideal society as Nozick has proposed in the prior two sections of *Anarchy, State, and Utopia*, then rationally minded enlightened individuals will choose to migrate en masse to such societies. There is, strictly speaking, no such thing as a utopia. Etymologically, utopia means "no place." This also implies the absence of change, as pointed out by Hanan Yoran.[9] Utopia lacks any specific content whatsoever. "Utopia," states Nozick, "is meta-utopia."[10] Against the grain of utopian thinking, which posits a design of a supposed social ideal, Nozick's proposal is an agonistic praxis of filtration, wherein the maximal range of social forms can be experimented with. Given the impossibility of knowing all human desires in advance, libertarian utopians must not interpret utopia as constituting some type of "design device," to which reality must be molded. Rather, meta-utopia is a "filter process" which "eliminates (filters out) many from a large set of alternatives."[11] A meta-utopia is a setting, an ecology within which evolution can spontaneously select from a variety of social norms, ideas and practices, until the most ideal social form is attained.

It is vital that any and all actors refrain from attempting to impose their ideals upon the different actors within this filtration process; otherwise, it is liable to become corrupted. For instance, legal measures meant to compel citizens of a society to remain put are clearly illegitimate. To qualify as "utopian," an association's stability must be based upon the voluntary consent of its members. Within a meta-utopia, "no one can impose his own utopian vision upon others."[12] Evolution, in Nozick's interpretation, would be a neutral process of selection that contributes to the constant improvement of utopias. Because—at least in theory—each society has a material and political interest in attracting as large a group of taxpaying, value creating citizens as possible, they will be forced to compete for the favor of citizens. Those societies and social models that fail to make the cut will, optimally, fade away into oblivion. Meta-utopia allows Nozick to prioritize the idea of freedom while also keeping his options open regarding the form of a future society. It permits him to maintain libertarianism as a specific form of community, a mode of life among others, while nonetheless extending it in the form of an implicit, universal, globalized framework. On the whole, global society can become libertarian while individual social worlds are free to institute radically different social norms. Furthermore, Nozick's meta-utopia also allows him to reconcile the dynamic and flexible aspects of utopian thought. As Bader explains, "Nozick's framework allows for but does not require change. It thereby reconciles a dynamic and flexible conception of society with the idea that a utopian society is in equilibrium and cannot be improved upon."[13] In a meta-utopia, individual societies can remain static, completely stable, without any willingness to change. But individuals are still permitted an exit, whether in terms of emigration (hard, or cold exit), or dreaming new worlds altogether (soft, or hot exit). Because of its supposed exteriority and neutrality to any particular social form, the meta-utopia as framework allows us to keep our civilizational options open to many different alternatives. Nozick even accounts for the possibility that not one individual society will opt for explicitly libertarian institutions: "Though the framework is libertarian and laissez-faire, individual communities within it need not be, and perhaps no community within it will choose to be so. Thus, the characteristics of the framework need not pervade the individual communities."[14] Libertarianism is thereby transformed into something akin to a transcendental category, an ideal which transcends any and all concrete manifestations. What matters for Nozick is that each and every individual be endowed with the opportunity, but not the obligation, to exit from dissatisfying social institutions. Whether through soft or hard exit, individuals must be able at least in theory to step out of communities they cannot assent to.

Human beings themselves are, when all is said and done, the sociobioculturally constructed products of evolution.[15] Individual communities are permitted to engage in as many experiments as they see fit. By a process of trial and error, humans can achieve social forms and ideals worth living for, without these ideals being imposed. Nozick differentiates between three types of utopians, namely "missionary," "existential" and "imperialistic" utopians. Missionaries are those who believe in spreading their message in a non-compulsory manner, without utilizing force. Existential utopians merely live as they please without especially popularizing their views, hoping that their example in itself will prove popular among the broader, as yet unconvinced population. Imperialistic utopians, however, attempt to force others to accept their worldview. This latter group, in whatever guise, "will oppose the framework so long as some others do not agree with them."[16]

So as to prevent atrocities committed by all those opposed to the tolerant meta-utopian framework, Nozick holds that in the case of such individuals and groups, force is required. One may add in passing that even libertarian groupings can be liable to become imperialistic, although spreading any ideology by force does seem to violate the Non-Aggression-Principle (NAP), one of the fundamental doctrines of modern libertarian thought. In Ayn Rand's simple formulation, the NAP states that "force may be used only in retaliation and only against those who initiate its use."[17] Earlier on Nozick himself states in no uncertain terms that a system of compulsory taxation constitutes "forced labour," because it is based on the government's threat of aggression against those who refuse to pay their tax burden.[18] Force is only permitted, in the case of the meta-utopia, if a threat arises that would undo the tolerant, diverse framework. "The structure itself," writes Nozick, "is diverse; it does not itself provide or guarantee that there will be any common goal that all pursue jointly."[19] Instead of a single goal toward which all human beings must strive, the meta-utopia provides a plurality of projects, goals and ideas.

Undoubtedly, this is a cornucopian concept. Nozick promises us that a neutral frame can indeed be erected within which evolutionary trial-and-error can select the most perfect society. It is the absence of a single norm or universal ideal that allows for the positing of diversity as the penultimate ideal. Here we arrive at the central paradox of the Nozickean ideal: "individual communities may have any character" in this utopia, provided that this character is "compatible with the operation of the framework."[20] Even communities prone to flagrantly and abominably violating the rights of their members are permitted, as long as free movement is guaranteed. Presumably, Nozick is hopeful that no human is so masochistic as to remain in a setting where they are tortured, abused or violated continuously in any other manner. Communities that abuse their members will find themselves bereft of citizens. Of course, the meta-utopia demands something much more than a minimal state on a global level, for the framework must be capable of compelling each and every community to accede to unlimited free access of persons to communities of their own choice. Such a capability implies large military might, capable of overriding nationalist or authoritarian regimes willing to prevent their citizens from leaving for greener pastures. Nozick himself admits that there are no simple answers to devising a neutral central authority that would somehow enforce the framework without thereby violating the freedom and autonomy of any single community. Such matters are left by Nozick to the pragmatism of everyday politics, leaving a rather unfortunate lacuna unresolved in the process.[21] A "central authority" is required, to handle conflicts between communities and to enforce "an individual's right to leave a community."[22]

The sole criteria of a global environment corresponding to a meta-utopia would therefore be freedom of movement. It is no exaggeration to say that Nozick's entire utopia is, for better or worse, dependent on this single, rather narrow type of freedom. As long as the soft or hard version of exit is available, at the minimum on the level of open possibilities, individuals are even permitted to renounce their own freedom. Infamously, Nozick even permits that a libertarian meta-utopia could even include contractural forms of slavery, so long as individuals assent to such relationships on a voluntary basis without the explicit or implicit threat of force.[23] Not so unusually for a utopian, Nozick too refrains from speaking much about the concrete reality of his utopia. In fact, the agonistic meta-utopia is even less concrete than many previous utopian constructs, precisely because it is not meant to compose anything more than an empty framework waiting to be filled with content. Puzzlingly, the promise of Nozick's cornucopian idea resides in its indeterminacy. Meta-utopia is a task, an ambiguous project waiting for fruition, but of whose fruits we can never be entirely sure of. Extending the metaphor of "growth" further, Nozick declares that "it is what grows spontaneously from the individual choices of many people over a long period of time that will be worth speaking eloquently about."[24] How utopia works out in the end is something permanently open to elaboration. The way concrete communities shall operate will be determined by spontaneous evolutionary processes outside the control of any and all participants. The mystery of the cornucopia is what is most inspiring about it. We do not, as yet, know what bountiful manna it shall sprinkle upon us. That being the case, it is worth reflecting upon what a meta-utopia might nevertheless look like in practice through the fictional register of superhero cinema. What will be of particular interest is what, if anything, such a superhero narrative can have to say about the political realm in general, as well as how fiction can better illuminate Nozick's concept.

James Wan's Aquaman *as Meta-Utopian Narrative*

Having elucidated Nozick's idea of the meta-utopia, the framework for the spontaneous selection among a range of concrete utopias and modes of existence, in the following I shall bring this concept into dialogue with the contents of James Wan's 2018 superhero film *Aquaman*, an adaptation of the DC Comics comicbook narrative of the same title. Such experiments are far from exceptional within the broader literature relating to the superhero genre. One particularly interesting example which comes to mind is that of Chris Murray's 2013 article, "Invisible symmetries," which convincingly utilizes examples from Scott Morrison's comicbooks to explain Isaiah

Berlin's differentiation of two types of freedom, without reducing the narrative to a merely instrumental illustration of philosophical concepts.[25] What we are interested in is how popular cultural narratives and philosophical concerns can be brought into a productive connection with one another. For meta-utopianism, as a doctrine or, better, outlook, necessitates a type of hermeneutical openness with regard to the works under debate. In my view, *Aquaman* may be read as a Nozickean narrative that affirms the need for respecting difference. Yet far from uncritically accepting Nozick for his word, the narrative of the film also teases out some of the limitations of a purely agonistic, neutral framework. In the final instance, the utopian framework cannot remain neutral. Hence, while highlighting the attractiveness and inspiring nature of meta-utopian diversity, *Aquaman* can also serve to tease out some of the limitations of the Nozickean position. As the film itself is an adaptation of a comic book series, the non-triviality of the genre must also be emphasized. According to art philosopher Aaron Meskin, "the art form of comics is a hybrid art form among whose ancestors is the art form of literature."[26] Registering the ontological hybridity of the comic book, it would seem, is the best aesthetics can do at this point. The jury is still out as to whether comic books even count as literature. Hannah Miodrag has nonetheless made an excellent methodological case for focusing upon the specifically textual element in comics. Text is what allows us to make sense of what is happening: pure visuality is never enough, and comic books as a genre usually make ample use of text. As Miodrag notes, commenting on a number of individual examples from the comic book genre, "it is simply not true that textual content is a definitively supplementary element, whose contribution could largely fade into the background while the visual content carries the burden of the narrative."[27] Narrative cannot take off without being re-codified into a language accessible to readers and, for that matter, viewers. Because *Aquaman* is based on a comic book narrative, methodologically it will be helpful to therefore focus mostly on the script, as well as statements made by the individual characters themselves, without excluding pictorial, extra-linguistic and even nonhuman dimensions. Through our creative "reading" of the film, we will shed new light on the idea of meta-utopia while also expanding the gambit of this concept.

The story begins with a transgression of boundaries. Atlanna (Nicole Kidman), Queen of Atlantis, flees from her arranged marriage, being washed up on the shore of a North American island. She has, to quote Arthur Curry/Aquaman (Jason Momoa), "left her whole world behind." This type of hard exit is an example of world-creating utopianism, as envisioned by Nozick. When customs or cultural norms oppose our own preferences, we have the right to leave such arrangements. We must recognize

Promotional poster for James Wan's DC blockbuster hit *Aquaman* (Warner Bros.), starring Jason Momoa and Amber Heard.

that in a Nozickian meta-utopian framework, everybody has the right to abandon constructs that are intolerable for them. A forced marriage surely must count, at least from a Western cultural perspective, as something intolerable for the compelled party. Similarly, people have a universal right to opt out of their own nation.[28] That being said, Nozick is pragmatic enough to account for the messiness of reality. There are cases when persons may be "viewed as owing something to the other members of a community he wishes to leave," as in cases of education or other expenses that have been invested in a certain person.[29] In such an instance, the community can feel aggrieved or injured, and may pursue actions intended to rectify the perceived damage it has suffered. Presumably, the cost of training a princess is exorbitant; therefore, Atlanna's escape from Atlantis is, for the Atlanteans, an affront and a great loss. From the Atlantean perspective, a debt has been incurred that must be repaid by sacrificing Atlanna's interests to the greater good.

Indeed, years later, she is abducted by Atlantis and "sacrificed" to the nonhuman, evolutionarily regressed inhabitants of "the Trench," terrible creatures who remind us of H.P. Lovecraft's "Deep Ones," reminiscent from *The Shadow Over Innsmouth*, the latter similarly being products of regression and genetic decay. Indeed, this is far from accidental, as Wan himself has acknowledged a debt to Lovecraft.[30] The film incidentally contains two explicit references to the horror author's work: Arthur's father has a copy of *The Dunwich Horror and Other Stories* on his table, and the pirate Black Manta (Yahya Abdul-Mateen II) quotes a line from "The Call of Cthulhu": "Loathsomeness waits and dreams in the deep, and decay spreads over the tottering cities of men." Arthur, i.e., Aquaman, is not unlike the comic book genre generally, a hybrid, a product of the lighthouse keeper Thomas Curry and Atlanna's illicit interracial cohabitation. He is "living proof our people can coexist," comments Aquaman. Incidentally, later on we learn that Aquaman has become a publically renowned "meta-human," whose actions are broadcast in the international media. Whenever he can, he assists human endeavors, having attained a mostly human identity. He belongs to the surface; however, the ambiguity of his identity is never entirely distant. Identity is a theme that is, indeed, always present in James Wan's films. We learn from an interview that the choice of casting Jason Momoa, himself multiracial and of several backgrounds, as Aquaman was no accident on Wan's part.[31] Diversity, however, extends far beyond merely ethnic heterogeneity. Rather, it is an acceptance of the irreducible differences of cultures, especially against the imperialistic claims of expansionist communities.

This is in evidence in the depiction of King Orm of Atlantis, who embodies the paradigm case of an "imperialistic utopian." Orm seeks to rebuild the unity of the seas, which has been undone by the more-than-legendary Fall of Atlantis. In this, the ruthless king is willing to stop at nothing. Interestingly, this expansionism is legitimated as a type of ecological self-defense. Orm's goal is to unite the undersea realms so as to wage war against "the surface," which, according to his interpretation of matters, is guilty of aggression, polluting as it does the seas with garbage. Pollution is, for Orm, an "atrocity" that demands vengeance.

We as viewers are treated to depictions of several different kingdoms. There is New Atlantis and the Kingdom of Xebel, undersea monarchies populated with technologically advanced humanoids adapted to life under water and apparently equipped with infinite energy and the ability to transform water into lasers. Then there is the Fishermen's Kingdom, a modification of what was originally called "Lemuria" in the comic book version of *Aquaman*, peopled by anthropomorphic, blue-skinned creatures. And there is the Kingdom of the Brine, inhabited by somewhat less sophisticated, albeit intelligent crustaceans, as well as the Trench, replete with genetically flawed amphibious monsters, crafted by the creator of the Aquaman comics Geoff Johns to resemble something from a Lovecraft story. And of course, we must also mention the human "surface" world, which, as Mera's ecologically aware monologue states, is replete with "disgusting cities whose sewers empty out into our ocean and whole mountains made out of trash," as well as "great factories that do nothing but belch out filth and melt ice caps." From an Atlantean perspective, which coincides interestingly with contemporary ecological sensitivities, it seems that the libertarian NAP is being constantly violated by the surface. Pollution, for Orm and like-minded Atlanteans, is an atrocity, an aggression which must be countered. Yet Orm's methods are underhanded, and we are keenly aware that ecological sensitivity is a thin mask disguising the imperialistic pretensions of New Atlantis. For Orm, those who follow different cultural norms or even fail to resemble the exteriors of Atlanteans are "less than Atlantean," to paraphrase the "less than human" epithet. Indeed, later on, King Nereus characterizes the residents of the Brine Kingdom as "savage brutes": the mask disguising cultural supremacism as universalism is a thin one at best. Orm is an imperialist utopian, seeking to create unity at the expense of difference. He has no respect for communities that differ from his own and is willing to destroy all that stand in the way of achieving the unity of the undersea realm. His goal, we learn, is to become "Ocean Master," emperor of the aquatic empire.

The issue at stake in *Aquaman* is that of neutrality. This is a crucial issue for the meta-utopia. How is the framework to guarantee the maintenance of the NAP, without becoming partial to one or another party? When confronted by Orm, Aquaman is insistent on his own neutrality. Rather than participating in an unjust war of aggression, Aquaman would rather prefer to halt the conflict altogether. As he states, "there are no sides in a war like this," implying that it would be a mistake to proceed with such a conflict. The war of conquest must be stopped, even if this implies taking sides against his own people. Neutrality is far from certain, and the framework, as we shall see, can easily be construed as something fundamentally non-neutral in character. While individual communities are diverse and are permitted by Nozick to follow non-libertarian ideals, a strong case can be made that the mere existence of a generally libertarian meta-utopian framework in itself already makes said framework a basically non-neutral institution. Who is to stop the aggressor? In my interpretation, Aquaman serves as a symbolic embodiment of the framework. When one community, say, Black Manta's pirates, or King Orm, threatens to disrupt the always tenuous boundary between cultures, Aquaman intervenes to save the integrity of the injured party. Then again, there are clear limitations even to Aquaman's abilities. Clearly, and this is a message made quite explicit by the film, even a meta-human superhero cannot save the oceans from environmental pollution. According to Scott Bukatman, the superhero film, as opposed to the comic book genre, is far too dependent on CGI (computer-generated imagery), resulting in a distancing between real-world embodiment and the fantasy on display in the cinema. Characters such as Aquaman metamorphose in impossible ways, alienating the viewer from the impossible visuality. In Bukatman's summation, "the superhero film is a bifurcated form—not even hybrid—between actor and action figure, between live action and CGI."[32] We must take issue with such a one-sided denigration of the superhero film genre. The predominance of CGI can be tiring at times, especially as compared with classical film aesthetics. But we cannot return to a presumed age of innocence prior to the advent of computer graphics, regardless of Bukatman's nostalgia. What CGI does add is a temporal discontinuity, privileging the moment. In Black Manta and Aquaman's epic struggle midway through the film, the narrative is punctuated with explosions. Moments of adversity open our perception to alternative futures, while also deafening the viewer in the process. It is precisely the impossibility of the narrative that makes such works open to utopian interpretations. As Nozick reminds us, it is very frequently the impossibility of a vision that inspires us to action: "without such visions impelling and animating the creation of particular communities with particular desired characteristics, the framework will lack life."[33] Visions, even impossible or counterintuitive glimpses of uncertain futures, are what drives agents to create new worlds. Aquaman's capabilities inspire us to emulate the impossible. Meta-humans, far from locking viewers into apathy, move everyday human beings to reach for the heights.

Of worlds, realms and kingdoms, there is no lack in *Aquaman*. How is the framework to prevent atrocities, invasions and aggressions? In the real world, we lack an Atlan's Trident, the legendary regal weapon that allows Aquaman to command all aquatic creatures through sympathetic emanations. As finite beings, we as real humans cannot hope to ever accomplish such a level of mastery as Aquaman does. As meta-human, the superhero extends his sympathy to all living creatures of the ocean, the Trench-dwellers included. Nozick's construct, however, does not lack a final arbiter of truth and justice. The final judge of a community's value, or even its right to exist, is no human institution. At first, we would be inclined to think that the meta-utopian framework itself is best suited to fill this purpose. But Nozick seeks to avoid the positing of any design apparatus that would construct communities through social engineering. Rather, evolution itself is the filtration device. As opposed to biological evolution, social evolution allows for certain experiments to be "retried," provided that their cost is not too prohibitive.[34] Commensurably, utopias incompatible with the realities of evolution may be retired. It is no exaggeration to say that what Nozick does is to exteriorize the State as final arbiter of power disputes, transforming Thomas Hobbes' Leviathan into a cosmic, self-organizing principle. Spontaneous evolution is far more powerful than any existing social form. Every society must adapt in various ways to its environment, otherwise, it is fated to collapse and disappear from history. *Aquaman* the film symbolizes the meta-utopian framework once it has come into connection with the power of evolutionary selection, the latter being embodied by the immense, sea-monster, Karathen, obviously modeled upon the kaijus of the Pacific Rim series of films and Lovecraft's Cthulhu.[35] The monster in *Aquaman* serves a type of political, or prepolitical filtration function. Ancient, pre-dating every human society, and impervious to any profane will power (with the exception of the godlike Aquaman-become-Ocean Master, of course) Karathen, similarly to evolution, is impartial. Communities either pay heed to its power, or face the consequences. The seabed is littered with the remains of heroes who have arrogantly presumed to cheat Karathen. Evolution filters out communities and norms that are unconducive to thriving humans. But more than this, it can eliminate also those cultures which pose a threat to the living environment as well. Nozick himself is open to Peter Singer's suggestion of attributing rights to nonhuman beings. As Nozick writes, "once they exist, animals too may have claims to certain treatment," although he does not elaborate on this point within *Anarchy, State, and Utopia*, going on to merely reject utilitarianism with regard to animals as inadequate without offering alternatives regarding animal rights.[36] Taking issue with Walter E. Block and Steven Craig's characterization of libertarianism as pertaining "only to intra human interactions," we suggest that animals and all other nonhuman agents too must fall within the purview of the NAP, if the doctrine of libertarianism is to have any relevance in the Anthropocene era.[37] Such a callous and speciesist position must be rejected in no uncertain terms. To claim that libertarianism pertains solely to humans is an abomination. Furthermore, it is not even necessary. Rather, one is inclined to think that the freedom of non-human animals would actually serve to enhance intra-human freedom. To cite a more constructive example, Julie Hiden has made an explicitly classical liberal case for extending the principle of non-aggression to include animals as well. Because one cannot know as which lifeform one shall be born, one must assent to extending the purview of non-aggression to, at the minimum, any living creature capable of suffering.[38] Let us return to Aquaman.

In the final instance, Aquaman is only capable of preventing Orm's imperialist plans for world domination by summoning the enormous might of Karathen. Nozick's meta-utopian framework is dependent upon the introduction of a cosmic principle, namely self-organizing evolutionary selection. What lends legitimacy to Nozick's ploy of adding a cosmic principle to a fundamentally deontological project of political philosophy is the need for a neutral third party. God would not do, as many individuals do not believe in such a transcendental category. Nozick seems to suggest, without actually saying as much, that evolution is the true transcendental principle, the real process that can actually and effectively weed out unviable societies. Nobody is capable of controlling or manipulating evolution in general. But what of those persons who, say, adamantly refuse to believe in evolution while sticking with their guns and believing in one God who governs the entirety of the cosmos? Similarly, Nozick's meta-utopia does not seem well equipped to handle general, all-round skepticism regarding the neutrality or good intentions of a universal, global meta-utopian framework. Aquaman is a nice person, charming and endowed with a self-deprecating sense of humor. But governmental institutions rarely behave in such a manner. It would be difficult indeed to find a governing body that displays the hallmarks of humility. Were it similarly good-natured to Aquaman, nobody would seriously hesitate to trust policing of inter-communal affairs to the Nozickean framework. Yet in practice, global policemen are rarely inclined to restrict their own power. And here we arrive at the weak points of Nozick's meta-utopia. Without disputing its inspiring nature, especially in relation to more homogeneous, authoritarian utopian conceptions, we must nonetheless account for some of the limitations of meta-utopia.

Some Problems with Meta-Utopia

One line of critique stems from Nozick's emphasis on the "stability" of a meta-utopia. As we have seen, it is the stability of a society that makes it a utopia in the Nozickian system. But Nozick does not adequately explain how such stability can be made compatible with the existence of a minimal state. At the very least, large-scale education would be required to instill citizens with a sense of justice. Moral education seems to be a key requirement of a Nozickian society.[39] Yet this would imply a need for a government considerably larger than a minimal one. More disturbingly, it may also be claimed with some basis that Nozick's meta-utopia does not exclude the possibility of potentially large-scale social disasters and calamities. If communities are allowed to fail, then these collapses can have serious humanitarian costs. As Mark Fowler warns, meta-utopia "is equally obliging, that is, to utopian dreams and social catastrophes, and indeed in this sense it could be called a 'framework for disaster' with as much truth as a 'framework for utopia.'"[40] As opposed to such pessimism, can it not be said that intolerant imperialistic utopianisms have already created a multitude of disasters? Without seeking to absolve Nozick of the charge of nihilism—evolution really is amoral, therefore making a political theory dependent upon a cosmic principle does seem nihilistic, which can be an issue for individuals with non-nihilist personal preferences—it must nonetheless be emphasized that reality as such can only ever fit ethical norms in a messy, indeterminate manner. In itself, the charge of leaving as much room for disaster as for utopia, leveled against Nozick by Fowler, must be regarded as not carrying much more weight than in any other case. Political philosophies generally do contain many elements that can and do go wrong during the process of practical application. As a matter of fact, Nozick is to be commended for at least accounting for the possibility of cultural, civilizational and social failures. Rather than seeking to impose a top-down design mechanism, Nozick asks us to entrust ourselves to the blindness of evolutionary contingency. We as humans must accept that we are powerless against Karathen.

More serious concerns have been raised by Bader and Chandran Kukathas. As Bader points out, Nozick does not prove exhaustively that the minimal state is actually the best context for realizing human potential. In certain cases, a "more-than-minimal" or even "less-than-minimal," i.e., nonexistent, state's performance can prove superior to that of a minimal state.[41] Nothing militates against choosing a social form or community which is composed of a non-libertarian system. Furthermore, transaction costs can occasionally prevent persons from pursuing their individual visions of the good.[42] In Aquaman, for instance, we learn that New Atlantis has strict border controls. As Mera tells Aquaman, "people try to sneak in all the time," only for the latter to express his ironic skepticism with regard to the truth value of her statement ("Yeah right"). Accordingly, government intervention to reduce the costs of migration seem warranted in a Nozickian framework, yet this would surely require a more-than-minimal state apparatus, to ensure free movement of people across all inter-communal borders. In other cases, a more-than-minimal government may be better equipped than a laissez-faire regime when it comes to helping citizens to experiment with their own lives, bodies and technologies. As Bader asserts, "providing incentives for experimentation may allow us to achieve a more optimal rate of experimentation and the provision of such incentives is a role that might be fulfilled by a more-than-minimal state."[43] Of course, governments historically have also provided many negative goods as well. It would be a highly difficult, morally deeply problematic and, for all intents and purposes, impossible to calculate the sum of all positive goods provided by the various historical forms of more-than-minimal governments and compare this with the sum of suffering caused by negative governmental goods such as wars and artificial famines. More troublingly, Bader also calls attention to the absence of any restriction on the right of individual communities within the meta-utopian framework to murder their own citizens. Even the grossest of individual rights violations are permitted by Nozick, with the proviso that citizens are allowed to leave as and when they see fit.[44] Yet even worse, Nozick does not seem to account for the uncertain of "voluntary" consensus within each individual community. Persons have a right to live in a community of their own choice, following ideals they wish to subscribe to. But seemingly voluntary assent can be the product of "brainwashing."[45] The grey zone separating voluntary participation from coercion is highly difficult to detect and threatens to undermine the entire Nozickian project. We ourselves, as living beings, are the products of biological and social evolutionary processes that transcend individual free will.

As Kukathas sees it, the root of the problems with Nozick's meta-utopia lie in Nozick's rejection of the possibility of anarchy.[46] For Nozick, the state is essentially analogous to a "client-service provider relationship," within which taxpayers consent to paying a certain amount of money in exchange for a guarantee of security.[47] Taxes, it must be emphasized, cannot be compulsory in a libertarian setting. Their payment must be commensurate with client satisfaction regarding the services of their government. Yet, as Kukathas emphasizes, the state has never been a neutral service provider. Rather, "the state as it exists now has a life, and interests, of its own."[48] The meta-utopia is, in Kukathas' interpretation, itself a type of globalized minimal state, a neutral body serving to coordinate the interests of rival communities, keeping the peace and maintaining order. But why even have a framework in the first place? Does utopia even need a governing body? Through evolutionary selection, utopian alternatives are generated and rejected, while the framework prevents excessive aggressions and malfeasance on the part of imperialistically oriented communities. Kukathas, however, is unconvinced that any governing, central institution is even required on a global level. "Couldn't this outcome [diversity—A.L.] be achieved just as well without any kind of state—without any kind of framework?"—he asks.[49] Social and natural history itself can be entrusted to select from among a variety of social alternatives, without recourse to any framework at all. If we accept an anarchist interpretation of reality, there is really no need to reject contingency by pinning our hopes on meta-humans and meta-utopias. Certitude can be found through accepting our own passive subordination to the power of chance. Perhaps it is within chance that true freedom can be uncovered, a freedom so complete as to be capable of surrendering itself to exigency. Nozick fails to show why we should prefer a minimal state to the anarchy of naked reality. As Kukathas summarizes, "a world without states might in fact be one in which the greatest variety of experiments might be conducted."[50] *Aquaman* highlights the limitations of meta-utopia. Instead of Orm's global empire, we are left with a variety of cultures and systems, each coexisting with each other in a fragile harmony. Difference and unity alike are preserved. In this sense, the film's ending is meta-utopian. Karathen, evolution personified, lunges out of the water toward a splendid sun like a new Leviathan, underwriting this fragile and complex new world order. However, as distinct from the film, in our own world we lack an impartial Ocean Master equipped with a metahuman sense of justice emanating from Atlan's Trident. Its great distance from pragmatic political realities seems to be an important limitation of the concept of meta-utopia.

Conclusions

Throughout this essay, we have shown some of the characteristics of Robert Nozick's idea of meta-utopia. Reading James Wan's film, *Aquaman* in a Nozickian spirit, I have emphasized both the inspiring and more ambiguous points of Nozick's utopian libertarianism. While avoiding the pitfalls of universalist and imperialistic utopianisms, the meta-utopia as a globalized framework for utopian experimentation nonetheless fails to prove more inspiring than an explicitly anarchist abandonment of any and all frameworks. Aquaman succeeds in halting King Orm's imperialist plans for global unification, but we as viewers are left unconvinced as to whether other factors could not have had the same effect. The absence of a framework too can be productive of difference. It would seem that Nozick is incapable of proving the superiority of the meta-utopian framework vis-à-vis anarchy, defined as the absence of any governing structure whatsoever. A minimal state could very well be less able to create new varieties of social experimentation than either a less-than-minimal (nonexistent) government or a more-than-minimal state geared to enhancing the capabilities of citizens.

Acknowledgments

The research and writing for this essay was supported by the ÚNKP-19-3 New National Excellence Program of the Ministry for Innovation and Technology.

Notes

1. Robert Nozick, *Anarchy, State, and Utopia* (London: Blackwell, 1999 [1974]), 297.
2. *Ibid.*
3. Nozick, *Anarchy*, 299.
4. Nozick, *Anarchy*, 300.
5. Ralf M. Bader, "The Framework for Utopia," in *The Cambridge Companion to Nozick's Anarchy, State, and Utopia*, ed. Ralf M. Bader and John Meadowcraft (Cambridge: Cambridge University Press, 2013), 257.
6. Nozick, *Anarchy*, 308.
7. Nozick, *Anarchy*, 304.
8. Nozick, *Anarchy*, 311–2.
9. "Utopia Has Not Known Any Development or Change." Hanan Yoran, "More's Utopia and Erasmus' No-Place." *English Literary Renaissance* 35.1 (2005): 17.
10. Nozick, *Anarchy*, 312.
11. Nozick, *Anarchy*, 314.
12. Nozick, *Anarchy*, 312.
13. Bader, "The Framework," 260.
14. Nozick, *Anarchy*, 320–1.
15. Nozick, *Anarchy*, 314.
16. Nozick, *Anarchy*, 320–1.
17. Ayn Rand, *The Virtue of Selfishness: A New Concept of Egoism* (New York: Signet, 1964), 112.
18. Nozick, *Anarchy*, 169.
19. Nozick, *Anarchy*, 325.
20. Nozick, *Anarchy*, 323.
21. Nozick, *Anarchy*, 329.
22. Nozick, *Anarchy*, 330.
23. Nozick, *Anarchy*, 331.
24. Nozick, *Anarchy*, 331–2.
25. Chris Murray, "Invisible Symmetries: Superheroes, Grant Morrison and Isaiah Berlin's Two Concepts of Liberty." *Studies in Comics* 4.2 (2013).
26. Aaron Meskin, "Comics as Literature?" *The British Journal of Aesthetics* 49.3 (2009): 234.
27. Hannah Miodrag, "Narrative, Language, and Comics-as-Literature." *Studies in Comics* 2.2 (2012): 275.
28. Nozick, *Anarchy*, 320–1.
29. Nozick, *Anarchy*, 330.
30. Patrick Cavanaugh, "'Aquaman' Director Comments on Film's Lovecraft Influence." 12.19.2018., comicbook.com, link: https://comicbook.com/dc/2018/12/19/aquaman-h-p-lovecraft-james-wan-comments-influence/; William Han, "H.P. Lovecraft, Aquaman, and What to Do with Racist Authors." March 4, 2019, exilesbazaar.com, link: http://www.exilesbazaar.com/home/h-p-lovecraft-aquaman-and-what-to-do-with-racist-authors.
31. Dino-Ray Ramos and Amanda N'Duka, "New Hollywood Podcast: 'Aquaman' Director James Wan Takes to the Seven Seas to Explore Cultural Identity," deadline.com, 12.19.2018., link: https://deadline.com/2018/12/new-hollywood-podcast-james-wan-aquaman-jason-momoa-saw-conjuring-representation-inclusion-diversity-1202522441/.

32. Scott Bukatman, "Why I Hate Superhero Movies." *Cinema Journal* 50.3 (2011): 122.
33. Nozick, *Anarchy*, 332.
34. Nozick, *Anarchy*, 317.
35. The phrase kaiju means "strange Monster," and refers to both the monsters of ancient legends, originating from the Chinese Classic of Mountains and Seas and the specific genre of monster films created in post-World War Two Japan. Too often, the political aspect of the kaiju is ignored, with American adaptations obscuring the concrete historical background of the genre. The experience of the monster is inseparable from the "nuclear Experience" of the American atomic bombings of Hiroshima and Nagasaki (cf. Jason C. Jones, "Japan Erased. Godzilla Adaptations and Erasure of the Politics of Nuclear Experience," in *The Atomic Bomb in Japanese Cinema. Critical Essays*, ed. Matthew Edwards [Jefferson, NC: McFarland, 2015]).
36. Nozick, *Anarchy*, 35–42.
37. Walter E. Block and Steven Craig, "Animal Torture." *The Review of Social and Economic Issues* 1.4 (2017): 92.
38. Julie Hilden, "A Contractarian View of Animal Rights: Insuring Against the Possibility of Being a Non-human Animal." *Animal Law*, 14 (2007): 21–3.
39. Mark Fowler, "Stability and Utopia: A Critique of Nozick's Framework Argument." *Ethics* 90.4 (1980): 561–2.
40. Fowler, "Stability," 560.
41. Bader, "The Framework," 279.
42. Bader, "The Framework," 280.
43. Bader, "The Framework," 282.
44. Bader, "The Framework," 283.
45. Bader, "The Framework," 275.
46. Chandran Kukathas, "E Pluribus Plurum, Or, How to Fail to Get to Utopia in Spite of Really Trying," in *The Cambridge Companion to Nozick's Anarchy, State, and Utopia*, ed. Ralf M. Bader and John Meadowcraft (Cambridge: Cambridge University Press, 2013), 289.
47. Kukathas, "E Pluribus Plurum," 295.
48. *Ibid*.
49. Kukathas, "E Pluribus Plurum," 297.
50. Kukathas, "E Pluribus Plurum," 301.

Works Cited

Bader, Ralf M. "The Framework for Utopia." In *The Cambridge Companion to Nozick's Anarchy, State, and Utopia*, edited by Ralf M. Bader and John Meadowcraft, 255–289. Cambridge: Cambridge University Press, 2013.
Block, Walter E., and Steven Craig. "Animal Torture." *The Review of Social and Economic Issues* 1.4 (2017): 82–95.
Bukatman, Scott. "Why I Hate Superhero Movies." *Cinema Journal* 50.3 (2011): 118–122.
Cavanaugh, Patrick. "'Aquaman' Director Comments on Film's Lovecraft Influence." December 19, 2018, comicbook.com, link: https://comicbook.com/dc/2018/12/19/aquaman-h-p-lovecraft-james-wan-comments-influence/, accessed October 10, 2019.
Fowler, Mark. "Stability and Utopia: A Critique of Nozick's Framework Argument." *Ethics* 90.4 (1980): 550–563.
Han, William. "H.P. Lovecraft, Aquaman, and What to Do with Racist Authors." March 4, 2019, exilesbazaar.com, link: http://www.exilesbazaar.com/home/h-p-lovecraft-aquaman-and-what-to-do-with-racist-authors, accessed October 10, 2019.
Hilden, Julie. "A Contractarian View of Animal Rights: Insuring Against the Possibility of Being a Non-human Animal." *Animal Law*, 14 (2007): 5–28.
Jones, Jason C. "Japan Erased. Godzilla Adaptations and Erasure of the Politics of Nuclear Experience." In *The Atomic Bomb in Japanese Cinema: Critical Essays* edited by Matthew Edwards, 34–56. Jefferson: McFarland, 2015.
Kukathas, Chandran. "E Pluribus Plurum, Or, How to Fail to Get to Utopia in Spite of Really

Trying." In *The Cambridge Companion to Nozick's Anarchy, State, and Utopia* edited by Ralf M. Bader and John Meadowcraft, 289–303. Cambridge: Cambridge University Press, 2013.

Meskin, Aaron. "Comics as Literature?" *The British Journal of Aesthetics* 49.3 (2009): 219–239.

Miodrag, Hannah. "Narrative, Language, and Comics-as-literature." *Studies in Comics* 2.2 (2012): 263–279.

Murray, Chris. "Invisible Symmetries: Superheroes, Grant Morrison and Isaiah Berlin's Two Concepts of Liberty." *Studies in Comics* 4.2 (2013): 277–306.

Nozick, Robert. *Anarchy, State, and Utopia*. London: Blackwell, 1999 [1974].

Ramos, Dino-Ray, and Amanda N'Duka. "New Hollywood Podcast: 'Aquaman' Director James Wan Takes to the Seven Seas to Explore Cultural Identity." deadline.com, 12.19.2018., link: https://deadline.com/2018/12/new-hollywood-podcast-james-wan-aquaman-jason-momoa-saw-conjuring-representation-inclusion-diversity-1202522441/, last accessed: 10.10.2019.

Rand, Ayn. *The Virtue of Selfishness. a New Concept of Egoism*. New York: Signet, 1964.

Yoran, Hanan. "More's Utopia and Erasmus' No-place." *English Literary Renaissance* 35.1 (2005): 3–30.

Occupy and Replace
A Migratory Reading of Possession in The Conjuring 2 *and* Annabelle: Creation

SHASTRI AKELLA

Introduction

The evil entities in *The Conjuring 2* (2016, directed by James Wan), and *Annabelle: Creation* (2017, directed by David F. Sandberg), possess the most vulnerable characters: in the former, Janet (Madison Wolfe), a child with a sleeping disorder is possessed by a human spirit, and in the later, the devil possesses Janice (Talitha Bateman), a disabled child. Further, Janet comes from a single parent, working class household and Janice is an orphan. If all horror gives "audiences an opportunity to process very real contemporary fears and political anxieties,"[1] then horror that endures in the collective imagination of a generation is reflective of their shared anxieties. In the '70s, films like *The Exorcist* (1973, directed by William Friedkin), which showed virgins as subjects of demonic attacks, brought to life the fear of the moral threats that the American family value faced, and in the '80s, films like *A Nightmare on Elm Street* (1984, directed by Wes Craven) showed children being killed by a psychopath and exposed parental fear about the mortal danger faced by the children of the latch-key generation.[2] In what follows, we will study the shared social anxieties that were present during both the temporal axes of each film: its narrative time (when it was set) and cinematic time (when it was released). The possession acts of Janet and Janice are studied through a Deleuzian lens and it is proposed that the possession acts lend themselves to a reading of the right-wing fear of the Outsider entering and altering Western spaces. This migratory reading is accompanied by works of migrant art that subvert the possession trope to centralize the voice of the Outsider in migrant narratives. The two human spirits in these films are controlled by more powerful entities: where the spirit in *The Conjuring 2* is controlled by the demon Vallac, in *Annabelle: Creation*, the spirit of a girl child is used by the demon to enter a home and the body of Janice. The conclusion, makes the case that the two human spirits in these films, controlled and manipulated by supernatural entities, serve as social allegories for those right-wing individuals who are manipulated by political and capitalistic forces. It is argued that, with radical empathy, the sort that is the goal of migrant art, such individuals might adopt more pluralistic perspectives.

The Entities: Historic and Territorial Approaches

The Conjuring 2 opens with Peggy Hodgson (Frances O'Connor), a recently divorced, single mother, moving into a dilapidated home with her children, Janet, Margret (Lauren Esposito), Johnny (Patrick McAuley) and Billy (Benjamin Haigh). On the one hand, at school, Billy is picked on because of his speech impairment and Janet is wrongly accused of smoking, and on the other hand, Peggy is, in her new home, struggling financially: her ex-husband has not paid child support in three months and she is unable to make her monthly rent. The ghost of Bill Wilkins (Bob Adrian), who shares the territory of the house with the Hodgson family, latches himself onto them. Their misfortunes, that have no resolution in sight, are the fissure through which he makes his entry. A broken family is the demoniac's ideal roosting place. From the "Murder House" season of *American Horror Story* (2012, directed by Ryan Murphy et al) to the more recent *Babadook* (2016, directed by Jennifer Kent), horror contains narratives of families where the cracks, whose causation remains unaddressed, serves as the gateway for the demoniac: secrets never communicated, conflicts never resolved, infidelity never addressed. If unhappiness and anxiety give the demoniac an entry point, in order for it to thrive, those conditions must persist.[3] Thus, it is in the interest of the demoniac to hold all possible solutions at bay, for it is "an unfreedom that wants to close itself off when confronted with the possibility of being healed."[4] Acts of possession are, therefore, as much territorial claims—over the geography of the house and the body—as they are acts of need: the demoniac extending the host family's anxiety, potentially to an indefinite point, so the conditions necessary for it to thrive persist.

The circumstances of the Hodgson family are exacerbated by their location: Ponders End, where their house is situated, is a neighborhood in Enfield, a borough of London and, formerly, an industrial area that thrived during England's post–World War II economic expansion.[5] Between 1973

Promotional poster for *The Conjuring 2* (New Line Cinema).

and 1975, however, the recession that hit England had two effects: on the one hand, the outsourcing of industrial production to countries like China became a more economically viable option, and on the other, there was an increase in the number of cheap migrant workers entering the U.K.[6] As a result, by the late 1970s, an era called the winter of discontent, and when the film's narrative is set, industrial neighborhoods like Ponders End suffered a significant economic slump (as is apparent from the condition of the house the Hodgson family is renting), and foreigners were perceived as a threat in two ways: migrants who entered the country "took" jobs that could have provided for a local, English family, and the outsourced jobs "took" resources from an English family and provided for a foreign family in their stead.[7]

Therefore, the new reality of England—demographic, economic—was at odds with the England located in the cultural consciousness of its citizens: the English generation of the early 1900s, raised to believe that they would have inherited the world, found themselves, instead, in a postcolonial world where they were stripped of that power and were responsible for making amends for their forbearers, so that they resented, but could not openly express their resentment for the "foreigner" problem.[8] It was a resentment concerned, therefore, with territory: who had the right to live in and make a living in a particular space, who had the priority to resources produced in and for that place.[9] The resentment produced what Friedrich Nietzsche calls ressentiment: the internalized failure to react to what is perceived as an unjust treatment of the self.[10] Such ressentiment is one of the two driving forces behind the entity in the *The Conjuring 2*. The house that the Hodgsons move into was formerly owned by Wilkins, and his spirit, present in the house, is resentful of the family that has taken what he believes to be rightfully his territory. Wilkins lived through both the economic expansion and eventual recession of Ponders End, and his ghostly appearance corresponds to description of the result of ressentiment: a slow rotting of the soul.[11] If a scholarly reading of the supernatural in supernatural narratives is necessarily informed by the shared social anxiety of the time,[12] Wilkins' spatial possessiveness—his need to evacuate the Hodgson family from his home—may be read as an allegory for ressentiment about the Outsider that thrived in the '70s.

Further, the migrant paranoia saw a resurgence after the Syrian refugee crisis in 2016, the year in which *The Conjuring 2* was released, lending the ghost of Wilkins to a migratory reading on the film's dual temporal axes: its narrative timeline and its release date. Migrants who are currently targets of hate crimes in Europe are predominantly Middle-Eastern refugees because the rise in their numbers coincided with the decline in the childbirth of white Europeans. The demographic shift is causing a noticeable shift in Europe's cultural reality. Mohammad, for instance, became the most common baby boy in Amsterdam even by 2014, before the Syrian refugee crisis.[13] The current of anxiety coursing through the European consciousness now is that Europe's cultural identity is on the brink of extinction.[14] The economic paranoia of the '70s has therefore become a cultural one, but the fear is still one of bodily displacement: where before Outsiders were seen as unjustly displacing locals from jobs, now Outsiders are seen as horrific replacements of the *local* in the *local*ity of cultural capital. Thus, in allegorical terms, possession, in which the spirit of the former "resident" occupies the body of the arriving Outsider, is a reactionary response to the invasions of the Outsider on the economic and cultural territory of the "resident." It follows, in other words, the logic that produced the original slight: corporeal possession is a reaction to territorial and cultural possession. It is an externalization of ressentiment.

In *The Conjuring* (2013), Ed Warren (Patrick Wilson) notes that demonic possession has three distinct stages: infestation, oppression, and possession.[15] In 2016, alt-right groups produced a video that predicted that the Islamization of Europe would take place in three stages that correspond to the stages of possession: Muslims enter a foreign space and lure the trust of those around them by presenting themselves as a peaceful community (infestation), they then start planting their cultural markers (mosques, shrines, public celebrations of Ramadan, etc.) that alter the native geography (oppression), and finally, they take over the space and enforce Islamic (Sharia) law on the locals, turning Europe to "Eurabia" (possession), the word coined in 2005, a space whose geography corresponds to Europe as it is present on the map but that is removed from the Europe as it exists in the cultural memory of locals.[16]

The liberal culture of the West, as it were, "finds itself in an existential battle with 'their' illiberal [Islamic] culture that can only be won in 'our' favor by neutralizing and dominating 'them.'"[17] The fixity and continued perpetuation of this perception may also be seen as the West's unwillingness to recognize that "there is more than one way of being modern, each being pegged to a society's particular historical trajectory and cultural specificity."[18] As a result, when Muslim migrants come in contact with Western citizens on their turf, what follows is an encounter between the perceived and entrenched perception, resulting in Xenoracism, a dangerous mixture of xenophobia and racism that "is meted out by the western nations of Europe which are seeking to preserve their national identities."[19] Seen in this light, the burkha ban, first put in place by France, maybe understood as a decision made:

> less out of an interest in women's rights than because they see it as the most visible symbol of the dilution of their culture by immigration. Given higher fertility

rates among Muslims, so goes the argument, immigration will purportedly culminate in making the majority (culture) a "minority in its own land."[20]

Thus, the narrative of supernatural-bodily invasion in *The Conjuring* 2 replicates the structures of perceived territorial-cultural invasion, serving an allegory for the reaction of the West to Muslim migrants. Across Europe, this counter-reaction took the form of a surge of violence against those who were perceived as non-secular Muslims: the ones who wore the hijab, went to pray in mosques, and those who spoke in Arabic.[21] Thus, the sartorial, architectural, and linguistic markers were targeted, and the violence that followed, verbal or physical, was often accompanied by slogans of "Go back home" or some variant thereof. The ghost of Wilkins, in a similar vein, says to Janet, "This is my home," "My house," and "You don't belong here." He at first haunts her in the nights when she sleepwalks and is at her most vulnerable. She ties herself to her bed, the binding of body to territory, so she may wake up if she starts sleepwalking and, in this way, avoid getting possessed, the binding of ghost to body. Further, as Janet is watching "The Christmas Carol," Wilkins changes the channel to a video of a royal celebration that, given the year (1977), is, or so one may safely assume, the silver jubilee of Queen Elizabeth II's ascension to the throne,[22] an event which, given the predominant sentiment of the time, was particularly well-received by those to whom the nominal monarchy was the one remaining vestige of the systemic power that in a postcolonial world had been dismantled.

The possession in *Annabelle: Creation* also begins with a violation of geography. After an orphanage is shutdown (an off-screen event), Sister Charlotte (Stephanie Sigman) and six orphan girls are left homeless, so that when the Mullins family offers them refuge, they gratefully accept the offer which comes with one condition: there are two areas of the house where the girls are prohibited entry, the bedroom of the Mullins and the locked nursery of their deceased daughter, Annabelle (Samara Lee), who died in a car crash twelve years prior. Janice is lured into Annabelle's room by the supernatural force that eventually possesses her: the door to the room becomes unlocked of its volition and the gramophone starts to automatically play an old tune, thus stoking her childish curiosity, an instinct which also nudges her to explore the room full of toys. When she opens the closet that houses the possessed doll, the evil spirit, at first, makes its presence known in the form of the girl Annabelle. "Will you help me," this disguised entity asks, and when Janice asks "What do you want?," it responds, "I want your soul."

Annabelle dies in 1943 and the girls from the orphanage move into the house of the Mullins in 1955. The film, thus, is set in the McCarthyism era of the U.S. when Senator Joseph McCarthy generated a widespread hysteria of communist invasion of the U.S.[23] He pointed, as evidence, on global atomic trends: "the Soviet Union had exploded its first A-bomb in 1945. That same year, China, the world's most populous nation, became communist. Half of Europe was under Joseph Stalin's influence, and every time Americans read their newspapers there seemed to be a new atomic threat."[24] This perceived influence of the Outsider on the American spirit led McCarthy to conducted background checks on several government employees, his method seen as a political counterpart to the Salem witch trials.[25] In 2016, shortly before *Annabelle: Creation* was released, President Trump "expanded his anti-terror policy—which has included a 'total and complete shutdown' of America's borders to Muslims—by calling for a revival of McCarthyism. 'In the cold war we had an ideological screening test…. The time is overdue for a new test. I call it extreme vetting,' he said in his speech."[26] The film's dual temporal axes (narrative, cinematic) allows the possessed Janet to be read as an allegory of the feared communist Outsider and the Muslim Other, the devil that takes on the guise of Annabelle to lure and then possess her as an allegory for the political reaction to the two Outsider figures, disguised in each case as a security measure. Further, the paranormal phenomena that animates the inanimate in Annabelle's room—the locked door, a sheet floating in the air, marionettes, light switches in a dollhouse, etc.,—turn the physical geography of the house into an Eldritch Space: a space that is physically located on the earth but that does not obey the laws of physics, kinesis, and spatial logic, and that, therefore, is also outside known geography.[27] Such spatial alterations produce a paranoia in its witness, weakening her, making it easier, therefore, to assume psychological and corporeal control of her, a strategy not unlike the one executed by both McCarthy and Trump whose visions of an altered America produced paranoia in their target audience. What begins with perceived geographic violation (infestation), leads at first to geographic aberration (oppression) and eventually to corporeal violation (possession).

From Reshaped Geographies to Contorted Bodies

After "contacting" Janet, who is a sleepwalker, Wilkins contacts Billy, his namesake, who has a speech impairment, thus further establishing the pattern of his choice of victim, a pattern that repeats itself in *Annabelle: Creation* where the devil, in the guise of Annabelle, chooses to lure Janice, the only girl among the orphans who is disabled. The entities thus choose victims whose sense of power, shaky at best (given their corporeal, psychological, and social circumstances) is easy to upend. This particular form of "centrality of the sentient body" shows that "spirit possession is an arena of sensuous mimetic production and reproduction, which makes it a stage for the production and reproduction of power," specifically, "colonial encounters and political power."[28]

In each film, the entity, after colonizing the body of its victim, engages the senses of the latter to exercise its power. In *The Conjuring 2,* Peggy, having witnessed paranormal disturbances in her house, seeks shelter with a neighbor. But the ghost of Wilkins, having latched himself onto Janet's body, no longer needs a shared geography to pursue them. He shows himself in the guise of the crooked man to Billy, and when a frightened Billy runs away and wakes up his family, they see the approaching, elongating shadow of the crooked man, and they hear a hoarse male voice. But the figure that appears before them is that of Janet, possessed now by the spirit of Will who produces, through her, the spatial violence that so far she has been the subject of: Janet, who is often suspended midair by the ghost, causes the fireplace grate to levitate. Janice (*Annabelle: Creation*), too, is physically violated by the devil after he lures her into the locked, forbidden geography of the nursery: she is clawed at, and thus marked; she is then flung into the air before being dropped to the floor; where before she walks with the aid of a stick, she now becomes wheelchair-bound. Thus, the bodies of the possessed children, Janet and Janice, are re-coded "in relation to the embodied presence of spirits,"[29] just as the bodies of the Outsider are re-coded—marked as Other and violated in some capacity—by oppressive sociopolitical forces. If, in ethnographic research, "mediums reported manifold somatic changes while possessed," we find that "bodiliness is altered" for the characters (Janet, Janice) when they become "the embodiment of [supernatural] spirits" and for the discriminated Outsider when they experience "the displacement or disembodiment of the quotidian self," experience.[30]

Once possessed, Janet and Janice are temporal and spiritual fusions: Wilkins, a ghost, occupies Janet, while the devil, a supernatural entity, occupies Janice. The entities exist outside the construct of human time, even as they communicate through the corporeality of their human hosts that is temporally bound. They are, we posit, assemblages, for an assemblage is necessary for the relation between two strata to come about and "for organisms to be caught within and [become] permeated by a social field that utilizes them."[31] The social field that permeates and utilizes the child characters are the supernatural entities that possess them. As assemblages, Janet and Janice each have "both territorial sides ... which stabilize it, and cutting edges of deterritorialization, which carry it away."[32] The recognizable forms of the girls and their speech constitutes the territorial side which makes them familiar to their families: Janice, for instance, references the promise that Linda (a fellow orphan) and she make of getting adopted as a pair. However, their possessions and resulting subjectifications—Janet, as a girl, talking in the voice of an older-man and the disabled Janice walking with ease—produces the effect of deterritorialization. Whereas the fact of their multiplicity, which makes them each an assemblage, is visible, the Hodgsons and Sister Charlotte, who are trying to *re*cover Janet and Janice respectively, "don't know yet what the multiple entails [for] it is no[t] attributed."[33] Sister Charlotte, for instance, is unaware, until the climactic act, that the devil has gotten hold of Janice. Each of the girls—as "an assemblage is precisely this increase in the dimensions of a multiplicity that necessarily changes in nature as it expands its connections."[34] Further, the entities that have a hold over them, causing their multiplicity, prevent clarity regarding what is causing the multiplicity by disorienting the spatial perception of fellow-characters: specifically, they "swindle ... of the very experience of difference, especially the difference of space" by "dissolve[ing] the mutually reinforced separation of inside and outside, Innenvelt and Umvelt, so that we have neither a determinate space to inhabit nor determinate principles of space to inhabit us."[35] To clarify the distinction between "inside" and "outside":

> we might follow Henry Allison here when he explains that "by 'outer sense' is meant a sense through which one can become perceptually aware of objects as distinct from the self and its states. Similarly, by 'inner sense' is meant a sense through which one can become perceptually aware of the self and its states."[36]

The external biological geography of the girls and their internal state (possession) are blurred in the subjective experience of witness characters when the latter is expressed through aberrations in the body without entirely defamiliarizing this known body. The hosts themselves, Janice and Janet, lose the clarity of their inner sense after the entity that has a hold over each of them turns them from cohesive, biological units to assemblages by "continually dismantling the organism" that is each of their body and by "attributing itself to subjects that it leaves with nothing more than a name."[37] They are visibly Janet and Janice, but other than these persistent corporeal and nominal identities, they—their behaviors of speech and actions—are unidentifiable with their histories that preceded their possession. Thus, the consequence of the geographic violation—Janet entering Wilkins' home and Janice Annabelle's room—is the "landscapification" of their bodies, for "the collapse of corporeal coordinates or milieus implies the constitution of a landscape."[38] The collapse of the identities of the girls and the entities, that gives the latter the corporality of the former, and the former the voice and physical capabilities of the latter, may be seen, returning to the allegorical, migratory readings of these films, as a reaction to the new "constitution of a landscape": the Outsider entering the landscape is punished by acquiring control over their corporeality and the torturous altering of their biological landscape. Contemporary border rhetoric contains examples of such mutilations that migrant bodies encounter upon their arrival in their host country: the undocumented Latin children arriving at the U.S.-Mexico border are kept in cages, thus becoming-animal; the migrants arriving in Australia are marooned on Manus Island, each of them becoming-castaway. Like possessed bodies, they are suspended between worlds: their old life left behind, their new life yet to come to fruition, the former present in the form of their bodies and remembered histories, the latter kept at bay through their subjectification that apprehends them and curtails their movement indefinitely. If Janet and Janice, under the control of entities, exist outside time—neither human nor spirit—the act of waiting in liminal border spaces (detention centers, airports, borderlands etc.), leaves migrants with the experience of being outside time.[39]

Gilles Deleuze notes that "the assemblage is fundamentally libidinal and unconscious," and, notably, to clarify what he calls an Oedipal statement, he presents, as an example, Franz Kafka's story "Jackals and Arabs" (1917) in which a pack of jackals, who perceives the Arabs as unclean, enlist the help of a European traveler to deterritorialize the desert landscape of the Arabs.[40] Aligning the European, perceived as superior, with the pack of wild animals, which are perceived as inherently native to the land, produces a "jackal-man"[41] assemblage that exemplifies the at once unconscious and libidinal desire to annihilate the Arab race that is perceived as neither native to the land nor as culturally and morally equal to the European. Kafka's fable is relevant to current state of European consciousness that has found its jackal-man in the form of a right-wing rhetoric that brings together the fear of becoming-Eurabia and a young generation that wants to annihilate the Arab body from European territory.

Vocal Possessions and Aural Testimony

In *The Conjuring 2*, when religious ceremony (exorcism) becomes the only recourse to free Janet from the force that has overtaken her, the church asks Ed Warren and Lorraine Warren (Vera Farmiga) to first verify the authenticity of the claim that Janet is possessed. Wilkins does speak to Ed through Janet, but when Ed is looking away. Consequently, the responses to Janet's aural testimony of her possession fall, as expected, into the stalk categories of believers (Maurice [Simon McBurney]) and skeptics (Anita [Franka Potente]), the two components of the dialectic serving, in my migratory reading of the film, as stand-ins for the sympathetic and skeptic reception of migrants, the latter often claiming that refugees make up a trauma narratives to leech off of the systemic benefits that Western countries provide, such as healthcare. Ed and Lorraine are, by extension of this reading, the filmic equivalents of asylum officers who test the authenticity of the claim an asylum-seeker makes about the well-founded fear in their homeland that they are fleeing. Lorraine says she "wants" to believe Janet's story, and she is indeed sympathetic to her, but she frets over her "inability to feel" the presence of the traumatizing entity, an experience which is not uncommon of asylum officers. Where in the case of the former, the demonic force controlling Bill keeps Lorraine from feeling Janet's trauma, in the case of the latter, hearing the same trauma narrative and handling more cases than they should has a benumbing effect on officers. The "inability to feel" is a function, that is, of the authoritarian systems that govern the supernatural and asylum processes respectively. And, as with asylum applicants, Janet's oppression—her possession—becomes proof of her innocence. It is the ghost of Wilkins that has control of Janet and not the other way around, so that Janet cannot, at will, bring forth the presence of Wilkins. The paradoxical and unfair nature of her oral testimony that is meant to bring her the relief she needs conjures up the immigration practice that England adapted after some migrants from "safe" countries try to get asylum (and get into Europe) by claiming that they are Syrian.[42] To determine if asylum-seekers are telling the truth about their country of origin, immigration officers use an accent test that checks if the asylum-seeker sounds Syrian.[43] As a critique of the vocal testimony-based asylum system, the Jordanian artist Lawrence Abu Hamdan produced sculptural forms called *Voiceprints* (2015).[44] He gives physical form to two sound-waves: they are different pronunciations of the word "you," both by Syrians from the same province, yet, both sounding and appearing different. The sculptures materialize the flawed ideology behind the accent test: the binding of territory to voice.[45]

From Despotic and Authoritarian Assemblage to Counter-Assemblage

The final acts of the films reveal that the spirits of Wilkins and Annabelle are controlled by the demon Vallac and the devil respectively. Where the spirits work as authoritarian assemblages, the demon and the devil work as despotic assemblages. These phrases:

> give the new semiotic system the means of its imperialism, in other words, the means both to crush the other semiotics and protect itself against any threat from outside. A concerted effort is made to do away with the body and corporeal coordinates through which the multidimensional or polyvocal semiotics operated. Bodies are disciplined, corporeality dismantled … deterritorialization pushed to a new threshold—a jump is made from the organic strata to the strata of significance and subjectification.[46]

The semiotics of what it means to be human (one's corporeal language consistent with one's history) is imperialized by the spirits and the demon/devil that deterritorialize and dismantle the bodies of Janet and Janice by decentralizing their presence in their corporeal coordinates and producing their unrecognizable, subjectified selves. Further, the coinciding of the names of Bill Hodgson and Bill Wilkins reflects the trouble they each have with the act of verbalization, the former because of a speech impairment, the latter because he is controlled by Vallac, causing, in each case, the erasure of individuation from voice. The two times that Bill is faced with the cross, he speaks broken phrases; further, Ed overlaps two separate recorded testimonies to discover that Wilkins' possession of Janet is orchestrated by Vallac. Where, typically, "an assemblage comprises two segments, one of content, the other of expression," and "an assemblage, in its multiplicity, necessarily acts on semiotic flows," Janet and Janice, as assemblages, constitute of three segments: the audible and visual expressions of the possessed characters, the characters who are doing the possession (Wilkins, Annabelle) and providing the "content" of how the girls act and what they say, and the entities who are controlling Wilkins and Annabelle (Vallac and the devil), the directors, if you will, of the acts possession.[47]

According to demonology lore, Vallac goes after treasures, in the vein, one may say, of England that entered third world countries. He targets the spirit of Wilkins, specifically, his weakness: he wants to regain possession of his home. Vallac may be seen as the right-wing ideology itself that controls vulnerable individuals by targeting their weakness. Similarly, in *Annabelle: Creation* the devil takes on the appearance of Annabelle to take advantage of her grieving parents: soon after the death of their daughter he talks to them through her spirit and asks for permission to move into the doll that the father had made, and once he gets their permission, he reveals his true form. If "there is no significance without a despotic assemblage, no subjectification without an authoritarian assemblage and no mixture between the two without assemblages of power,"[48] then the subjectifications of Janet and Janice take place through the authoritarian assemblages of Wilkins and Annabelle, who in turn are controlled by Vallac and the devil who assign the acts of possession—of turning the bodies of the girls to assemblages—their underlying significance. Possession, thus "acts through signifiers and acts upon souls and subjects" of Janet and Janice.[49]

Therefore, the two films discussed share a DNA: by the final acts of both stories, there is compassion for Janet and Janice as well for the souls of Billy and Annabelle (and for her parents) who are, at first, perceived as evil. In the allegorical reading of this concluding narrative "turn," we claim that there needs to be an empathetic, open-minded approach to individuals who identify as conservative, for even when there are those in that faction whose hatred of difference is irredeemable, the vast majority of right, research shows, constitutes of individuals who have been manipulated by political forces that have taken advantage of their unfortunate circumstances. For instance, Matt Eich, a photojournalist, photographed families who were affected by the bust of the coal industry in Ohio. He writes: "from the 1820s to the 1960s, mining corporations stripped Appalachia of its resources. After taking all that they could, the companies left, leaving former boomtowns with little but their cultural identity."[50] Under Obama's regime, "like many other members of the country's white working class, [Eich's subjects] felt that the country has abandoned them,"[51] a fact which Trump used to his advantage by acknowledging their existence in his 2016 political campaign: he promised the revival of the coal industry, for instance. Eich, on the other hand, simply "hung around for years observing, and listening to what they had to say. It was a very basic act, but also, in its way, a radical one."[52] It is an act of radical empathy, and if political (Democratic) and social (left-wing) had expressed radical empathy with people like Eich's subjects, they might have arrived at a different conclusion in the 2016 elections. Radical empathy is a physical manifestation of a cerebral phenomenon, an act that simultaneously illuminates, in our brains, the ventral component of the Medial Prefrontal Cortex which creates an awareness of the self, and its dorsal component that creates an awareness of the other, while producing physical sensation.[53] This radical empathy, if extended toward those controlled by more powerful ideologies, enables us to look beyond the conservative veneer. It serves as a counter-assemblage which brings together groups of people who have not engaged with each other so far to produce a pluralistic dialogue that counters the authoritarian and despotic assemblages that are acting upon those people.

An example of such an assemblage is the artwork produced by Tibetan artist Gonkar Gyatso. After China invaded Tibet, Gyatso fled the country and eventually landed in London where, in the wake of the support for the exiled Dalai Lama, he was expected to produce tradition Buddhist iconography in his art. As a resistant response, he created *Dissected Buddha* (2003),[54] a mixed-media collage painting in which a life-sized silhouette of the Buddha is filled with and possessed by stickers that are iconic representations of the places his globalized excursions took Gyatso to—London tubes, Statue of Liberty, McDonalds, Tibetan monasteries, and Superman, among others. Placed one next to the other inside the body of the Buddha, these metaphoric stand-ins for geographic and cultural encounters contextualize and illuminate each other by association; the statue of liberty, for instance, appearing next to the London underground within the context of migrant art, turns from a tourist spot to the reminder that Ellis island was, between 1892 and 1954, the portal of entry for immigrants where they were issued or denied visas upon arrival. The overwhelming sensorial counter-assemblage demonstrates, through its accumulation "of disparate parts, operating without any discernible logic," the experience of "absolute simultaneity" that is innate to the artist's migratory experience.[55] By incorporating instead of rejecting the iconic meditative form of the Buddha that was expected of him, Gyatso shows that the Buddha is neither removed from nor exclusively his aesthetic identity, but rather is a part of it. This counter-assemblage speaks to the audience that had imposed the expectation of Buddha's iconic presence in Gyatso, and in doing so it also tells the migrant narrative through a striking visual language. The precise semiotics of the counter-assemblage that brings conservative and liberal ideologues are, it is acknowledged, uncertain, but like Gyatso's artwork, it begins with a decision to not reject, up front, an idea of a different ilk, and it is realized through imagination.

In conclusion, possession, the act of corporeal invasion, in *The Conjuring 2* and *Annabelle: Creation* is a reaction to acts perceived as geographic invasion: Janet and Janice entering the house of Billy Wilkins and the room of Annabelle respectively. The narrative and cinematic temporality of the films allow for a migratory reading of possession, the act functioning, allegorically speaking, as a reaction to the unwelcome arrival of certain migrants. Where possession turns the bodies of hosts to assemblages, works of migrant art produce counter-assemblages that are acts of radical empathy meant to turn the act of looking to a *felt* experience for viewers. Such empathy, if extended, through imagination, to those who have been manipulated by authoritarian and despotic forces to make conservative decisions, will bridge gaps and produce stronger communities. That, we can all agree, is necessary, critical even, in our current political moment.

Notes

1. Michael Dango, "2017, the Year in Horror," *LA Review of Books*, January 31, 2018, https://lareviewofbooks.org/article/2017-the-year-in-horror/.

2. Joseph LeDoux, "Why We Enjoy Horror Movies," in *It's Alive: Classic Horror and Sci-Fi Movie Posters from the Kirk Hammett Collection*, ed. Daniel Finamore (New York: Rizzoli Electa, 2017), 13–25.

3. Soren Kierkegaard, *The Concept of Anxiety*, trans. by Alastair Hannay (New York: Liveright, 2015), 34–35.

4. Soren Kierkegaard, *The Concept of Anxiety*, trans. by Alastair Hannay (New York: Liveright, 2015), 34–35.

5. Daniel James, "Boroughs of London: Before and After Recession," *Daily Mirror* (British Newspaper Archive), March 25, 1979, https://www.britishnewspaperarchive.co.uk/search/results/1951-03-02?NewspaperTitle=Daily%2BMirror&IssueId=BL%2F0000560%2F19510302%2F&County=London%2C%20England.

6. Daniel James, "Boroughs of London: Before and After Recession," *Daily Mirror* (British Newspaper Archive), March 25, 1979, https://www.britishnewspaperarchive.co.uk/search/

results/1951-03-02?NewspaperTitle=Daily%2BMirror&IssueId=BL%2F0000560%2F19510302%2F&County=London%2C%20England.

7. Markus. M.L. Crepaz, *Trust Beyond Borders: Immigration, the Welfare State, and Identity in Modern Societies* (Ann Arbor: University of Michigan Press, 2008), 52–92.

8. Ron Ramdin, *Reimaging Britain: Years of Black and Asian History* (London: Pluto Press, 1999), 306–350.

9. Achille Mbembe, *Notes on Postcolony*, trans. A.M. Berrett (Berkeley: University of California Press, 2001), 123.

10. Guy Elgat, *Nietzsche's Psychology of Ressentiment* (Abingdon: Routledge, 2019), 34.

11. Stefano Tomelleri, *Ressentiment: Reflections on Mimetic Desire and Society* (East Lansing: Michigan State University Press, 2015), 19.

12. Fredric Jameson, *Allegory and Ideology* (New York: Verso Books, 2019), 113.

13. Leo Lucassen, "To Amsterdam: Migration Past and Present," in *New York and Amsterdam: Immigration and the New Urban Landscape*, ed. Jan Rath, Jan Willem Duyvendak, Nancy Foner, and Rogier van Reekum (New York: NYU Press, 2014.)

14. Leo Lucassen, "To Amsterdam: Migration Past and Present," in *New York and Amsterdam: Immigration and the New Urban Landscape*, ed. Jan Rath, Jan Willem Duyvendak, Nancy Foner, and Rogier van Reekum (New York: NYU Press, 2014).

15. *The Conjuring*, directed by James Wan (2013, LA: Warner Brothers), DVD.

16. Bat Ye'Or, *Eurabia: The Euro-Arab Axis* (Madison: Fairleigh Dickinson University Press, 2005).

17. Samuel P. Huntington, *The Clash of Civilizations and the Remaking of World Order* (New York: Simon & Schuster, 1996), 93.

18. Tariq Ramadan, *Islam, the West and the Challenges of Modernity* (Leicestershire: The Islamic Foundation, 2009), 27.

19. Peter O'Brien, *The Muslim Question in Europe* (Philiadelphi: ,Temple University Press, 2016), 9.

20. Peter O'Brien, *The Muslim Question in Europe* (Philadelphia: Temple University Press, 2016), 9.

21. Riham Alkousaa, "Violent Crime Rises in Germany," Reuters, January 3, 2018. https://www.reuters.com/article/us-europe-migrants-germany-crime/violent-crime-rises-in-germany-and-is-attributed-to-refugees-idUSKBN1ES16J.

22. Lauren Hubbard, "Queen Elizabeth's Silver Jubilee Celebration," *Town and Country*, December 1, 2019. https://www.townandcountrymag.com/society/tradition/g29415467/queen-elizabeth-silver-jubilee-celebration-25th-anniversary-throne-photos/.

23. *U.S. History*, s.v. "53a. McCarthyism," 2008, https://www.ushistory.org/Us/53a.asp.

24. *U.S. History*, s.v. "53a. McCarthyism," 2008, https://www.ushistory.org/Us/53a.asp.

25. *U.S. History*, s.v. "53a. McCarthyism," 2008, https://www.ushistory.org/Us/53a.asp.

26. James Nevius, "McCarthyism Redux: The Long View of Trump's Immigration Plan," *The Guardian*, August 16, 2016. https://www.theguardian.com/commentisfree/2016/aug/16/donald-trumps-extreme-vetting-plan-immigration.

27. H.P. Lovecraft, *Eldritch Tales* (London: Gollancz, 2011), ix–xiii.

28. Paul Stoller, *The Taste of Ethnographic Things: The Senses in Anthropology* (Philadelphia: University of Pennsylvania Press, 1989), 101–112.

29. Barley Norton, *Songs for the Spirits: Music and Mediums in Modern Vietnam* (Urbana: University of Illinois Press, 2009), 54–78.

30. Barley Norton, *Songs for the Spirits: Music and Mediums in Modern Vietnam* (Urbana: University of Illinois Press, 2009), 54–78.

31. Gilles Deleuze and Felix Guattari, *A Thousand Plateaus: Capitalism and Schizophrenia*, trans. Brian Massumi (Minneapolis: University of Minnesota Press, 1987), 149–167.

32. Gilles Deleuze and Felix Guattari, *A Thousand Plateaus: Capitalism and Schizophrenia*, trans. Brian Massumi (Minneapolis: University of Minnesota Press, 1987), 149–167.

33. Gilles Deleuze and Felix Guattari, *A Thousand Plateaus: Capitalism and Schizophrenia*, trans. Brian Massumi (Minneapolis: University of Minnesota Press, 1987), 149–167.

34. Gilles Deleuze and Felix Guattari, *A Thousand Plateaus: Capitalism and Schizophrenia*, trans. Brian Massumi (Minneapolis: University of Minnesota Press, 1987), 149–167.

68   Migratory Anxieties and Diasporic Communities

35. Gregory Flaxman, *At the Edges of Thought: Deleuze and Post-Kantian Philosophy* (Edinburgh: Edinburgh University Press, 2015), 307–329.
36. Henry. E. Allison, *Kant's Transcendental Idealism: An Interpretation and Defense* (New Haven, CT: Yale University Press, 2004), 275–304.
37. Gilles Deleuze and Felix Guattari, *A Thousand Plateaus: Capitalism and Schizophrenia*, trans. Brian Massumi (Minneapolis: University of Minnesota Press, 1987), 3–26.
38. Gilles Deleuze and Felix Guattari, *A Thousand Plateaus: Capitalism and Schizophrenia*, trans. Brian Massumi (Minneapolis: University of Minnesota Press, 1987), 149–167.
39. Gloria Anzaldúa, *Borderlands / La Frontera: The New Mestiza* (San Francisco: Aunt Lute Books, 2012), 3–18.
40. Gilles Deleuze and Felix Guattari, *A Thousand Plateaus: Capitalism and Schizophrenia*, trans. Brian Massumi (Minneapolis: University of Minnesota Press, 1987), 3–26.
41. Gilles Deleuze and Felix Guattari, *A Thousand Plateaus: Capitalism and Schizophrenia*, trans. Brian Massumi (Minneapolis: University of Minnesota Press, 1987), 3–26.
42. Alan Travis and Rebecca Smithers, "Accents on Trial," *The Guardian*, October 22, 2003. https://www.theguardian.com/politics/2003/oct/22/schools.immigrationandpublicservices.
43. Alan Travis and Rebecca Smithers, "Accents on Trial," *The Guardian*, October 22, 2003. https://www.theguardian.com/politics/2003/oct/22/schools.immigrationandpublicservices.
44. Lawrence Abu Hamdan, "The Freedom of Speech Itself," 2014. http://lawrenceabuhamdan.com/#/the-freedom-of-speech-itself/.
45. Lawrence Abu Hamdan, "The Freedom of Speech Itself," 2014. http://lawrenceabuhamdan.com/#/the-freedom-of-speech-itself/.
46. Gilles Deleuze and Felix Guattari, *A Thousand Plateaus: Capitalism and Schizophrenia*, trans. Brian Massumi (Minneapolis: University of Minnesota Press, 1987), 208–231.
47. Gilles Deleuze and Felix Guattari, *A Thousand Plateaus: Capitalism and Schizophrenia*, trans. Brian Massumi (Minneapolis: University of Minnesota Press, 1987), 208–231.
48. Gilles Deleuze and Felix Guattari, *A Thousand Plateaus: Capitalism and Schizophrenia*, trans. Brian Massumi (Minneapolis: University of Minnesota Press, 1987), 232–309.
49. Gilles Deleuze and Felix Guattari, *A Thousand Plateaus: Capitalism and Schizophrenia*, trans. Brian Massumi (Minneapolis: University of Minnesota Press, 1987), 232–309.
50. Matt Eich, "Carry Me Ohio: The Place That Taught Me to See," October 16, 2014. https://medium.com/vantage/i-spent-10-years-photographing-appalachia-d5692dfec5bf.
51. Matt Eich, "Carry Me Ohio: The Place That Taught Me to See," October 16, 2014. https://medium.com/vantage/i-spent-10-years-photographing-appalachia-d5692dfec5bf.
52. Kate Linthicum, "'I Feel Forgotten': A Decade of Struggle in Rural Ohio," *New Yorker*, October 18, 2016. https://www.newyorker.com/culture/photo-booth/i-feel-forgotten-a-decade-of-struggle-in-rural-ohio?verso=true.
53. Simon Baron-Cohen. *The Science of Evil: On Empathy and the Origins of Cruelty* (New York: Basic Books, 2012), 17–44.
54. Joyce Lau, "Tibetan Artists Rise to the Fore," *The New York Times*, October 8, 2014. https://www.nytimes.com/2014/10/09/arts/international/tibetan-artists-like-gonkar-gyatso-are-rising-to-the-fore-in-contemporary-art.html.
55. Gilles Deleuze and Felix Guattari, *A Thousand Plateaus: Capitalism and Schizophrenia*, trans. Brian Massumi (Minneapolis: University of Minnesota Press, 1987), 208–231.

Works Cited

Alkousaa, Riham. "Violent Crime Rises in Germany." *Reuters* 2018. https://www.reuters.com/article/us-europe-migrants-germany-crime/violent-crime-rises-in-germany-and-is-attributed-to-refugees-idUSKBN1ES16J, accessed August 15, 2019.

Allison, Henry E. *Kant's Transcendental Idealism: An Interpretation and Defense.* New Haven: Yale University Press, 2004.

Anzaldúa, Gloria. *Borderlands/La Frontera: The New Mestiza.* San Francisco: Aunt Lute Books, 2012.

Baron-Cohen, Simon. *The Science of Evil: On Empathy and the Origins of Cruelty.* New York: Basic Books, 2012.
Crepaz M.L., Markus. *Trust Beyond Borders: Immigration, the Welfare State, and Identity in Modern Societies.* Ann Arbor: University of Michigan Press, 2008.
Dango, Michael. "2017, the Year in Horror." *Los Angeles Review of Books.* January 31, 2018. https://lareviewofbooks.org/article/2017-the-year-in-horror/.
Deleuze, Gilles, and Felix Guattari, *A Thousand Plateaus: Capitalism and Schizophrenia.* Translated by Brian Massumi. Minneapolis: University of Minnesota Press, 1987.
Eich, Matt. "Carry Me Ohio: The Place That Taught Me to See." October 2019. https://medium.com/vantage/i-spent-10-years-photographing-appalachia-d5692dfec5bf, accessed September 25, 2019.
Elgat, Guy. *Nietzsche's Psychology of Ressentiment.* Abingdon: Routledge, 2019.
Flexman, Gregory. *At the Edges of Thought: Deleuze and Post-Kantian Philosophy.* Edinburgh: Edinburgh University Press, 2015.
Hamdan, Lawrence Abu. "The Freedom of Speech Itself." 2014. http://lawrenceabuhamdan.com/#/the-freedom-of-speech-itself/, accessed September 14, 2019.
Hubbard, Lauren. "Queen Elizabeth's Silver Jubilee Celebration." *Town and Country,* December 1, 2019, https://www.townandcountrymag.com/society/tradition/g29415467/queen-elizabeth-silver-jubilee-celebration-25th-anniversary-throne-photos/, accessed September 18, 2019.
Huntington, Samuel P. *The Clash of Civilizations and the Remaking of World Order.* New York: Simon & Schuster, 1996.
James, Daniel. "Boroughs of London: Before and After Recession." *Daily Mirror* (British Newspaper Archive), March 1979, https://newspaperarchive.com/browse/uk/, accessed November 4, 2019.
Jameson, Fredric. *Allegory and Ideology.* New York: Verso Books, 2019.
Kierkegaard, Soren. *The Concept of Anxiety,* translated by Alastair Hannay. New York: Liveright, 2015.
Lau, Joyce. "Tibetan Artists Rise to the Fore." *New York Times,* October 8, 2014. https://www.nytimes.com/2014/10/09/arts/international/tibetan-artists-like-gonkar-gyatso-are-rising-to-the-fore-in-contemporary-art.html, accessed September 1, 2018.
LeDoux, Joseph. "Why We Enjoy Horror Movies." In *It's Alive: Classic Horror and Sci-Fi Movie Posters from the Kirk Hammett Collection,* edited by Daniel Finamore, 13–25. New York: Rizzoli Electa, 2017.
Linthicum, Kate. "'I Feel Forgotten': A Decade of Struggle in Rural Ohio." *New Yorker.* October 8, 2016. https://www.newyorker.com/culture/photo-booth/i-feel-forgotten-a-decade-of-struggle-in-rural-ohio?verso=true, accessed September 25, 2019.
Lovecraft, H.P. *Eldritch Tales.* London: Gollancz, 2011.
Lucassen, Leo. "To Amsterdam: Migration Past and Present." In *New York and Amsterdam: Immigration and the New Urban Landscape,* edited by Jan Rath, Jan Willem Duyvendak, Nancy Foner, and Rogier van Reekum, 34–56. New York: NYU Press, 2014.
Mbembe, Achille. *Notes on Postcolony,* translated by A.M. Berrett. Berkeley: University of California Press, 2001.
Nevius, James. "McCarthyism Redux: The Long View of Trump's Immigration Plan." *The Guardian.* August 16, 2016. https://www.theguardian.com/commentisfree/2016/aug/16/donald-trumps-extreme-vetting-plan-immigration, accessed August 25, 2019.
Norton, Barley. *Songs for the Spirits: Music and Mediums in Modern Vietnam.* Chicago: University of Illinois Press, 2009.
O'Brien, Peter. *The Muslim Question in Europe: Political Controversies and Public Philosophies.* Philadelphia: Temple University Press, 2016.
Ramadan, Tariq. *Islam, the West and the Challenges of Modernity.* Leicester: Islamic Foundation, 2009.
Ramdin, Ron. *Reimaging Britain: Years of Black and Asian History.* London: Pluto Press, 1999.
Smithers, Travis, and Rebecca Smithers. "Accents on Trial." *The Guardian,* October 22, 2003. https://www.theguardian.com/politics/2003/oct/22/schools.immigrationandpublicservice.

Stoller, Paul. *The Taste of Ethnographic Things: The Senses in Anthropology.* Philadelphia: University of Pennsylvania Press, 1989.
Tomelleri, Stefano. *Ressentiment: Reflections on Mimetic Desire and Society.* East Lansing: Michigan State University Press, 2015.
Ye'Or, Bat. *Eurabia: The Euro-Arab Axis.* Madison: Fairleigh Dickinson University Press, 2005.

Aquaman and American White Supremacy

Luis A. Grande Branger

Introduction

Warner Bros. and DC Comics have tried to reproduce the success of the Marvel Cinematic Universe through films such as *Batman vs. Superman* (Zack Snyder, 2016), *Justice League* (Zack Snyder, 2017), *Wonder Woman* (Patty Jenkins, 2017), *Shazam* (David Sandberg, 2019), etc.; and even though it is arguable the extent to which they have managed to establish a solid diegetic universe within their films, certainly, the audience and the critics' acceptance has increased with the latest installments of the franchise. One of these movies is James Wan's 2018 release *Aquaman*, which although far from perfect, is one of the most successful films of this universe, the one with the greatest potential and with the most thought-provoking discourse.

It would be fair to admit that the action scenes in *Aquaman* are very well executed and are possibly the best ones in the Warner Bros./DC Cinematic Universe—much of this is due to the great camera movement and cinematography work already known to be part of Wan's filmography. However, the greatest achievement of Wan's debut in the superhero genre is his depiction of the underwater realm. Everything that has to do with the kingdom of Atlantis, the beautifully well-crafted art direction that accompanies it and its political intrigue, although with a few clichés and hackneyed themes, is attractive and deep—no pun intended—since, as will be examined in this work, it mirrors some elements of our contemporary political reality. The political discourse presented in the film is displayed through this plot, which makes the underwater city, and ultimately, the film itself, more interesting. This discourse is the central focus of my analysis.

The film is not without its shortcomings. While the political drama within the Kingdom of Atlantis is interesting, the script is not as complex.

It is full of "one liners" that, without the film's context to aid in filling them with meaning and depth, become empty and without forcefulness. The biggest pitfall in the script, however, is Aquaman himself. This is not a critique of Jason Momoa's histrionic ability but rather the way in which his character was written. The actor cannot do much with his character, since Arthur Curry does not really do much in the plot. He simply accompanies Mera (Amber Heard), while she and Vulko (Willem Dafoe) manage to sit Arthur on the throne. Aquaman's greatest achievement is embodying an instrument of strength—or "a blunt instrument" as he puts it—and being able to communicate with animals—a power he simply inherited. The character's arc is not without merit, for Arthur's character does grow throughout the course of the film, he learns a few things on his journey, yet by the end of the film his character has ultimately changed very little. This is particularly frustrating given the history of mockery targeted at the comic character for not being as resourceful and powerful as his Justice League teammates,[1] and the achievement of the comic book writers in the 1980s of finally depicting a well-written hero after almost forty years of criticism for being an undeveloped character.[2] This lack of huge character arc evolution likely occurs because within the discourse, the figure of Aquaman functions, not as an active character pursuing an ideology, but as a metaphor of the ideology itself. We will further explore this theory later.

Nevertheless, the film survives all these flaws because it brings light to a pertinent and relevant issue in today's society: the American discussion about race, immigration, nationalism and white supremacy which is one of the most important topics in contemporary U.S. politics. This national debate was one of the major talking points of Donald Trump's 2016 presidential campaign and it has been a frequent subject of his speeches during his presidential term. Immigration has also been one of the most heated topics brought by liberal critics of the president, especially because of the treatment of illegal immigrants by border security forces.

This debate has become more heated through the years, resulting in a severe polarization of the country and generating the creation of extreme groups on both sides. We argue that James Wan's *Aquaman* metaphorically depicts the political climate and gives a hopeful message presenting a way for minorities to earn respect and recognition in our society, ending the fight around this very controversial topic.

A Vast Sea of Signs

James Wan's *Aquaman* is particularly interesting for addressing the rising racial tensions in our society's contemporary political reality.

Superhero films are often underestimated and viewed as meaningless fantasy movies whose only purpose is to merely entertain the masses and generate vast amounts of money. Renowned film director Martin Scorsese made news headlines when he said that Marvel movies were not "real cinema" and even compared superhero films to theme parks.[3] Amid the controversy, other laureated film directors like Francis Ford Coppola agreed with Scorsese's words. In addition, various celebrated filmmakers like Ken Loach, Lucrecia Martel, Ridley Scott and David Cronenberg have shown disdain for the genre expressing that "it's for kids" and that "it's not about communicating."[4] In reality, the superhero genre is rich in symbolism and discourse, which is the core of our analysis of James Wan's film. It is important to acknowledge that superhero films do communicate a wide variety of messages, including political discourse, relevant to the present time. These messages are no longer sequestered to teenage bedrooms or dusty boxes filled with comics from the past, "superheroes have gone from garnering a narrow audience of children and a few nostalgic adults to achieving worldwide acclaim as a wildly successful, multibillion-dollar enterprise with a level of popularity never seen before."[5] In other words, the messages in these films are reaching millions of people around the world. Therefore, we should be more attentive of the discourses and the messages within the narrative of these films rather than being dismissive.

As with any other movie, the narrative in Wan's film presents a series of signs that can be interpreted in order to understand the discourse and the ideology contained in the story of *Aquaman*. For this purpose, we can have a semiotic approach, which means the "analysis of the concrete vehicles of the signs—texts and images—as carriers of culture, ideology or myths."[6] What is the underlying political message of the film? In several European countries, extreme nationalist and white supremacist groups have been opposing immigrants and refugees from non–European countries. As the global nonprofit media corporation Public Radio International says in an article on their website, "Most of the Western world—from Switzerland and Germany to the United States, Scandinavia and New Zealand—has witnessed a potent nationalist strain infecting society in recent years."[7] However, media coverage has heavily focused on the United States specifically, given the prominence of the figure of Donald Trump. It can be argued that the discourse of Wan's *Aquaman* can be applied to today's discussion on race in the entire world, but like the media, it is also focused on the recent American debate. We believe this, not only because we can identify several signs within the narrative of *Aquaman* that reference the political debate specifically in the United States—and we will point them out in the next segments—but because this film is a Hollywood blockbuster, produced by the American company Warner Bros. Stuart Hall's theory of codification and decodification of meaning suggests that during the production of mediatic content, meaning is codified based on the knowledge structures, production relationships and technical infrastructure of all those involved in the realization of these materials.[8] Hence, this film was made within the American cultural frame and therefore it was most probably created with the American political climate as a source of inspiration.

With attention to what Stuart Hall proposes, during the reception of media content, audiences decode meaning using the same codes: knowledge structures, production relationships and technical infrastructure of each person receiving the discourse.[9] When someone is building meaning out of media content, that person will use all their personal experiences and cultural baggage as reference to interpret every sign they are exposed to.[10] We also recognize that polysemy and the diversity of interpretations are part of the limitations of semiotic analysis.

In order to avoid these problems, we can take Roland Barthes' approach of finding the anchoring relationship between the text and images of the mediatic content that is the focus of our analysis, in order to read the meaning originally conceived at the time of its creation.[11] Within the dialogues said throughout the film, we can find pieces of information that allow us to make connections between the plot and the cultural frame of the creators of the movie, and therefore, attempt to recognize the semiotic code used to build meaning during the creation of the film.

Furthermore, Hall explains that within a society there will be preferred readings, common to a larger group of individuals, since members of the same community are more likely to share the same codes.[12] Given the international media exposure of American politics and its racial debate, it is possible that most people would have the same reading.

The Legend of King Arthur

In the film, Arthur's father explains that our hero's name came to him as an inspiration by the legend of King Arthur. Indeed, Aquaman's heroic journey is similar to the Arthurian legends. The need to look for a mystical weapon that only the true king can use to claim the throne—the trident is the new Excalibur—and the unlikely hero who is the rightful heir to the throne and earns his place as king, precisely by getting that mystical weapon are elements originally present in the British myth. Beyond this first level of significance and the intertextuality between Wan's film and the Arthurian literature, we believe that Aquaman is also an embodiment that represents an entire ideology.

To begin with, it is crucial to evaluate the casting decision behind the selection of Jason Momoa as Arthur Curry. Created in 1941, Aquaman has always been a white, blue-eyed blond man, but for the Warner Bros./DC Cinematic Universe's version, Momoa was chosen for the role. Some critics saw Arthur Curry's ethnicity change as a case of woke-washing, that is, "the appropriation of ethical and progressive values as a form of advertising just to make more profit while hiding the dark side of conventional capitalistic business management,"[13] in a similar way that some companies have started to use ecofriendly practices and special labeling for their products as a marketing strategy. However, the decision was mostly praised by media because it was assumed as an act of inclusiveness of non-white representation in the superhero genre. In a response to a tweet thanking Wan for making a mixed Aquaman, the director tweeted: "Arthur's the very definition of biracial. Half Surface Dweller, Half Atlantean. Momoa's mixed heritage perfectly aligns with this. As the world becomes increasingly diversified/mixed, it's great to have a character modern kids can identify with. This was an important msg for us."[14]

However, how much of this decision was under Wan's control? After all, Momoa was casted as Aquaman for Zack Snyder's films *Batman vs Superman* and *Justice League*, and according to Deborah Snyder, producer of every film of the Warner Bros./DC Cinematic Universe, she and her husband Zack chose the Hawaiian actor because they were fans of *Game of Thrones* (2011–2019) and seeing him as Khal Drogo in the HBO series, made them believe that he was the right actor to play the aquatic superhero.[15] On the other hand, when asked about how much agency he had on the casting decision, Wan said: "I was kept in the loop by DC and Warner Bros., and they really wanted my input,"[16] so he was already on board in the cinematic universe at that point. Regardless if Wan chose Momoa as part of his discourse or if he created his work using the actor's ethnicity as his base, it may be argued that Momoa's skin color goes in concordance to a discourse present in the film for which Arthur Curry needed to be a character of evidently mixed race. Thus, the Hawaiian star, Jason Momoa is perfect for the role.

In the comic books, Aquaman's origin has been rewritten several times since his first appearance in November 1941's *More Fun Comics #73*. Initially, the hero was simply a human being who obtained his abilities thanks to Atlantean knowledge discovered by his father. In 1959's *Adventure Comics #260* his origin was completely rewritten making him the offspring of the Atlantean queen Atlanna and a human lighthouse keeper named Tom Curry, making Arthur (Aquaman's real name) half human and half Atlantean. In this version, Tom Curry had another son named Orm, a human who despises his half-brother and later becomes one of his greatest archenemies, the Ocean Master. In 1989's *The Legend of Aquaman Special* (or *Aquaman Special #1*), his origin was once again rewritten, making him fully

Atlantean, but raised by Tom Curry, a human, and his blond hair, seen by the superstitious Atlanteans as a sign of a curse. In 2011's *New 52*, a relaunch of the DC Comics superhero universe, Aquaman's origin was rewritten one more time, creating a very similar story to the 1959 one, focusing on Arthur's duality. In this version, however, Orm is Atlanna's son, an Atlantean who hates Arthur and also becomes the Ocean Master.[17] James Wan's film is heavily based on this version, but there is even more emphasis on the mixed heritage of the character, as it can be seen with the change of Aquaman's appearance from white and blond to Momoa's Hawaiian heritage, and the portrayal of all the Atlanteans as Caucasians while Arthur's father is played by Temuera Morrison, a dark-skinned New Zealand Maori actor.

Let us summarize the origin of Arthur Curry in the film. His father is a human who lives in a lighthouse on the coast, and his mother Atlanna (Nicole Kidman) was the queen of Atlantis. In the words of Arthur himself, this was a forbidden love that should not have existed, but from the love of these two individuals, Aquaman was born. Being half human and half Atlantean, Arthur is called several times in the film with the pejorative term "half-breed" and even "mongrel" at an important point of the story. Mongrel is the word or name by which mestizo stray dogs that are not purebred are known. It is also a term used by the infamous organization the Ku Klux Klan and many other groups that support white supremacy, to refer to any person who is not Caucasian, but of mixed race. In fact, George Lincoln Rockwell, who became commander of the American Nazi Party, uses this word several times in his book *White Power* (1966) in a degrading way for people of mixed race, such as when he says: "At the leftwing meeting, you will see swarms of racially alien people—Jews, 'niggers' and mongrels of all sorts. Most of them will be racially repulsive."[18] It is important to stress that the use of the word Mongrel to refer to Aquaman—as was the decision to change the character's historical Caucasian race to a character that is mixed—was deliberately included to reference and incorporate the significant debate on race that is present in America today.

Purebloods vs. Half-Breeds

The political landscape of the kingdom of Atlantis is presented to us as one in which an Atlantean faction believes that humans are a danger to their society. Their ideology is that the human race has spent enough time committing atrocities against the seven underwater kingdoms. Likewise, this faction believes that, since humans are a violent and aggressive race, they will eventually attack them, so humanity represents a direct danger to the population of the seven kingdoms. Therefore, it is imperative that the kingdoms of the seas unite to attack the humans before the surface world inhabitants do so first. The leader that represents this faction is King Orm, a pure Atlantean, half-brother of Aquaman. Orm is played by a blond and extremely pale Patrick Wilson. His paleness is significant in the same way Jason Momoa's mixed race is an important element in the ideological message of the film.

On the other hand, the other Atlantean faction does not see humans as a threat. Moreover, their members see no distinction between the Atlantis population and humans. The Atlanteans originally lived on the surface until, at a time when the rest of humanity still believed that the earth was flat, the Atlanteans, out of greed, ended up at the bottom of the ocean and once there, changed until they were able to breathe under the water, acquired super strength, among other evolutionary traits. This fact is used by the members of this faction of the kingdoms of the seven seas as an argument to seek the union between Atlantis and humans. Aquaman is the person who the members of this faction have decided to place as a leader to represent them, because Arthur is half Atlantean and half human.

In order to compare Aquaman's discourse with America's contemporary debate on race, we must understand the historical moment that the United States is going through. American public opinion is polarized, engaged in a social debate about what it means to be "American" and the opinion about any individual who does not fit that definition (for a large portion of the population, this means immigrants, Black people and other people of color, Muslims, communists, vegans, etc.). The divided population is forced to take sides in the dispute over which country they live in. Is the United States a pure and proud nation of Americans or a mixed and united land of immigrants?

U.S. vs. Them

As analyzed earlier, the United States of America is engulfed in a heated debate about race, immigration and nationalism that has resulted in a growing right-wing, conservative, white supremacist and an extreme nationalist movement. Behind this growth is the perceived notion that "whiteness" is under attack and that, even though Caucasian people are still a large majority in the U.S. (76.5 percent according to the 2018 U.S. Census), white people will soon become a minority and this demographic change "will lead to an extermination of the white race and culture."[19]

This is not merely an academic discussion but instead, it has evolved into rallies, protests, public manifestations, and sadly, fatal events including cars running over people and mass shootings. On August 12, 2017, with chants saying, "you will not replace us," a white supremacy rally opposing the removal of the statue of a Confederate general from a local park, took place in Charlottesville, Virginia. A group of people decided to act and counter-protest this event, and then, a white man deliberately drove his car into the crowd, killing one protester. According to a report published by the Anti-Defamation League, "white supremacists have committed at least 73 murders since Charlottesville, 39 of which were clearly motivated by hateful, racist ideology. These numbers include the deadly white supremacist shooting rampages in Parkland, Pittsburgh, Poway and El Paso."[20]

Patrick Wood Crusius, the killer of the El Paso massacre, wrote a manifesto titled "The Inconvenient Truth About Me" before going on his shooting rampage against Latinos in a Walmart store. In the pages of this text, we can read his justification for this violent act, when he says: "this attack is a response to the Hispanic invasion of Texas. They are the instigators, not me. I am simply defending my country from cultural and ethnic replacement brought on by an invasion."[21] He also wrote about how immigrants will raise unemployment, shortage of resources, the decimation of the environment and how America would be destroyed from the inside out if this "invasion" is not stopped. In the Manifest, Wood Crusius exclaims: "America is full of hypocrites who will blast my actions as the sole result of racism and hatred of other countries, despite the extensive evidence of all the problems these invaders cause and will cause,"[22] so we can see that in his mind, his actions were justified as an act of self-preservation.

Likewise, other white supremacy and alt-right supporters believe that their nation is in danger due to non-white immigrants, Muslims, Jews, etc.,[23] echoing the general anti–Islam sentiment[24] following the 9/11 World Trade Center terrorist attacks[25] and Donald Trump's America first rhetoric,[26] anti-immigration politics[27] (aiming for the stop of illegal immigration)[28] and declarations about Latino criminal gangs[29] and Muslims.[30] They usually speak about Latino criminal gangs like MS-13 in California, drug cartel activity on the border with Mexico, and ISIS or terrorist attacks made by Islamic extremists around the world, as proof that the United States is under a real threat. To them, wanting to segregate and even attack non-white people is an act of defense. This is why they also support Trump's immigration bans and the controversial idea of building a wall between the United States and Mexico.

On the other side of the debate, even though there is support for some form of regulations on immigration, liberals have adopted a more lenient position regarding the issue.[31] They have also included Muslims in their ranks, like Democrat Congresswoman Ilhan Omar and other Muslim activists,[32] promoting the idea that Islam is not an anti–American religion.[33] One of the strongest arguments against harsh anti-immigration policies and sentiments in the United States is that America was colonized by Europe—during a time when humanity believed that the earth was flat, similarly to the moment in which Atlanteans fell to the bottom of the ocean in Wan's film—and after subsequent waves of immigration, especially throughout the early 1900s, many people tout the now popular saying that America is a nation of immigrants. Another argument of those who oppose the views of the alt-right on immigration is that, while it is true that some immigrants have shown violent and dangerous behaviors (gangs, criminals, terrorist attacks, etc.), we cannot judge all nations, beliefs and races by the acts of some of their individuals.

According to the Migration Policy Institute:

> Despite the attention Trump has dedicated to immigration matters ... the fragmented nature of the U.S. political system has made it difficult for his administration to pursue some of its most ambitious aims. Congress has thus far shown little inclination to pass major immigration legislation, and the courts have halted or slowed key initiatives, including early iterations of the travel ban and the separation of families as part of a "zero-tolerance" border policy.[34]

This has frustrated some white supremacist Trump supporters who believe that, despite the President's intentions of defending their country, the political system has allowed the Democratic Party and even some Republicans to stop Donald Trump from doing what is needed in order to make America safe. Patrick Wood Crusius calls these politicians traitors in his manifesto.[35]

Make Atlantis Great Again?

Politics and superheroes have always been connected. "Since their inception in 1938, superheroes have consistently closely followed American ideals, values, fears, and aspirations, frequently changing to adjust to their times."[36] Like Captain America, Superman, Batman and most superheroes during the golden age of comic books (1938–1956), "Aquaman's World War II adventures revolved around fighting America's real-world enemies, the Nazis and the Japanese."[37] In this way, comic books were used as a way to spread American values.

How do American politics, more specifically, the national race debate in the United States fit into Wan's *Aquaman*? King Orm represents white nationalism and the idea of the United States as a pure nation, whose citizens have an identity separate from the rest of the planet, which they must be proud of and must defend against those who do not share it. Arthur Curry, on the other hand, represents the idea of the United States as a hybrid nation, enriched by the mixture of cultures. A nation that should feel affinity for all the inhabitants of the planet because in reality we are all human. As Atlanna answers when Arthur asks her what could be greater than a king: "a hero. A King only fights for his nation. You fight for everyone," Aquaman represents the idea that the United States needs to care not only for their citizens but also, for every human being on Earth. The battle between Aquaman and his half-brother is the struggle between American extreme nationalism and the ideology of pro-immigration that rejects all nationalism. More specifically, the film is a metaphor for the debate between Conservatives and Liberals in the United States on nationalism, U.S. citizenship, immigration, security policies and foreign relations.

Signifying the conservative, right-wing, nationalist and white supremacist side there is King Orm, his ideas of blood purity and his fear mongering about the surface dwellers. Orm justifies his desire to attack and obliterate humans by stating from the beginning that he is "not trying to start a war" since "the war has already begun." He denounces that the surface dwellers have polluted the waters, poisoned the Atlanteans, killed off marine species and that they represent a danger to their society. When Aquaman confronts him for the first time, Arthur tells him that he is there to stop a maniac from destroying the world. Orm's answer to this claim is "Ah I see, and how do you plan to stop the atrocities that the surface continues to commit?" This is exactly the same sentiment that Wood Crusius expressed in his manifesto and is shared by many alt-right anti-immigration policy supporters in America. Additionally, in the movie, Orm expresses to King Nereus (Dolph Lundgren) his frustration about how he is unable to keep his kingdom safe because he is shackled by the ancient laws of Atlantis, in the same way some Trump supporters—including Wood Crusius—feel that the traitorous Senate has not allowed their president to defend America.

Furthermore, Orm is very proud of being a pureblood, a characteristic that makes him "the natural choice to lead" as he mentions to King Nereus. He believes that being anything other than a true Atlantean is something to be ashamed of. He even says: "I have been ashamed of my mother for defiling herself with a surface-dweller. Ashamed of the fact that I have a half-breed brother." This echoes the white supremacist sentiments about other races being inferior and repulsive. At one point during the film, Mera reproaches her father because even though he knows that the surface dwellers did not start the war he still wants war, to which he answers that it is time the surface knows its place in the world. In this sense, the film goes even further to suggest that some white nationalists—the Atlanteans—do not really believe that non-white people started anything, but they simply want to keep the status quo in which they maintain their superiority in numbers, privilege and power—over other races.

The film also alludes to the immigration policy in the United States. In a scene in which Mera and Aquaman are entering Atlantis, Mera speaks about the customs and border control. About how there is a giant wall surrounding Atlantis—could this be a jab at Donald Trump's idea of building a wall on the border?—and how people try to sneak into Atlantis all the time. She suggests that Atlantean security forces would not allow Arthur to enter, but that he does not need to worry since he is entering in her vehicle and she has diplomatic immunity and clearance. Later, border defense patrols eventually find Arthur and detain him for illegal entry.

Vulko and Mera signify the liberals' view on race, immigration and nationalism. They are both Atlanteans and both are connected to Orm's regime. Vulko is his Vizier and Mera is her fiancée—a politically driven marriage to create an alliance within Ocean Kingdoms, since she is the daughter of King Nereus. Vulko, who has trained Arthur since he was a child to become the next king of Atlantis, is the representation of the pro-immigration liberal while Mera starts out as a moderate conservative and evolves throughout the film by embracing liberal ideology. At first, she believes in peace among surface dwellers and Atlanteans, even though she thinks the surface is indeed inferior to the people of the oceans. Through her journey, Mera begins to understand that she was wrong to judge a place before she had seen it. She changes her mind about the humans because, although they have hurt the kingdom of the seven seas and are violent with each other, not all of them deserve the punishment of Atlantis. This lesson reaches its climax when Arthur teaches Mera that the surface world is full of beautiful things (presented to us in a slightly sweetened sequence of the couple in Italy, just before Black Manta's fight).

Mera personifies white Americans that, even though they believe accepting immigrants could harm their country (in economic, cultural or even endangering ways), they believe in the moral obligation of helping those in need. There is a scene in which she says: "my obligation is to my family and my nation and I have turned my back on both. Sometimes you have to do what is right, even if your heart aches against it." With these words, she reminds Arthur that she is first and foremost an Atlantean and she is loyal to her people, but nevertheless, she is helping to stop the war between the two species, and this is why she aides him, a half-breed, to become king.

The Half-Breed Solution

It can be argued that Wan not only accurately represents the American debate on race, nationalism and immigration on his film, but he also gives us a solution to this issue. Aquaman must become the king of Atlantis, that is, we must embrace the idea that we are all humans and nationalism is becoming more and more irrelevant in a globalized world full of constant mass immigration.

Throughout the film, Wan makes sure we understand that the mixed race of Arthur is what makes him great and fit to lead the future of Atlantis. During the first minutes of the film, after Arthur's parents meet and their relationship starts, we are shown a shot of a copy of H.P. Lovecraft's *The Dunwich Horror* (1929). The presence of this book has sparked many debates on the Internet regarding its symbolism and why the director decided to include it and make such an emphasis on it. *The Dunwich Horror* is a book about hybrid creatures and the fight between two brothers. This is clearly a foreshadowing of what is to come in the film. Moreover, a December 2018 article on *Slate Magazine* talked about how even though this was an homage from Wang, honoring Lovecraft's influence on him and his film, it was also Wan's personal spin on Lovecraft's use of hybrid creatures. The article proposed that the famous Rhode Island writer, being a xenophobic and a racist who based large part of his work on the fear of hybrid mixed creatures, would have hated the movie, because:

> Where Lovecraft saw the offspring of two societies as a sign of decay, the film positions Aquaman, born Arthur Curry (Jason Momoa), as a character whose background makes him uniquely qualified to both heal the rifts in the undersea kingdom and end the battle between the worlds of land and sea. His mixed-race background isn't a curse, as Lovecraft would no doubt have seen it, but a blessing.[38]

Wan tweeted a response to this article saying "For all the reasons you pointed out in your article, AQUAMAN would've been the ultimate horror movie/story for Lovecraft. And I'm OK with that."[39] During the film, this can be perceived in scenes like the one in which Arthur's mother explains that he is the living proof that the people from the ocean and the surface can coexist, and he can unite their worlds one day, or the scene in which Mera tells Arthur "you think you're unworthy to lead because you are from two different worlds, but that's exactly why you are worthy."

However, Wan does not imply that liberals, minorities and immigrants should fight conservatives, alt-right white supremacist and nationalists on their terms, because they would simply lose the battle. As Vulko puts it early in the movie, right after Arthur accepts to fight King Orm in a challenge for the throne: "How can you be so foolish to let Orm bait you into a fight?" "You are a formidable fighter on land, but here, you are out of your element, literally." The film proposes that giving into the fight against discrimination, hate and fear is foolish because it would legitimize those narratives and discourses. In this sense, we believe Wan's film is making a statement against the Antifa movement, a leftist group who believes that right-wing ideologies should be opposed through actions that can include the use of violence, rather than through electoral means. Antifa believes that people with hurtful ideologies should be attacked and that they should not be able to spread their ideas through any means. Under the "punch a Nazi" banner, the Antifa movement experienced a sudden rise in the United States after Charleston as a response to the growth of the white supremacy nationalism of the right.[40]

Wan's film suggests a different tactic, telling liberals, minorities and immigrants that they need to follow the route described by Mera when she tells Aquaman that he needs to show up and claim the throne to defeat Orm. They need to show up and make their existence real, their identities validated as real actors in society in order to defeat white supremacy. Not by force, as seen in the challenge scene between Aquaman and Orm, but as Vulko puts it: "by winning the hearts and minds of the Atlantean people." Simply put, Wan's film is saying that minorities need to earn the trust of the people by being activists, by being part of the community and the government, taking the throne not by force but "by winning hearts and minds" through democracy. That is, according to the director our best chance and it is why Arthur says to the oceanic monster, the Karathen: "I came because the Trident is our only hope." The Trident of the ancient King Atlan is the object that will allow Arthur to be seen as worthy of acceptance by the Atlanteans.

In this sense, Wan's solution is more aligned with Martin Luther King, Jr.'s pacifist way of solving the segregation of the Black people, than it is with Malcolm X or Angela Davis' ideas of fighting through actions that include the use of violence. Doctor King believed that "the Negro's great stumbling block in the stride toward freedom is not the White Citizens Councilor or the Ku Klux Klanner but the white moderate who is more devoted to order than to justice; who prefers a negative peace which is the absence of tension to a positive peace which is the presence of justice."[41] What King meant with this is that a peaceful way was preferable in order to gain the support of the white moderate who would disapprove of violent tactics, and this is Wan's statement in the film as well.

In the end, Aquaman arrives with the formerly lost Trident of King Atlan, commanding every aquatic species, proving that he is the legitimate king of Atlantis and worthy of the throne. The Atlanteans recognize him as king and they accept him as one of them. Consequently, the soldiers of the ocean army put down their weapons and the war ends. Subsequently, Orm decides to challenge him and Aquaman fights him again, but this time it is not under the sea, but on the surface, where he is able to defeat him. However, Arthur does not kill his brother, instead he spares his life. Then, Atlanna arrives and tells his son Orm: "you're both my children and I love you so much. But you were misguided. Your father taught you that there were two worlds. He was wrong. The land and the sea are one." Then, just before the guards take him, Arthur tells his brother: "when you're ready, let's talk." Wan is letting us know that white supremacy is not about being evil but about being misguided, and that the only way we can heal as a nation is through conversation and dialogue, but for that to happen, both sides need to be ready.

An Asian-Australian Tale

We believe it is noteworthy to mention that this movie is significant in James Wan's filmography, even though *Aquaman* is undeniably the complete opposite of his usual style. The film is the second one that he directs outside the genre for which he is renowned—the first one being the seventh installation of the *Fast & Furious* franchise—since Wan is known as a master of horror films, specifically, a very unique type of low budget horror movies that rely more on practical effects than on special effects generated by computers. The last decade trend of impressively well written, low budget horror films that include great films like *Get Out* (Jordan Peele, 2017), *Us* (Jordan Peele, 2019), *The Purge* franchise (James DeMonaco, 2013–2019) and other movies, owe their existence and success to the triumph of Wan's films *Saw* (2004) and *Insidious* (2010). However, we believe that *Aquaman* is remarkable among the works of James Wan because it tells us a lot about him and about how he feels about his own mixed-race heritage.

For director Wan, *Aquaman* is possibly not only a metaphor for the debate about immigration in the United States, but a very personal film given his own identity. Wan is an Australian of Malaysian Chinese descent, so he, like Arthur Curry, is a non-white person in a mostly white country. Moreover, even though he was born in Malaysia, he was raised in Australia and he admits that his upbringing has deeply influenced him. In a 2019 interview he said that his Australian identity is important in making him who he is today, and who he is as an artist.[42] Given that it was only after the huge success of *Aquaman* that some Australians have started recognizing Wan as an outstanding Australian director, he probably understands very well how it feels to be of mixed culture and to feel that your fellow countrymen fail to see you as one of their own.[43]

It is also important to point out that there is a subplot in *Aquaman* which also has to do with another relevant issue about race in the United States. This is the presence of the only two Black characters in the film: Black Manta and his father. These pirates can be seen as a symbol of how white people have created a system in which Black communities are disadvantaged and driven to crime as a means for survival, but that entire subplot is worthy of its own essay because it would be necessary to carefully analyze every detail, and connect the semiotic codes within the narrative to the reality of poor Black communities in the United States in order to understand the discourse and ideology behind it. Therefore, we have merely suggested this theme for another piece, by highlighting its importance and connection to the main discourse, since it brings up a discussion about how part of the violence and poverty that is pervasive in Black communities, and is pointed out by right wing conservatives to generate fear of Black people, could actually be a repercussion of a long history of white people's actions (slavery, segregation, redlining, etc.).[44] This adds a new dimension to the conversation about the interactions between different races in the United States.

Mirroring the way in which early comic book superheroes fought against Nazis and the Japanese as a symbol of American values, *Aquaman* is a captivating political film and its discourse about how minorities can end the debate on race in the United States, while emerging victorious is its most relevant and thought-provoking element. This is particularly important today since this debate has become so intense in the United States that it has led to protests, outbreaks of violence and even death. In the same way Mera and Vulko fight against Orm's regime for the recognition of Aquaman as the ruler of Atlantis, liberal Americans are living through a heated fight to end racism and white supremacy. This dispute is being fought in different ways. In some cases, through violence, riots and "punching Nazis," and in other cases, through protests, peaceful demonstrations, non-violent resistance and civil disobedience. It is also being fought through the removal and the renaming of monuments, like statues and landmarks honoring Confederate generals[45] and Ku Klux Klan leaders[46] to further cement the idea that America is a nation of immigrants that embraces individuals of all races and religions and rejects white supremacy and nationalism as fundamental American values. It can be argued that, with his film, James Wan proposes that, the only way for minorities to win is through pacifist means. He warns minorities to not engage in violence, but to earn their rightful place by gaining a political force and "win the hearts and minds" of white Americans.

Notes

1. Duncan Norris, "Aquaman and Lovecraft: An Unlikely Mating." *Lovecraft Annual* 13 (2019): 189–203, 189.
2. Doug Singsen, "Critical Perspectives on Mainstream, Groundlevel, and Alternative

Comics in the Comics Journal, 1977 to 1996." *Journal of Graphic Novels and Comics* 8, no. 2 (2016): 156–72. https://doi.org/10.1080/21504857.2016.1247372, 163.

3. N. Pope, "All the Directors and Actors Who Agree with Scorsese About Marvel." Esquire, November 20, 2019. Accessed June 29, 2020. https://www.esquire.com/uk/culture/a29545222/scorsese-marvel-directors-actors-agree-coppola-loach-cronenberg-aniston/.

4. Pope, "All the Directors and Actors Who Agree with Scorsese About Marvel."

5. Talia Smart, "Superhero Popularity in Past and Present America." *PIT Journal* 7 (2016). Accessed online June 29, 2020. https://pitjournal.unc.edu/article/superhero-popularity-past-and-present-america.

6. Klaus Bruhn Jensen and Mariano Sánchez Ventura, *La comunicación y los medios: Metodologías de investigación cualitativa y cuantitativa* (México, D.F.: Fondo de Cultura Económica, 2014), 60.

7. A. Jipson and P.J. Becker, "White Nationalism, Born in the USA, Is Now a Global Terror Threat." Public Radio International, March 20, 2019. Accessed August 23, 2019. https://www.pri.org/stories/2019-03-20/white-nationalism-born-usa-now-global-terror-threat.

8. Stuart Hall, "Encoding, Decoding." in *The Cultural Studies Reader*, edited by Simon During (London: Routledge. 1980).

9. Hall, "Encoding, Decoding."

10. I am aware of the fact that, since I lived in Florida from 2012 to 2017, and experienced Donald Trump's electoral campaign and triumph while residing in the United States, I am decoding with my own personal experience within the American cultural frame.

11. Roland Barthes, *Retórica de la imagen. Lo obvio y lo obtuso: Imágenes, gestos, voces* (Barcelona: Paidós, 1995).

12. Hall, "Encoding, Decoding."

13. Venice Diplomatic Society, "What Is Woke Washing?" Accessed September 23, 2019. https://www.venicediplomaticsociety.com/blog/what-is-woke-washing.

14. James Wan, Twitter post, December 11, 2018.

15. M. Wood, "Why Jason Momoa Was Hired as Aquaman, According to Zack Snyder," Cinemablend, October 8, 2018. Accessed October 2, 2019. https://www.cinemablend.com/news/1724049/why-jason-momoa-was-hired-as-aquaman-according-to-zack-snyder.

16. J.J. Medina, "*Aquaman*: How Much Input James Wan Had in Jason Momoa's Casting," LRM Online, December 17, 2018. Accessed October 2, 2019. https://lrmonline.com/news/aquaman-how-much-input-james-wan-had-in-jason-momoas-casting/.

17. T. Salan, "Origins Explained—Exploring the Evolution of Aquaman." SuperHero-Hype, December 19, 2018. Accessed June 13, 2020. https://www.superherohype.com/comics/429729-origins-explained-aquaman.

18. George Lincoln Rockwell, *White Power*, Place of publication not identified. Revisionist Books, 2016.

19. A. Jipson and P.J. Becker, "White Nationalism, Born in the USA, Is Now a Global Terror Threat."

20. Anti-Defamation League, "Two Years Ago, They Marched in Charlottesville. Where Are They Now?" August 8, 2019. Accessed August 23, 2019. https://www.adl.org/blog/two-years-ago-they-marched-in-charlottesville-where-are-they-now.

21. T. Feeley, "Walmart Shooter Manifesto," Information Clearing House, August 7, 2019. Accessed September 18, 2019. http://www.informationclearinghouse.info/52053.htm.

22. T. Feeley, "Walmart Shooter Manifesto."

23. Anti-Defamation League, "White Supremacists Double Down on Propaganda in 2019." February 11, 2020. Accessed June 13, 2020. https://www.adl.org/blog/white-supremacists-double-down-on-propaganda-in-2019.

24. Batem Al Atom, "Examining the Trends of Islamophobia: Western Public Attitudes Since 9/11." *Studies in Sociology of Science* 5, no. 3 (2014): 83–88.

25. Bryan D. Byers, and James A. Jones, "The Impact of the Terrorist Attacks of 9/11 on Anti-Islamic Hate Crime." *Journal of Ethnicity in Criminal Justice* 5, no. 1 (2007): 43–56. https://doi.org/10.1300/j222v05n01_03.

26. Michael Magcamit, "Explaining the Three-Way Linkage Between Populism, Securitization, and Realist Foreign Policies: President Donald Trump and the

Pursuit of 'America First' Doctrine." *World Affairs* 180, no. 3 (2017): 6–35. https://doi.org/10.1177/0043820017746263.

27. N. Martinez, "Facebook Let Trump's Campaign Run Over 2,000 Ads Referring to Immigration as an 'Invasion.'" Media Matters for America, August 5, 2019. Accessed June 13, 2020. https://www.mediamatters.org/facebook/facebook-let-trumps-campaign-run-over-2000-ads-referring-immigration-invasion.

28. P. Rucker, "'How Do You Stop These People?': Trump's Anti-Immigrant Rhetoric Looms Over El Paso Massacre." *The Washington Post*, August 4, 2019. Accessed June 13, 2020. https://www.washingtonpost.com/politics/how-do-you-stop-these-people-trumps-anti-immigrant-rhetoric-looms-over-el-paso-massacre/2019/08/04/62d0435a-b6ce-11e9-a091-6a96e67d9cce_story.html.

29. J.H. Davis and N. Chokshi, "Trump Defends 'Animals' Remark, Saying It Referred to MS-13 Gang Members." *New York Times*, May 17, 2018. Accessed June 13, 2020. https://www.nytimes.com/2018/05/17/us/trump-animals-ms-13-gangs.html.

30. J. Johnson and A. Hauslohner, "'I Think Islam Hates Us': A Timeline of Trump's Comments About Islam and Muslims." *The Washington Post*, May 20, 2017. Accessed June 13, 2020. https://www.washingtonpost.com/news/post-politics/wp/2017/05/20/i-think-islam-hates-us-a-timeline-of-trumps-comments-about-islam-and-muslims/.

31. David Macdonald, "Political Trust and Support for Immigration in the American Mass Public." *British Journal of Political Science*, 2020, 1–19. https://doi.org/10.1017/s0007123419000668.

32. S. Crabbe-Field, "Islam and Liberalism." *Democracy Journal*, June 21, 2016. Accessed June 13, 2020. https://democracyjournal.org/magazine/41/islam-and-liberalism/.

33. Saba Fatima, "Liberalism and the Muslim-American Predicament." *Social Theory and Practice* 40, no. 4 (2014): 591–608. www.jstor.org/stable/24332365. Accessed June 13, 2020.

34. S. Pierce, J. Bolter, and A. Selee, "U.S. Immigration Policy Under Trump: Deep Changes and Lasting Impacts," migrationpolicy.org, August 16, 2018. Accessed June 13, 2020. https://www.migrationpolicy.org/research/us-immigration-policy-trump-deep-changes-impacts.

35. T. Feeley, "Walmart Shooter Manifesto."

36. Richard A. Hall. *The American Superhero: Encyclopedia of Caped Crusaders in History* (Santa Barbara: Greenwood, 2019).

37. Hall. *The American Superhero: Encyclopedia of Caped Crusaders in History*.

38. K. Phipps, "*Aquaman* Owes Lot to H.P. Lovecraft. It's Also His Worst Nightmare," *Slate*, December 18, 2018. Accessed October 2, 2019. https://slate.com/culture/2018/12/aquaman-movie-hp-lovecraft-racism-miscegenation.html.

39. James Wan, Twitter post, December 18, 2018.

40. L. O'Brien, "The Nazi-Puncher's Dilemma." *HuffPost*, December 20, 2017. Accessed June 13, 2020. https://www.huffpost.com/entry/nazi-punch-antifa_n_59e13ae9e4b03a7be580ce6f.

41. M. Harriot, "In His Own Words: Martin Luther King, Jr., on White Privilege, Police Brutality, Reparations and More," The Root, January 21, 2019. Accessed August 20, 2019. https://www.theroot.com/in-his-own-words-martin-luther-king-jr-on-white-privi-1831933703.

42. E. Chew, "*Aquaman*'s James Wan Is the Most Successful Aussie Director You've Never Heard Of." Junkee, 2019. Accessed September 25, 2019. https://junkee.com/james-wan-interview/188927.

43. Chew, "*Aquaman*'s James Wan Is the Most Successful Aussie Director You've Never Heard Of."

44. Ronald W. Walters, "The Impact of Slavery on 20th- and 21st-Century Black Progress." *The Journal of African American History* 97, no. 1–2 (2012): 110–30. https://doi.org/10.5323/jafriamerhist.97.1-2.0110.

45. I. Pereira, "Here's Where Confederate Statues and Memorials Have Been Removed in the U.S." *ABC News*, June 12, 2020. Accessed June 15, 2020. https://abcnews.go.com/U.S./confederate-statues-memorials-removed-us/story?id=71200382.

46. G. Garrison, "Petition: Rename Edmund Pettus Bridge for John Lewis." *al*, January 15, 2020. Accessed June 15, 2020. https://www.al.com/news/2020/01/petition-calls-for-renaming-edmund-pettus-bridge-for-us-rep-john-lewis.html.

Works Cited

Al Atom, Basem. "Examining the Trends of Islamophobia: Western Public Attitudes Since 9/11." *Studies in Sociology of Science* 5, no. 3 (2014): 83–88.

Anti-Defamation League. "Two Years Ago, They Marched in Charlottesville. Where Are They Now?" ADL, August 8, 2019. https://www.adl.org/blog/two-years-ago-they-marched-in-charlottesville-where-are-they-now, accessed August 23, 2019.

Anti-Defamation League. "White Supremacists Double Down on Propaganda in 2019." ADL, February 11, 2020. https://www.adl.org/blog/white-supremacists-double-down-on-propaganda-in-2019, accessed June 13, 2020.

Barthes, Roland. *Lo Obvio Y Lo Obtuso: Imágenes, Gestos, Voces*. Barcelona: Paidós, 1995.

Byers, Bryan D., and James A. Jones. "The Impact of the Terrorist Attacks of 9/11 on Anti-Islamic Hate Crime." *Journal of Ethnicity in Criminal Justice* 5, no. 1 (2007): 43–56. https://doi.org/10.1300/j222v05n01_03.

Chew, Erin. "*Aquaman*'s James Wan Is the Most Successful Aussie Director You've Never Heard Of." Junkee, January 8, 2019. https://junkee.com/james-wan-interview/188927, accessed September 25, 2019.

Crabbe-Field, Sophia. "Islam and Liberalism." *Democracy Journal*, June 21, 2016. https://democracyjournal.org/magazine/41/islam-and-liberalism/, accessed June 13, 2020.

Davis, Julie Hirschfeld, and Niraj Chokshi. "Trump Defends 'Animals' Remark, Saying It Referred to MS-13 Gang Members." *New York Times*, May 17, 2018. https://www.nytimes.com/2018/05/17/us/trump-animals-ms-13-gangs.html, accessed June 13, 2020.

Fatima, Saba. "Liberalism and the Muslim-American Predicament." *Social Theory and Practice* 40, no. 4 (2014): 591–608.

Feeley, Tom. "Walmart Shooter Manifesto." Information Clearing House, August 7, 2019. http://www.informationclearinghouse.info/52053.htm, accessed September 18, 2019.

Garrison, Greg. "Petition: Rename Edmund Pettus Bridge for John Lewis." al, January 15, 2020. https://www.al.com/news/2020/01/petition-calls-for-renaming-edmund-pettus-bridge-for-us-rep-john-lewis.html, accessed June 15, 2020.

Hall, Richard A. *The American Superhero: Encyclopedia of Caped Crusaders in History*. Santa Barbara: Greenwood, 2019.

Hall, Stuart. "Encoding, Decoding." In *The Cultural Studies Reader*, edited by Simon During, 90–103. London: Routledge. 1980.

Harriot, Michael. "In His Own Words: Martin Luther King, Jr., on White Privilege, Police Brutality, Reparations and More." The Root, January 21, 2019. https://www.theroot.com/in-his-own-words-martin-luther-king-jr-on-white-privi-1831933703, accessed August 20, 2019.

Jensen, Klaus Bruhn, and Mariano Sánchez Ventura. *La Comunicación Y Los Medios: Metodologías De Investigación Cualitativa Y Cuantitativa*. México, D.F.: Fondo de Cultura Económica, 2014.

Jipson, Art, and Paul J Becker. "White Nationalism, Born in the USA, Is Now a Global Terror Threat." Public Radio International, March 20, 2019. https://www.pri.org/stories/2019-03-20/white-nationalism-born-usa-now-global-terror-threat, accessed August 23, 2019.

Johnson, Jenna, and Abigail Hauslohner. "'I Think Islam Hates Us': A Timeline of Trump's Comments About Islam and Muslims." *The Washington Post*,. May 20, 2017. https://www.washingtonpost.com/news/post-politics/wp/2017/05/20/i-think-islam-hates-us-a-timeline-of-trumps-comments-about-islam-and-muslims/, accessed June 13, 2020.

Macdonald, David. "Political Trust and Support for Immigration in the American Mass Public." *British Journal of Political Science* (2020): 1–19. https://doi.org/10.1017/s0007123419000668.

Magcamit, Michael. "Explaining the Three-Way Linkage Between Populism, Securitization, and Realist Foreign Policies: President Donald Trump and the Pursuit of 'America First' Doctrine." *World Affairs* 180, no. 3 (2017): 6–35. https://doi.org/10.1177/0043820017746263.

Martinez, Natalie. "Facebook Let Trump's Campaign Run Over 2,000 Ads Referring to Immigration as an 'Invasion.'" Media Matters for America, August 5, 2019. https://

www.mediamatters.org/facebook/facebook-let-trumps-campaign-run-over-2000-ads-referring-immigration-invasion, accessed June 13, 2020.

Medina, Joseph Jammer. "*Aquaman*: How Much Input James Wan Had in Jason Momoa's Casting." LRM Online, December 17, 2018. https://lrmonline.com/news/aquaman-how-much-input-james-wan-had-in-jason-momoas-casting/, accessed October 2, 2019.

Norris, Duncan. "Aquaman and Lovecraft: An Unlikely Mating." *Lovecraft Annual* 13 (2019): 189–203.

O'Brien, Luke. "The Nazi-Puncher's Dilemma." *HuffPost*, December 20, 2017. https://www.huffpost.com/entry/nazi-punch-antifa_n_59e13ae9e4b03a7be580ce6f, accessed June 13, 2020.

Pereira, Ivan. "Here's Where Confederate Statues and Memorials Have Been Removed in the US." ABC News, June 12, 2020. https://abcnews.go.com/US/confederate-statues-memorials-removed-us/story?id=71200382, accessed June 15, 2020.

Phipps, Keith. "Aquaman Owes a Lot to H.P. Lovecraft. It's Also His Worst Nightmare." *Slate*, December 18, 2018. https://slate.com/culture/2018/12/aquaman-movie-hp-lovecraft-racism-miscegenation.html, accessed October 2, 2019.

Pierce, Sarah, Jessica Bolter, and Andrew Selee. "U.S. Immigration Policy Under Trump: Deep Changes and Lasting Impacts." migrationpolicy.org, August 16, 2018. https://www.migrationpolicy.org/research/us-immigration-policy-trump-deep-changes-impacts, accessed June 13, 2020.

Pope, Nick. "All the Directors and Actors Who Agree with Scorsese About Marvel." *Esquire*, November 20, 2019. https://www.esquire.com/uk/culture/a29545222/scorsese-marvel-directors-actors-agree-coppola-loach-cronenberg-aniston/, accessed June 29, 2020.

Rockwell, George Lincoln. *White Power*. Place of publication not identified. Revisionist Books, 2016.

Rucker, Philip. "'How Do You Stop These People?': Trump's Anti-Immigrant Rhetoric Looms Over El Paso Massacre." *The Washington Post*, August 4, 2019. https://www.washingtonpost.com/politics/how-do-you-stop-these-people-trumps-anti-immigrant-rhetoric-looms-over-el-paso-massacre/2019/08/04/62d0435a-b6ce-11e9-a091-6a96e67d9cce_story.html, accessed June 13, 2020.

Salan, Taylor. "Origins Explained—Exploring the Evolution of Aquaman." SuperHeroHype, December 19, 2018. https://www.superherohype.com/comics/429729-origins-explained-aquaman, accessed June 13, 2020.

Singsen, Doug. "Critical Perspectives on Mainstream, Groundlevel, and Alternative Comics in the Comics Journal, 1977 to 1996." *Journal of Graphic Novels and Comics* 8, no. 2 (2016): 156–72. https://doi.org/10.1080/21504857.2016.1247572.

Smart, Talia. "Superhero Popularity in Past and Present America." *PIT Journal* 7 (2016). https://pitjournal.unc.edu/article/superhero-popularity-past-and-present-america, accessed] June 29, 2020.

Venice Diplomatic Society. "What Is Woke Washing?" February 20, 2019. https://www.venicediplomaticsociety.com/blog/what-is-woke-washing, accessed September 23, 2019.

Walters, Ronald W. "The Impact of Slavery on 20Th- and 21St-Century Black Progress." *The Journal of African American History* 97, no. 1–2 (2012): 110–30. https://doi.org/10.5323/jafriamerhist.97.1-2.0110.

Wan, James. Twitter post, December 11, 2018. ⊠ https://twitter.com/creepypuppet.

Wood, Matt. "Why Jason Momoa Was Hired as Aquaman, According to Zack Snyder." Cinemablend, October 8, 2018. https://www.cinemablend.com/news/1724049/why-jason-momoa-was-hired-as-aquaman-according-to-zack-snyder, accessed October 2, 2019.

A Gendered Cinema of Violence and Horror

Make Technology Suffer

The Hypermasculine in Death Sentence, Furious 7 *and* Macgyver

Fernando Gabriel Pagnoni Berns

One of the most spectacular scenes in James Wan's *Death Sentence* (2007) occurs when Nick Hume (played by Kevin Bacon) is hunted down by a gang of ruthless criminals. Intent on killing him, a deadly game of hide-and-seek plays out on the highest floor of a five-story parking garage. During a brutal fight with Jamie (Dennis Keiffer), a car with both Nick and Jamie in it starts to move toward the edge of the parking lot's upper floor. Jamie, trapped by the seatbelt, dies when the car drops down to the streets below. Nick saves himself by jumping from the car through the shattered windshield. The scene is re-interpreted in Wan's *Furious 7* (2015), with Brian O'Conner (Paul Walker) replacing Kevin Bacon. There is a huge mountainside chase (one of the film's highpoints) which climaxes with Brian's spectacular escape from a bus that is teetering over the edge of a precipice. He runs up the side of the vehicle as the bus plunges off the cliff.

In both scenes, the (hyper)masculinity of both Nick and Brian overcome physics. It can be argued that Wan had *Death Sentence* in mind when directing his own take on the popular *Fast & Furious* franchise. In fact, *Death Sentence* may be read as the dark reflection of *Furious 7*. In *Death Sentence*, (anti)hero Nick Hume is forced to fight against a brotherhood of men who serve as the film's main villains. In Wan's *Furious 7*, Deckard Shaw (Jason Statham) is the main villain, a lonely and ruthless assassin who fights the brotherhood of male heroes. Each film is an exact reversal of the other. Yet, both stories share similarities: on one hand, both films have a masculine kinship as a form of homosociability and, on the other, a hypermasculine domination of technology epitomized by car and gun culture.

This recurrence to male kinship and dominance of technology as a form of masculine empowerment continues in Wan's pilot for the new iteration of the popular TV series *MacGyver* (CBS, 1985–1992). Wan serves as co-producer of the series, while directing the show's pilot. In this scenario of hypermasculinity and domination of technology, it is not surprising that Wan shifted the main lead, "Mr. Wizard" Angus MacGyver (Lucas Till) from being an unpretentious man (as in the original) to a debonair "ladies' man" in the remake. Furthermore, his relationship with Jack Dalton (George Eads) emphasizes a male bonding completely absent in the original series.

In his non-horror films, Wan depicts male bonding enacted through two main lines: on one hand, as spectacle of hypermasculinity, a term we will define later in this essay. On the other hand, and in connection with the above, the spectacle of hypermasculinity takes place vis-à-vis with a strong mastering of technology. This mastering includes both car culture, heavily associated with issues of hypermasculinity[1], and guns culture.

Amid a new milieu that questions notions of hypermasculinity as toxic, unattractive, misogynistic and passé, Wan evokes the hyper male as a form of cinematic spectacle. He does so reacting against the "softening" of masculinities[2] taking place in the last years, when the intricate nexus of discourses, identities, and notions of power surrounding men's subjectivities were discussed and rescued from fixity. It is not as simple as naming Wan as a misogynistic director; however his work does emphasize how social discourses on masculinity still circulate and are still linked to forms of technology coded as "brute" or "hyper," such as big guns or "muscle cars." Wan rescues this association and turns it into a visual spectacle, offering viewers and scholars alike the channel to discuss the construction of masculinities.

The director returns to the 1980s to bring back an era in which to be a "man" means an experience shared by those who "properly" belong. In this essay, I will discuss how the hypermasculine ethos is coded through an extreme mastering of technology—meaning, car and gun culture—in *Death Sentence*, *Furious 7* and *MacGyver*'s pilot.

Hypermasculinity and Male Kinship

It is widely known that such terms as masculine and feminine are gendered and socially constructed categories rather than manifestations of some "essence" attached to biological sex. This essay will analyze men in relationship with issues of hypermasculinity; thus, it is important to acknowledge that the dominant form of masculinity was, up to the 1990s, conceptualized through the notion of "hegemonic masculinity," a term mostly incapable of dealing with real masculinities except in negative ways: masculinity is socially constructed as what is not. The concept of hegemonic masculinity is derived from Raewyn Connell who points to masculinity as a social and discursive construction, rather than a set of given (i.e., "essential") biological facts. Masculinity, as a cultural text, is produced through a "reproductive arena" meaning, "the various practices, performances, and social processes that get culturally attached to reproductive differences."[3] For Connell, hegemonic masculinity legitimates "the dominant position of men and the subordination of women"[4] or, more specifically, the dominant position *of certain men*. Even if the concept has been "historically and contextually mobile,"[5] hegemonic masculinity "refers to the most culturally exalted forms of masculinity configurations that justify dominance and inequality"[6] such as superior rational intellect, emotional control or strength, all issues perceived as forms of superiority over women. Expelled from hegemonic masculinity are "less manly" things such as artistic taste, need of care or the showing of feelings, thus sustaining a clear line dividing men from their "weaker" counterpart, women and/or emasculated (symbolically castrated/effeminate) men.

Within the limits of hegemonic masculinity lies the concept of "hypermasculinity," that is to say, the excess of masculine attributes and the idea that ideal manhood resides "in the exercise of force to dominate others."[7] Hypermasculinity exaggerates the "essential" masculine attributes such as force, musculature, aggression, violence and a reckless inclination to danger.

Arguably, this was the masculinity that prevailed in the "macho" 1980s in the bodies and personas of Sylvester Stallone and Arnold Schwarzenegger, who helped to "man up" America. With "cowboy" Ronald Reagan as President, America was ready for a new period of hypermasculinity after two decades of "disorder" as the 1960s and the 1970s seemingly were. Stallone and Schwarzenegger's characters, with their bulging bodies, sent the message that America has "lost its masculine edge in the peace movement of the late 60s" and they, together with Reagan's "macho" image,[8] will re-direct the nation toward a brand new era of masculinity and order.

Masculinity, so related to violence in the 1980s, seemed to change from the spectacle of hypermasculinity toward a more "feminized" man in the 1990s.[9] The "hard bodies" of the Reaganomic era such as those of Stallone or Schwarzenegger were replaced by the suave figure of the yuppie in thrillers such as *Pacific Heights* (John Schlesinger, 1990) or *Sliver* (Phillip Noyce, 1993). The neoliberal thinking tried to reconfigure itself and found its place within this new decade through new forms of masculinity and discussion on violence, both in and out of the screen. The new millennium further brought new discussions on gender, especially after the advent of what is currently timidly called the "Fourth Wave Feminism." The replacement of fixed notions of what it takes to being a woman or a man are brought to the spotlight and widely discussed to access to more nuanced versions of the gender binary. Masculinity is more in flux than ever before, lifting some of the social pressure exerted upon men to act "manly" enough. Macho versions of masculinity are increasingly being viewed negatively, as these conceptions are related to violence, misogyny and toxicity.[10]

It is in this new scenario that James Wan recuperates the bodies and hypermasculinity of the 1980s.[11] Rather than doing so in a parodic way that read hypermasculinity through the lens of male ageing as *The Expendables* (Sylvester Stallone, 2010; Simon West, 2012) does, Wan brings back the macho in an unaltered way. Jason Statham (who also worked on *The Expendables'* franchise), Dwayne "The Rock" Johnson, Paul Walker and Vin Diesel evoke the bodies and personas of Stallone, Schwarzenegger, Chuck Norris or Jean-Claude Van Damme so popular in the 1980s. There is an exception, however: unlike the characters made famous by Schwarzenegger or Stallone such as Cobra, Rambo, the Terminator or Rocky, this new iteration on hypermasculinity strongly prefers male bonding and masculine kinship. In this setting, car culture and gun culture work as scenarios which allow the perfect circulation of male bonding without the main risk that comes with male-to-male kinship: the threat of homoeroticism or suspicious homosociability. Symbols heavily associated with masculinity, especially with hypermasculinity such as cars and/or big guns serve as a way to, at least to some extent, "clear the air" of any suspicion of homosexuality.

In her classic text *Between Men: English Literature and Male Homosocial Desire* (1992), Eve Kosofsky Sedgwick focuses on the existence of homosexual desire evident through different forms of male bonding. Sedgwick identifies different forms of male kinship that are inextricably linked to societal and cultural fears of homosexuality, the latter hanging upon any form of male-to-male relationship like a haunting. She argues that the boundaries between the social and the sexual are never entirely clear and are continually in a flux state. The dangerous passage from the homosocial to the homosexual must be disrupted to preserve "healthy" notions of masculinity; thus radical forms of dispelling any form of the homoerotic is required.[12] Hypermasculinity is the formula, as exacerbates the heterosexual masculine, even if the displays of oiled bulging muscles and broad shoulders could be interpreted as queer topography.[13] Still, the adding of layers of hypermasculinity tries to preserve within the boundaries of heterosexuality any practice of male bonding.

Recent studies define kinship as the analysis made on western human binding practices and how they are imagined and performed in society and culture. Michael Kimmel and Amy Aronson describe male bonding as a "distinct psychological and social attachment based on the parties' shared maleness" that differentiates from simple friendship via "a somewhat restricted axis of connectedness."[14] David Jackson, evoking John Stoltenberg, further adds that "male bonding is how men learn from each other that they are entitled under patriarchy to power in the culture. Male bonding is how men get that power, and male bonding is how it is kept."[15] Larry May notes that "male bonding is made easier because there is an 'Other' that males can bond 'against'"[16] and that this other is, mostly, the stereotype of the "female." The latter, however, may be read as a little reductionist, as the masculine can be constructed in negative ways with many other things that are not the female (for instance, gay men, non-human animals or, as we will see, technology). What remains crucial is that other thing (human or non-human) has to be coded as inferior or sub-par somehow. Following the latter, critical kinship studies seek "to examine how technologies of human kinship are part and parcel of the construction of humanness (which is positioned in opposition to those who are not considered human)."[17] In other words, human relationship between peers is defined, in part, on exclusion, on what is either not human or less-than-human. This "lack" of humanity has historically involved women, the LGBT community, Afro-Americans, animals and, of course, technology. Thus, the human must hold a grip on all things coded "sub-par" to show potency.

The latter is especially urgent for male communities, culturally obliged as they are to recurrently assert their right to power. The mastering of technology indicates not just the affirmation of masculinity, but the enthroning of hypermasculinity. In this scenario, car culture and gun culture add complex layers to the construction of hegemonic masculinity. On the one hand, technological productions such as guns and cars are phallic extensions of male psyche. As British theorist Richard Dyer explained, "one of the striking characteristics about penis symbols is the discrepancy between the symbols and what penises are actually like. Male genitals are fragile, squashy, delicate things."[18] However, when represented in popular culture, "the soft, vulnerable charm of male genitals is evoked as hard, tough, and dangerous. It is not flowers that most commonly symbolize male genitals but swords, knives, fists, guns."[19] Guns, especially big ones, still stand for extensions of male embodiment. If gun culture has been exaggerated to sell products, "it continues to shape American culture and masculinity."[20] Same thing with cars, still a particularly salient symbol of masculinity and also a "significant aspect in television and film."[21]

On the other hand, the relationship of masculinity with car or gun culture is not, in James Wan's cinema, predicated upon simple cohabitation. The hypermasculine subject must show a complete control and management of the technology of guns and cars. These material objects were not made to be just appreciated or caressed. This kind of relationship indicates common masculinity. The abuse and even destruction of guns and cars is what may be read as hypermasculine. It is amid the wreckage that the heart of hypermasculinity shines as truly superior to other forms of masculinity.

The latter is the kind of relationship that the hyper macho characters in Wan's films share with technology. They love it but, at the same time, they destroy it at the end of the scene. Doing less will mean *care and sentiments* for inanimate objects, something foreign for people like the brotherhood of *Furious 7* or *Death Sentence*. Like the (hyper)men of the 1980s, technology is an extension of male power to make destruction but, also, the same objects of consumption are not free from being destroyed. Understanding guns and cars as objects invested with gender codes (and riffed with destruction) through which men create intimate bonding can also help comprehend men's lure to narratives of hypermasculinity.

Male Kinship Amid the Wreckage: Gun Culture

Death Sentence opens with a montage of scenes of the Hume family's life as shown through their home videos. The collage, which encompasses different times in the everyday of the family, is very telling regarding gender binarism. Nick is teaching his sons Brendan and Lucas (still little kids), how to be good in sports (hockey) and how to ride a bicycle. As a way to encourage his kids, Nick is seen riding the bicycle with just one leg, the other out of the pedal and artistically elevated in a form of showmanship. Nick is showing his kids (and audiences alike) his complete mastering of the bicycle. When Lucas, not as good as his father, falls over in the grass, viewers hear a female voice soothing the little boy. The voice belongs to Helen Hume (Kelly Preston), Jordan's mother and Nick's wife. While the man of the house teaches "manly" practices such as sports, the home video shows Helen comforting her boys or teaching Lucas how to paint with brushes. The collage officiating as introduction sustains the common misconception that projects on fathers the passing of knowledge on sports while women transmit "sensible" practices such as art. By request of Helen, Nick applauds his son's efforts on painting; however, he quickly asks him (with a note of mockery in his voice), "what the heck is it?," a subtle form of downplaying the importance of artistic practices. Another cut reveals Brendan as a teenager (Stuart Lafferty) after winning a hockey competition, proudly showing his trophy to the camera (and to his father holding it). As teenagers, Brendan and Lucas (Jordan Garret) show their mutual love and respect through innocent banter and mild insults. Neither Nick nor Helen approves of this behavior, but they do not seem to give much thought to this kind of brotherly kinship, nonetheless. When the brothers get up from the dinner table, Nick indicates they must take out the empty plates. They do so, but only to give the dishes to their mother: for in the Hume family, teenage boys do not rinse plates.

Brendan is good at hockey and his father is proud of him. When Brendan mentions to his father his intention of attending university in Canada, Nick is reluctant: "Canada is far." Brendan mentions that both Nick and Helen will still have Lucas with them. Nick dry answer's is telling: "now there's a comfort." Nick is quick to point out that his answer is just a joke, but the gag reveals deep seated gender anxieties within the father: his "chum," his partner in bonding is Brendan, the kid who excels in sports. Lucas also plays hockey, but has been established earlier in the film that he is not as good as his older brother and, as such, he is coded emasculated (at least, in his father's eyes). Lucas addresses this fact when he mentions to his family that, since he is not a good sportsman, neither Nick nor Helen should lose their time taking him to hockey practices. After admitting that Canada and hockey may be a good choice, Nick tells Brendan to keep the secret: "Don't tell mom." At this earlier stage, the female has been already excluded from bonding.

Masculine kinship is reflected darkly in the gang of thugs that will assault and kill Brendan one night when both father and son stop at a gas station. After Brendan gets in the drugstore to buy foodstuff, a gang of thugs raid the place. Brendan is killed even when the boy is paralyzed and offers no resistance. Actually, his killing is part of a rite of initiation into manhood: to be considered as part of the gang of hypermasculine thugs, young Joe Darley (Matthew O'Leary) must kill someone. Anyone. If not, Joe does not belong. "Do this or you're not one of us. Do it," pushes one of the hooded thugs. Brendan is the victim, his death just the ticket into masculine kinship. As Nick simply puts it; "Are you saying that Brendan was killed so that some asshole could feel more like a man?" The other members of the gang consider Joe now "a man" and "an adult" after the killing and cheer him as a hero. After a truncated trial, Heco (Hector Atreyu Ruiz), the gang's leader (his Latin, muscular body filled with tattoos, another form of male/tribal kinship), expresses how proud he is of Joe. Before the murder, Nick told his son how proud he was of him (regarding Brendan's status as a sportsman). Both young boys, Brendan and Joe, made their "fathers" proud through the display of hard masculinity.

After the jury declares Joe "not guilty," the film begins to narrate Nick's ascension to hypermasculinity as he becomes a vigilante who makes his own justice. The first thing he does after the trial is rummage through his tool shack searching for a weapon to kill Joe. Nick evaluates the potentialities that each gardening tool (each one framed in close shot) has of becoming a deadly weapon. Finally, he chooses a rusty hunting knife, an item made to kill or, at least, wound. Nick is still unable to master technology right to the point of turning it completely in his favor; at the end, gardening tools remains inoffensive home appliances and Nick kills Joe with the knife. It is after this brutal murder that the ascension of Nick to hypermasculinity really starts.

Nick rises from his pain to exert power upon a network of inanimate objects that become extensions of his hatred and increasing hypermasculinity. It may be valuable to point here to what philosopher Bruno Latour calls *quasi humans* objects.[22] Because humans are always immersed within networks of actants (objects of technology that serve to interact with the world), what is human or nonhuman cannot be clearly pointed. There are not pure subjects or pure objects. Instead, Latour argues, we live in a world populated by quasi-subjects and quasi-objects. Latour analyzes the bumper-sticker phrase "Guns don't kill people, people kill people." For him, a person with a gun is a different kind of subject than without it. And the gun becomes, also, different: it turns to be an extension of the (human) desire to hurt, to kill or, at least, to warn or scare. Thus, the gun becomes a "quasi-human" actant, an object which has lost some of its inertness to be imbedded now with human subjectivity. "The gun is no longer the gun-in-the-armory or the gun-in-the-drawer or the gun-in-the pocket, but the gun-in-your-hand, aimed at someone who is screaming."[23] The gardening tools remains gardening tools because Nick is yet unable to turn them into murder weapons. They resist him, so he chooses something basic as a knife, even when he weighted the potential of each item before deciding for the obvious.

Agency over the objects becomes powerful after Joe's murder. Nick, at first, is traumatized; but as the gang threatens his family first and later kills his wife, Nick starts to use any inanimate object as a weapon, the material world around him becoming an extension of his rage, desire for vengeance and fear. He uses a car's door to slam the face of one of the thugs hunting him through the city and later traps the same man with a seatbelt before driving the car toward the edge of the five-story parking garage. In the middle of a home invasion, Nick defends himself with a baseball bat and pulls the rug from under one of his assailants, making him fall. Later, he uses one of the doors of his house to slam the face of one of the assailants the same way he used the car's door before.

It may be argued that using home appliances as murder/defense weapons is a well-known trope in many horror/thriller films. Indeed, the hero turning the tables on his/her attackers is part of the narrative of genre cinema. However, Nick's self-confidence increases exponentially after the killing of his son and, especially, after the killing of his wife later in the film. Nick awakes from his brief coma (after being shot by the criminals) with a new confidence acquired overnight. He suddenly navigates the criminal underworld with ease, slamming (again) the head of criminals on bar counters.

What is more striking, however, is the easiness in managing guns that Nick has acquired. For a man laboring in life insurances, Nick is depicted during the film's climax as a hyper-macho who knows how to shoot with rifles and revolvers like a professional. The final sequence of *Death Sentence* depicts Nick battling the gang amid an abandoned building; Nick rolls through the floor avoiding bullets, shoots from distance with excellent aim and kills each different member of the gang the same way Stallone or Schwarzenegger did in the 1980s. It seems that objects, especially guns, became "quasi-human" actants, extensions of Nick's body and fury. It remains unclear if the objects subsume to him due his hypermasculine persona or if his macho prowess is reached thanks to the use of objects. The distinction is impossible as both, Nick's new hypermasculinity and the mastering of technology go inextricably hand in hand in the film. The gore spilled in this last sequence (which rivals any horror film) legitimates Nick's position as hyper male. Not even a gunshot tearing apart some of his neck slows him down, as if the mild-mannered man is now protected by some kind of super strength.

There are two implications on the film's last scene; first, that even if severely bleeding, Nick survives. He makes it home and watches home videos while sitting on the couch, where he is found by detectives. Second, that he has succeeded in "passing" some of his hypermasculinity to his "weak" son Lucas. Detective Wallis (Aisha Tyler), the woman in charge of investigating Brendan's death, says to Nick that his son, who was in a coma after being shot, is stirring and moving now. He will be fine.

Gun culture appears prominently through the film, mostly in a vis-à-vis relationship with car culture. The man leading the gang (and, also, Joe's father) is Bones Darley (John Goodman), who uses his body car shop as a façade to sell guns to anyone who can pay the price. Through both, Bones and the gang, car culture and gun culture collapse together as scenarios for displays of hypermasculinity and male kinship.

Male Kinship Amid the Wreckage II: Car Culture

With *Death Sentence* in his filmography, Wan was an apt choice for another sequel in the *Fast & Furious* series even when the film seemed at odds with his previous work as a horror director. *Furious 7*, like the other films in the popular franchise, is loaded with explosions, gunfire and technological destruction. And, like the other films in the franchise, Wan's addition is based on hypermasculinity.

Furthering the parallels with *Death Sentence*, *Furious 7* begins with images of mild-mannered masculinity. Brian O'Conner, one of the main heroes of the franchise, has been emasculated as depicted in the beginning of the film. After a prologue where Deckard Shaw swears vengeance at the side of his hospitalized brother's bed (a scene that mirrors that of Nick Hume swearing vengeance at the side of his hospitalized son's bed, thus furthering the parallel between the two films),[24] a conversation between Dominic Toretto (Vin Diesel) and Letty Ortiz (Michelle Rodriguez), and a close shot of a young woman's behind (a visual signpost that tells audiences they are watching a "macho" movie), the film cuts to Brian at home with his family. The montage emphasizes the juxtaposition of "weak" masculinity against hypermasculinity. The sequence begins with a close shot of Brian's eyes. He looks concentrated in what he is doing: his hands gripping the steering wheel, his foot balancing on the accelerator pedal, Brian is ready to start the car and run through the streets. Indeed, Brian pushes down the accelerator and moves the car … just mere meters, only the necessary amount to park at the front of his son Jack's kindergarten. Through the montage, Brian did fall from the macho ideal of race daredevil to the emasculated image of paternal figure taking his little kid to school. This emasculation is aggravated by the car: rather than subsuming to Brian's will, the car traps him inside. He does not know how to open the doors and struggles with the seatbelt. Unlike the race cars he drove in the past, this new car is a "family-friendly" one, meaning, big space at the back and not that much capacity for speed. The young teacher receiving Jack mentions that, eventually, Brian will understand how the car actually works. Brian's statement, "I fears so," is a clear reference to his disgust or, better say, fear of adapting to home life. Even if happy with his wife and kid, it is clear that Brian feels he does not belong anymore with the gang of (hypermasculine) friends; further, he misses that life. He is now trapped into marital status and the new car is an extension of his feeling of entrapment.

Brian's wife, Mia Toretto (Jordana Brewster) mentions to his brother Dominic that life in family is just a "deadweight" for Brian. Brian hates the tranquility of marriage. Interestingly, it is not so much the cars that he misses most but, according to Mia, "the bullets." Through Mia's words, car culture and gun culture collapse together once again, both framing practices of hypermasculinity bonding. Unlike cars and guns, both easily controllable, family life is foreign to a "testosterone" man like Brian. When his infant son Jack throws a toy car through the air, the kid yells that his car "flies." Brian takes the toy from the floor and teaches his son that cars do not fly, but immediately corrects himself: "this did fly." To any member of the gang of heroes of the *Fast & Furious* franchise, objects are always performing feats foreign to their nature as inanimate things. When Mia's house explodes due to a bomb sent by Deckard Shaw, Brian successfully protects his son by sheltering him within the car. In Brian, Dominic and Luke Hobbs' (Dwayne Johnson) hands, cars always become other things, extensions of their capacity to protect, attack or perform their excessive masculinity. After the explosion, Jack is taken from the car unharmed.

After destroying Brian's house, Deckard makes his presence known to every member of the brotherhood. This leads to increasingly violent car chases, as Dominic and Brian, together with Letty, roam the world looking for Ian. The car scenes comprise the majority of the film. As usual in the franchise, the cars violate any speed limits and any traffic lights, get smashed into each other in spectacular (and slow motion) fashion and resist any kind of torture or abuse exerted upon them, including being dropped from an airplane. In most of the scenes, the cars become, at the end, a mess of glass and steel. Unlike the cars, Brian, Dominic and Luke come out from the wreckage mostly unscathed. The men of *Furious 7* do not only drive cars at high speed and in reckless ways (all signposts of masculinity according to traditional discourses). They have mastered technology right up to the point of turning cars into toys to be destroyed, shattered and punished. The male bonding is predicated upon this sameness, as all the men use, abuse, and destroy their toys at the end of each action scene. They not only dispel any suspicion of homoeroticism through the masculine practices of car/gun culture, but they also reaffirm their manly superiority exaggerating their mastering of technological things.

The only hero hurt in the film, Luke, is hospitalized after a brutal fight with Deckard. These are hypermachos confronting each other using their bare fists. There is no technology involved, so there are no "things" involved. Both men are leveled. Dominic visits Luke at the hospital and mocks his friend after noticing that Luke is eating Jell-O. The soft consistency of the dessert seems to parallel Luke's new soft condition as an emasculated man. Still, the show Luke is watching on the TV set in his room is the 1970s classic *The Incredible Hulk* (CBS, 1977–1982): the screen depicts Lou Ferrigno (as Hulk) growling at the camera, his green muscles showing through his tattered clothes. Like Hulk, Luke's big muscles are showing through the plaster and bandages, as he keeps his wide chest naked. It is an incredible man watching another incredible man, the viewer admiring the joint hypermasculinity through a mediated bonding. At the end of the film, Luke will get up from his bed in the hospital and fight Deckard again, now to win.

Hypermasculinity permeates the whole film. One of the film's highlights is the battle sequence taking place in Abu Dhabi, in the United Arab Emirates. There, Dominic and Brian steal a car containing a hacking device they need to locate Deckard through the world. After a fight against security guards, both men steal the rare and expensive car, a Lykan HyperSport. It is interesting to note the prefix "hyper" again in the name of the machine. The Lykan HyperSport is a car that Dominic caresses while lamenting that such a beautiful piece of technology is hiding at the top of a building rather than running free through the streets. This reveals sentiments that code the sports car as something alive, an animal/human-like creature that has its (his?) own needs. Like any living creature, it needs to run free through the sun-drenched desert. Security guards chase Dominic and Brian after they steal the car and, when cornered on one of the highest floors of the building without further place to go, they drive the car through the windows. Rather than dropping to their death, they jump into a nearby building. After discovering that the brakes do not work, they jump into yet another building. The towers in question are an immense five-tower skyscraper complex called Etihad Towers. Three of the five-tower complex are literally violently "penetrated" by the "hyper" sports car driven by the two hypermasculine men. The car turned into a phallic weapon; the towers are violated one by one. To emphasize the mastering that both men have upon technology, the hyper car ends the scene literally transformed into metal trash after falling from one of the buildings. Dominic and Brian jump from the car safely; they are unharmed with just some dust covering their expensive tuxedoes. Like the men, the car was coded "hyper" but, unlike the duo, the car becomes wreckage. The car is a "quasi-human" object but its human-like quality has to be halted to highlight Dominic and Brian's total mastering of technology, an issue that elevated them to the category of hyper-macho. The caressed car returns to its proper state at the end.

    Car culture is not solely highlighted in *Furious 7*. The first sign of the gang of thugs that will kill Brendan in *Death Sentence* is visually depicted with cars. Nick is driving home with his son when he spots a black car moving recklessly through the streets. The night is pitch black and the car has the front lights turned off. Furthermore, the black car has red flames painted upon the hood, a sign of car culture and a heavy contrast with Nick's (boring) gray car. Reading about causatives of premature deaths in men, Nick learns that, together with smocking and mental stress, "driving cars" is measured a high risk. The scene takes place immediately after the title credits, so Nick is still considered the perfect father with the perfect family and the epitome of the mild-mannered citizen. "Driving cars" is a practice associated with risk and, as such, hypermasculine. It is ironic, then, that in *Death Sentence*'s climax, Nick gets into the gang's lair driving his car through the front doors, even taking one of the goons with him (and destroying the car in the act).

    Male bonding and the mastering of technology is evoked, once again, in the pilot episode that Wan helmed for *MacGyver*. If the interest of Wan in MacGyver may be baffling for some people, as the director is widely recognized by his horror background, the series opens the space for one of the director's trademarks: visual displays of hypermale bonding and the mastering of technology. Unlike the original *MacGyver*, this new iteration of the hero prefers to work within a brotherhood (what has led critics to call this remake "MacGyver: Impossible"[25] an allusion to the popular TV show *Mission: Impossible* [CBS, 1966–1973]). The new MacGyver is a brilliant young man who is recruited by a branch of the government that operates secretly. Like in the old show, MacGyver is a genius improvising with the materials at hand, turning any innocent item into a weapon. Basically, this is what Nick, with less sophistication, does in *Death Sentence*. Unlike the previous incarnation, the pilot leaves clear how manly (and heterosexual) the new MacGyver is. In one of the pilot's first scenes, MacGyver is talking with his girlfriend and fellow agent Nikki Carpenter (Tracy Spiridakos): a brief flashback inserted at the middle of the conversation shows MacGyver making love to Nikki against the sophisticated computers she uses to track criminals. MacGyver says, "There's no one better on a keyboard," and then the episode suddenly cuts to them making love on her work computer, producing a visual disruption that downplays Nikki's skills as a hacker.

Angus MacGyver is the logical followup to the kind of men depicted in the previous two films. The pilot's first scene begins with MacGyver arriving at a high-society party driving a luxurious car which seems lifted from the *Fast & Furious* franchise. As MacGyver still prefers to make his own weapons rather than using firearms, gun culture is replaced by the mastering that he has upon any inanimate object, a feature that is the trademark of the character. Paper clips, powders, liquids and tin foil become bombs while stainless plates become weapons; every object "softens" into MacGyver's hands to become something else, something that only MacGyver can see. Arguably, this feature was part of the charm of the character's previous incarnation, but his propensity for "showing off" via expensive cars and clothes, and an active sexual life codes this new version as a unique persona closer to Dominic Torello or the hypermen of *Death Sentence* than an evocation of the old character. Furthermore, this new incarnation has his own brotherhood: MacGyver does not work alone, but together with his "chump" Jack Dalton, who had shared with him a time in the military and who now "guards his back." Their bonding evokes the gangs where hypermasculinity circulated freely in *Death Sentence* and *Furious 7*. The last scene of the pilot depicts MacGyver and Dalton consolidating their bonding with the adding of hacker Riley Davis (Tristin Mays) within the circle.

In these scenarios of hypermasculinity, women hold a position of authority but clearly marginal and closer to passivity. Riley is a hacker and her character mirrors that of Megan (Nathalie Emmanuel) in *Furious 7*. Like men, women also master technology, but their relationship with the technological is less complex: first, their task is more passive, as hacking involves patience, little physical movement and calmness, all characteristics commonly associated with femininity. Second, the computers at their hands serve exactly as computers rather than becoming something else. Thus, computers resist being subsumed into something else while a stainless plate becomes a weapon at MacGyver's skillful hands or a car an arm of destruction for Nick or Brian. Three, the computers are not smashed by the female users at the end of each scene, as the women are completely dependent on these technological devices. Thus, women are marginalized: they do not completely belong to the brotherhood created through male bonding (as they are only marginal in the adventures); neither have they had the capacity to turn the objects into extensions of their selves. Meanwhile, even the God's Eye, a specialized hacking device that the government asks Dominic and Brian to find in *Furious 7* is described as a "tracer on steroids." Everything the men touch or want somehow becomes hyper.

Conclusions

In one of the last scenes of the *MacGyver* pilot, the leading hero escapes from a jeep within seconds before the car explodes in pieces. Men escaping from cars at the last minute are a common staple in James Wan's films. At the end of each escape scene, the car is always destroyed. The driver, however, leaves unharmed. This answers social and cultural construction on manhood since "media culture, gun culture, gang culture, sports, and military culture produce ultramacho men as an ideal."[26] Wan's version of masculinity, however, does not rest solely on the basis of technology defining part of masculinity. The existence of expensive, luxurious and strong pieces of technology works not only to serve men (as computers work to serve women), but to be completely destroyed at the end by them. Thus, (1) the machines serve men complying with their functions, (2) become something else (like weapons) after becoming quasi-human objects and are (3) finally destroyed as a material conclusion of the hypermasculinity of their users and the reaffirmation of the little value held by all considered "things." The abuse and destruction of technology as an issue shared by hypermen results from an anxiety about maleness: social, material and cultural contexts are increasingly being co-opted by technology. Masculinity, as overpowering, interacts with this new world but just to some extent; at the end, brute force and the material body and the hard flesh prevails, while cars are destroyed and guns offer no resistance or complexity for men. There is a fascination and revulsion toward these "quasi-human" objects, and the "human" part must be obliterated, "thingified" at the end.

Evoking the 1980s, Wan imagines a world where hypermasculinity lies at the center. His filmic universe offers a recreation, an ideological bubble free from the constrains of political correctness of the new millennium, where there is a general rejection of the notion that masculinities can be conceived of exclusively as relationships of power and taming. In this scenario, Wan offers viewers a time capsule that works as an anachronism at the same time while pointing to the still current ways in which manhood is imagined in relation to technology.

NOTES

1. Karen Lumsden, *Boy Racer Culture: Youth, Masculinity and Deviance* (New York: Routledge, 2013).
2. Eric Anderson and Rory Magrath, *Men and Masculinities* (New York: Routledge, 2019), 101.
3. C.J. Pascoe and Tristan Bridges, "Exploring Masculinities: History, Reproduction, Hegemony, and Dislocation," in *Exploring Masculinities: Identity, Inequality, Continuity, and Change*, ed. C.J. Pascoe and Tristan Bridges (New York: Oxford University Press, 2016), 12.
4. Raewyn Connell, *Masculinities* (Cambridge: Polity Press, 2005), 77.
5. Pascoe and Bridges, *Exploring Masculinities*, 18.
6. *Ibid.*
7. Varda Burstyn, *The Rites of Men: Manhood, Politics, and the Culture of Sport* (Toronto: University of Toronto Press, 2000), 192.
8. Patrice Oppliger, *Wrestling and Hypermasculinity* (Jefferson, NC: McFarland, 2004), 55.
9. Hilary Neroni, *Violent Woman: Femininity, Narrative, and Violence in Contemporary American Cinema* (Albany: SUNY Press, 2005), 174.
10. See Valerie Frankel's excellent edited collections *Fourth Wave Feminism in Science Fiction and Fantasy*, Vol. I and II (Jefferson, NC: McFarland, 2019) for more on the relationships between gender awareness in the new millennium and popular culture.
11. In fact, the macho body and attitudes of some main characters is not the only link attaching Wan with the 1980s, as *Death Sentence* is another film in the long chain of films rotating around vigilantism, a cycle of stories where women where associated with "whiteness, purity and religion" (Westwell 55). The cycle was especially popular through the Reaganomic era.
12. Eve Kosofsky Sedgwick, *Between Men: English Literature and Male Homosocial Desire* (New York: Columbia University Press, 1992).
13. Thomas Piontek, *Queering Gay and Lesbian Studies* (Urbana: University of Illinois Press, 2006), 58.
14. Michael Kimmel and Amy Aronson (eds.), *Men and Masculinities: A Social, Cultural, and Historical Encyclopedia. Volume 1: A-J* (Santa Barbara: ABC-CLIO, 2004), 488.
15. David Jackson, *Unmasking Masculinity: A Critical Autobiography* (New York: Routledge, 2015), 168.
16. Larry May, *Masculinity and Morality* (Ithaca: Cornell University Press, 2018), 93.
17. Damien Riggs and Elizabeth Peel, *Critical Kinship Studies: An Introduction to the Field* (New York: Palgrave Macmillan, 2016), 11.

18. Richard Dyer, "Male Sexuality in the Media," in *The Sexuality of Men*, ed. A. Metcalf and M. Humphries (London: Pluto Press, 1985), 30.
19. *Ibid.*
20. Scott Melzer, *The NRA's Culture War* (New York: New York University Press, 2012), 28.
21. Mark Moss, *The Media and the Models of Masculinity* (Lanham, MD: Lexington, 2011), 142.
22. Bruno Latour, *We Have Never Been Modern* (Cambridge: Harvard University Press, 1993), 53.
23. Latour, *We Have Never Been Modern*, 179–80.
24. After swearing vengeance at the hospital, Nick starts his complete transformation into hypermasculinity. Equally, Deckard Shaw retires from the hospital not before causing complete destruction (with grenades) of the entire place. It may be argued that, after a scene of male sensibility and pain, both Nick and Deckard are reconstructed via hypermasculinity, thus recuperating something lost through their tears.
25. https://www.highdefdigest.com/blog/macgyver-2016-pilot-recap-guy-hero-good/. Accessed August 30, 2019.
26. Douglas Kellner, "Guys and Guns (Still) Amok: School Shootings, Domestic Terrorism, and Societal Violence in the Age of Obama," in *Gun Violence and Public Life*, ed. Ben Agger and Timothy W. Luke (New York: Routledge, 2014), 94.

Works Cited

Anderson, Eric, and Rory Magrath. *Men and Masculinities*. New York: Routledge, 2019.
Burstyn, Varda. *The Rites of Men: Manhood, Politics, and the Culture of Sport*. Toronto: University of Toronto Press, 2000.
Connell, Raewyn. *Masculinities*. Cambridge: Polity Press, 2005.
Dyer, Richard. "Male Sexuality in the Media." In *The Sexuality of Men*, edited by A. Metcalf and M. Humphries, 28–43. London: Pluto Press, 1985.
Frankel, Valerie, ed. *Fourth Wave Feminism in Science Fiction and Fantasy*, Vol. I and II. Jefferson, NC: McFarland, 2019.
Jackson, David. *Unmasking Masculinity: A Critical Autobiography*. New York: Routledge, 2015.
Kellner, Douglas. "Guys and Guns (Still) Amok: School Shootings, Domestic Terrorism, and Societal Violence in the Age of Obama." In *Gun Violence and Public Life*, edited by Ben Agger and Timothy W. Luke, 79–105. New York: Routledge, 2014.
Kimmel, Michael, and Amy Aronson, eds. *Men and Masculinities: A Social, Cultural, and Historical Encyclopedia. Volume 1: A–J*. Santa Barbara: ABC-CLIO, 2004.
Kosofsky Sedgwick, Eve. *Between Men: English Literature and Male Homosocial Desire*. New York: Columbia University Press, 1992.
Latour, Bruno. *We Have Never Been Modern*, translated by Catherine Porter. Cambridge: Harvard University Press, 1993.
Lumsden, Karen. *Boy Racer Culture: Youth, Masculinity and Deviance*. New York: Routledge, 2013.
May, Larry. *Masculinity and Morality*. Ithaca: Cornell University Press, 2018.
Melzer, Scott. *The NRA's Culture War*. New York: NYU Press, 2012.
Moss, Mark. *The Media and the Models of Masculinity*. Lanham, MD: Lexington, 2011.
Neroni, Hilary. *Violent Woman: Femininity, Narrative, and Violence in Contemporary American Cinema*. Albany: SUNY Press, 2005.
Oppliger, Patrice. *Wrestling and Hypermasculinity*. Jefferson, NC: McFarland, 2004.
Pascoe, C.J., and Tristan Bridges. "Exploring Masculinities: History, Reproduction, Hegemony, and Dislocation." In *Exploring Masculinities: Identity, Inequality, Continuity, and Change*, edited by C.J. Pascoe and Tristan Bridges, 1–34. New York: Oxford University Press, 2016.
Piontek, Thomas. *Queering Gay and Lesbian Studies*. Urbana: University of Illinois Press, 2006.
Riggs, Damien, and Elizabeth Peel. *Critical Kinship Studies: An Introduction to the Field*. New York: Palgrave Macmillan, 2016.
Westwell, Guy. *Parallel Lines: Post-9/11 American Cinema*. London: Wallflower Press, 2014.

State of Exception in *Saw* and *Death Sentence*

Choose Your Type of Antihero

Emiliano Aguilar

A prominent aspect of post–9/11 American cinema is the "Us versus Them" rhetorical stance through which George W. Bush proclaimed that "a democratic society moves forward and embraces progress,"[1] thus characterizing the terrorists assaulting U.S. as part of an "undemocratic past."[2] This successful Manichean rhetoric invites receivers to accept the suspensions of rights and laws of citizens of the world, while fostering public support and legitimacy of this "state of exception." Since the terrorist attacks of September 11, 2001, and after years of philosophical relativism, the clear-cut dichotomy of "good versus evil" is reinstated as justification to war efforts and states of exception. It is again "Us" versus "Them" after the ending of the Cold War dichotomy of freedom versus evil communism.

Citizens are inclined to condemn terrorism by granting the power to prevent, investigate, and resolve any form of international violence to the judicial and state powers, even if doing so means the installation of an estate of exception, meaning, a prerogative power through which a sovereign nation may act "to secure the common good in moments of emergency and not seek particular permissions"[3] to do so. Still, we may ask to what extent a power can suspend all human rights in the name of ethics without becoming a monster itself.

James Wan's cinema seems to predicate on the political and moral reinstatement of good and evil as labile categories. In *Saw* (2004) and its many sequels, a psychopath imprisons unsuspecting victims and subjects them to innumerable tortures, putting their lives at stake. In the first film, the main antagonist, John "Jigsaw" Kramer (Tobin Bell), labels these tortures as "challenges"; if the subject under torture passes the challenge, he or she will obtain freedom and redemption from a spoiled life. The film revolves around a man who erects himself as judge and who has the power to teach others the real value of life. To do so, he is ready to suspend all forms of freedom, even if he insists that his gruesome scenarios give the victims choices. Three years later, Wan returns to the same themes in his thriller *Death Sentence* (2007). The film narrates the despair of a working and successful father whose son is taken from him by a cold-blooded murder perpetrated by a gang of young criminals. After law is revealed as unable of providing the deserved punishment, he will seek his own kind of justice: revenge by his own hand. The protagonists of both films fit in the "long tradition of male characters fed up with democratic institutions, determined to set their own rules"[4] so typical of Western cinema and, specifically, of the vigilante cinema, a cycle in which the legal system fails to provide support, thus obliging the main antiheroes to take the law into their own hands.

These questions about the limits of justice and the main character's freedom of action imply a certain commitment in the architecture of the films. Already from its conceptual elaboration, some films flirt with philosophical questions as both, cinema and philosophy, "manifest attitudes towards their subject matter, and both invite their audiences to do the same."[5] With each film inviting the viewer to take on the world within the story—either accompanying the two leading middle-class men imprisoned in *Saw* or the exemplary father figure in *Death Sentence*—the narrative "encourages the spectator"[6] to "adopt a similar attitude"[7] and, thus, embrace a state of exception. The films leave little space to do differently: the focal point of *Saw* is the two imprisoned men (even if the action follows other events as well), while Nick Hume (Kevin Bacon), the grieving father of *Death Sentence* leads the narrative. The main (anti)heroes invite viewers to assume their ideological point of views. The excess of gore and violence, however, may be read as a way to distance the viewer, even if, in the context of the postmodern narrative, new technologies are leading violence in the screen to the category of "spectator sport."[8] Furthermore, the differences between the two main antiheroes indicate an ideological divide: while Jigsaw acts, he believes so, for the betterment of society as a whole, Nick does not escape the logic of individualistic revenge. In this sense, the ends of both films, similar and dissimilar at the same time, are signposts that indicates the embracing and rejection of liberal ideas on law and justice. In fact, Jigsaw does not see his actions as part of a revenge plan, but communitarian justice. Analyzing the relationships between state and individual violence, Rachel M. Stein explains how a state can rely on a citizen's desire for revenge. According to Stein, at the individual level (i.e., not as a community assessment), revenge is thought of as "a core value."[9] Since violence is often created as a weapon in response to physical harm, its use is

Promotional poster for Wan's vigilante action crime drama *Death Sentence* (Hyde Park Entertainment, 2007), starring Kevin Bacon. The film was loosely based on Brian Garfield's 1975 novel of the same name.

often considered "an act of moral virtue,"[10] unlike state violence, closer to terrorism.

My reading of both films will follow two purposes: one, illustrating how both *Saw* and *Death Sentence* are representatives of a post–9/11 filmmaking revolving around issues of state of exception. Second, how the films invite spectatorial identification and the embracing of politics of exceptionalism. Because both *Saw* and *Death Sentence* use scenes of graphic violence, this work will take into account the "bodily impact of the image and responses by the cultural meaning or significance of images"[11] to understand the aspects of spectatorial identification that are put into play in Wan's films. My analysis will consider two films belonging to different genres (one horror, the other labeled as a vigilante thriller) but whose treatments of justice, vengeance and the state of exception deserve careful examination.

Let the Exception Begin

In his *State of Exception* (2005), Giorgio Agamben explains that in special situations resulting from political crises, states may take exceptional measures whose jurisdiction is strictly in charge of the political field (rather than juridical), enthroning the state of exception as "the legal form of what cannot have legal form."[12] Thus, according to the author, the state tries—and, in terms of political strategy, succeeds—to justify extraordinary measures that may undermine such important rights as freedom of expression or freedom over bodies. Agamben argues that between these two positions, public law and politics, as well as between the legal and human life itself, an ambiguous space rises, from which can be thought the notion of "act politically"[13] (meaning, an act that involves some kind of "choice or decision"[14] with deliberation, that is, an intentional decision coming from a free subject), for example, escaping Constitutional restraints as a way to increase anti-terrorist actions. This is inconsistent with America's constitution as a liberal democracy, as rights believed inherent to humans are momentarily suspended (in a political, social and juridical limbo) as a way to face the crisis. Thus, it is not surprising that the first example that Agamben mentions is the use of such measures as applied by the Nazi regime to justify social segregation of the Jewish community in Germany in the 1930s. Agamben also cites as example the arrest warrant issued in the U.S. after the 9/11 attack on "noncitizens suspected of involvement in terrorist activities"[15] deleting "any legal status of the individual" and producing "a legally unnamable an unclassifiable being."[16] In sum, life itself reaches a degree of "maximum indeterminacy."[17] Further, Agamben calls the "estate of exception" the norm in the history of civilization rather than the exception, as believed.

What emerges from this analysis "is that the state has routinely suspended its own rule of law to preserve the rule of law, and the traditional model of the state needs to be understood in these terms."[18] Agamben takes the notion of the sovereign as a conceptual limit to argue that the defining characteristic of sovereignty is that the sovereign determines when law is applicable and what it applies to. In doing so, the sovereign must also create the conditions required for law to operate since the law presupposes normal conditions for its operation. In other words, the laws are flexible enough to be declared, at least momentarily, suspended. "What is at issue in the sovereign exception is not so much the control or neutralization of an excess as the creation and definition of the very space in which the juridico-political order can have validity."[19] The state of exception is not simply chaos as if any sense of law is lifted. State of exception "is not simply outside the realm of the law, but is in fact created through the law's suspension."[20] Agamben highlights the idea that these states of emergency are a "voluntary creation."[21] Undoubtedly, for a state of exception to be carried out, there must be a state or regulatory body that dictates that decision, and also a receiver who complies with that rule. It may be argued that, when following all the rules dictated by Jigsaw, the different characters in the *Saw* franchise comply with the state of exception created by Kramer. After all, they always can reject playing the "game," for example, disobeying the instructions dictated through the tape recorder. The gang of thugs hunted down by Nick in *Death Sentence*, on the other hand, engage in a cat and mouse game with the vigilante rather than recur to the cops, even if Nick is the person who is operating outside the law.

The narrative proposed by *Saw*, as a microcosm that operates under its own rules, behaves analogously to the state of exception. Jigsaw's plans run parallel to the instauration of a state of exception. He kidnaps, imprisons and tortures people under the general idea he is making a better community through reformation. Jigsaw decides to punish the ethical misbehavior of some citizens of America, but the implementation of his ideas lies outside the legal-constitutional law as long as it deprives human beings of their freedom or subjects them to torture that in everyday situations (under the Law) are punishable. For democracies under state of exception, torture is analyzed and allowed under a scale that allows a cost-benefit measurement. Jigsaw's tortures are particularly relevant in years in which the circulation of images depicting real scenes of torture and humiliation in Abu Ghraib and Guantanamo were released on a daily basis. The disturbing images from Guantánamo were dated January 2002, while photographs and videos taken in Abu Ghraib belonging to an internal Army investigation,[22] were made public at the beginning of March 2003. Thus, Wan's film circulates torture "as a fantasy motif"[23] with "all-too-clear resonance"[24] regarding reality. Thus, Jigsaw's decisions regarding kidnapping and torture imply a personal ethos which distances from the Law system to impose new rules provided by the kidnaper/judge. This situation mirrors the Bush-Cheney era, as Dick Cheney, one of the champions of torture, justified dismissing human rights "in cause of good because it is punishing evil,"[25] thus echoing Jigsaw's sentiments.

In the film's first scene, Adam (Leigh Whannell) wakes up submerged in a bathtub full of water, his foot tied to a chain. A male voice speaks in the dark, and when the lights are turned on by the invisible kidnapper, Adam and viewers alike see another man chained to a pipe against the wall, bathed in sweat. In the middle of the room, on the floor, lies a lifeless body, with a shattered skull, a tape player in one hand and gun in the other. It is assumed the man is a victim of suicide. Although both men still do not know why they are imprisoned and who put them into this dire scenario, the chained subjects already have the answer to the puzzle proposed by the film: the only possible solution lies in self-inflicted damage. The corpse (later revealed as Jigsaw himself, who is alive) discloses this. The only real escape seems to lie in suicide, the violation and/or suspension of all laws of human life. Agamben, following Émile Durkheim, notes the relationships between state of exception and suicide, as the diminution of society's regulative influence on individuals parallels a rise in the suicide rate.[26] When the law falls, anomie prevails and life may become a source of anxieties. On the other hand, self-aggression refers to systematic acts of violence by a state against its citizens, particularly during periods of extreme political instability or civil war. Jigsaw has established a micro-nation where the citizens (the kidnapped subjects) are brutalized rather than protected by the state. Rather than rights-bearing subjects, they become objects of a scrutinizing, punishing gaze.

In different scenes through the franchise, Jigsaw states his main principle: he does not kill, but gives his prisoners (all of them wrongdoers, at least, according to his point of view) the chance to choose between redemption or death. Many of his victims, however, have no recourse but to kill themselves, little by little, like Mr. Hindle (Michael Emerson) who, injected with poison by Jigsaw, is obliged to kidnap and kill Detective Tapp (Danny Glover) as part of the "game," only to be killed in turn by Adam. In a later scene, Lawrence (Cary Elwes) cuts off his own foot with a saw in order to try to escape. This self-aggression is achieved when, by exceeding the interest of the victim by his or her own wellbeing, he or she uses self-inflicted violence as a mean to an end "outside"[27] itself, in this case, escape from confinement. This parallels real practices sustained, for example, by detainees in Guantanamo, who go so far as inflicting self-harm as a way to escape imprisonment, as their own form of *habeas corpus*. "Enduring a state defined by unfreedom, the prisoners seek a form of negative freedom from life—life that is unlivable, that is not life at all."[28]

Through elaborate strategies Jigsaw puts the weapons in the hands of those in need of moral and ethical re-education. This re-education parallels the reaffirmation of paternalism or attempts "to preserve the patriarchal order."[29] As a consequence of the terrorist attacks, the Bush Administration created the Office of Homeland Security "to implement the emergency abridgement of civil liberties on the grounds that the post 9/11 represented an indefinite state of exception,"[30] triggering thus a series of policies based upon the notion of "Homeland-as-Home, the United States as fatherland, and Bush as its paternalistic guardian."[31] Within this scenario, the American citizens become children whose parents are "exemplary national figures"[32] who are doing "their patriotic duty."[33]

The state of exception is assimilated by Mandy (Shawnee Smith), a drug addict who survived the gauntlet created by Jigsaw and declares to the police that she is grateful to him because "he helped me" to understand the consequences of her addiction, a fact which leads her to reintegrate (apparently) to society. In the aftermath, however, that reintegration into society is not fruitful; Mandy will follow Jigsaw's steps and will become an extension of his plans rather than a subject with a will of her own. Like the exemplary "good" citizen of the state of exception, she complies with the (suspension of) rules rather than reclaim her role as a rights-bearing citizen.

A clear-cut illustration of the state of exception takes place when the detectives searching the missing persons find Jigsaw's lair and a man about to be drilled by a mechanic contraption. There, Jigsaw proposes to save the subject's life only if the detectives find "the key in the box." "What's more important? To arrest me, or the life of another human being?" says the hooded villain. As punishment for saving the subject (by cheating), Jigsaw cuts Detective David Tapp' throat. The other detective dies shattered by shotgun shots after crossing a booby-trap room. Later, David takes justice into his own hands and tries to capture the criminal outside the sphere of law, since he has been momentarily removed from the police force. Agamben states that the state of exception has the characteristic of being the "suspension of the juridical order."[34] So, it is possible to argue that not only Jigsaw installs an estate of exception when he declares that laws prohibiting torture should be momentarily lifted, but Detective Tapp as well; the latter also acts on his own behalf for—theoretically—a common good to society, although at that point he has already transformed the investigation into a personal account to settle down.

Sean Carter notes that the state of exception is both "visible and hidden,"[35] as well as regulated and unlimited. In *Saw*, these properties are applied in their own way: each victim is exposed to exemplary and (supposedly) justified punishment. The rules are clear, as dictated by Jigsaw to his victims. He, however, remains invisible. The kidnappers never really see the face of their judge, who cloaks himself under a puppet (Billy the Puppet), a wild boar mask, or presents himself as a disemboweled voice coming out from a tape recorder. Likewise, every detail is planned and under control, although not by federal laws, but internal laws of the game established by Jigsaw himself and with absolute validity within the space of torture. This regulation is based on compliance with severe surveillance of the subjects under torture being judged by Jigsaw, the latter taking full advantage of the state of exception, laminating another layer onto the escalating capacity of inspection. Within this state of exception, nobody can escape the rules that establish that torture and severe surveillance are acceptable. Jigsaw created a panopticon made up of surveillance cameras, high technology and recording. Adam, one of the kidnapped men, calls the cell phone "the most beautiful invention of this planet" denoting human dependence on technology. Ironically, he is undergoing imprisonment due his voyeurism, as he is a photographer who spies on unsuspected victims.

The most disturbing aspect the film offers is the fact that Jigsaw finally gets his way and, at the end of the film, he is free from any form of punishment. He has created his own version of the state of exception and, as such, he seems impervious to (common) juridical laws. He has been in the room with the kidnapped men all the time, thus enhancing his presence within this state of exception (but, at the same time, remaining invisible through faking his death). Before leaving, he reveals to Adam the fact that escape is impossible. Finally, Adam is re-punished and locked up for trying to cheat (trying to escape) on laws which have suspended human rights, thus allowing torture.

We have seen how a subject can configure a state of exception all of his own dismissing established rules of welfare, although building rules and laws valid for his own ethos. But, what happens when a citizen who is victim of criminal violence decides to apply his own rules within the same universe in which Law has failed him? If Jigsaw can be considered a monster, a simple citizen trying to ignore rules to apply his own version of vigilantism may be closer to viewers' sympathy, both complicit in the rise of new forms of (justified) exceptionalism.

Sometimes, Just Chaos

Nick Hume is a mild-mannered executive with a perfect life and a perfect family until one terrible night he witnesses his teenage son being killed by a thug. This event will change him forever, inserting in him a "self-destructive spiral of vengeance,"[36] justifying his vigilante actions as a form of "a motivated, post-traumatic and justifiable response"[37] to the lack of a strong state that can guarantee the safety of citizens. His focus lies in clear-cut revenge; soon enough, however, he will embark on a crusade akin to that sustained by Jigsaw: clean America of people undeserving of life. To do this, torture and killing is allowed.

Wan's film is based on Brian Garfield's homonymous novel, which previously inspired *Death Wish* (Michael Winner, 1974), a key film in the vigilante cycle that "mutates the interesting ambiguity of cop movies like *Dirty Harry* (1971) into an uncomfortable lynch mob attitude."[38] *Death Sentence* updates through extreme violence the concept of revenge, turning the avenger into a dubious hero who follows the basic premise of the cycle: "the avenging hero gets it right."[39] Generally, the narrator's omniscient point of view "subdues the fear of unjust revenge with the promise that the heroic avenger will get the right man"[40] at the end, a way of protecting citizens from the weakness of common State justice.

Like in *Saw*, *Death Sentence* offers an image of the justice as fallible at the moment of protecting families and individuals. After his son is brutally and senseless killed (the killer ends a life just as a way to be allowed entrance into a gang), the laws simply proved to be imperfect for Nick. Rather than serving the life sentence he expects, Joe Darley (Matthew O'Leary), the murdering thug, goes free, unpunished. At this point, it is worth stating that Joe goes free due to Nick's lies. After learning Joe will receive just a couple of years in prison, Nick decides to withdraw his testimony. Nick has decided that law is inefficient to stop crime; at the same time, he has decided to enact his own form of justice: killing Joe.

Indeed, law seems unable to protect the citizens against the horrors of violence. When the leader of the gang, Billy (Garrett Hedlund), threatens to kill Nick's family, Detective Wallis (Aisha Tyler) assures him that law and justice will protect them. That hope, however, will prove to be ephemeral, as Nick's family is, indeed, brutally killed with the exception of Nick's son Luke (Jordan Garret), who remains in coma. Police inefficiency is noticeable again when Nick successfully escapes custody, returning to his home after illegally buying some guns.

Speaking to his comatose son Luke, at his bedside at the hospital, Nick makes a mea culpa: "I'm so sorry that I wasn't a better father," and "so sorry I could not protect all of us." These words anticipate the outcome, as Nick will establish his own state of exception: all common laws made for the betterment of society are suspended so justice can be enacted. State-as-paternal-figure is unable to protect, neither to do justice. Thus, rules must be downplayed to secure, ironically, a (very subjective) form of justice.

There is a sub-cycle of vigilante films in which the main arc is built upon the redemption of the main antihero. Carter places films like *Rendition* (Gavid Hood, 2007) or *Iron Man* (Jon Favreau, 2008) in that category, as the (anti)heroes, still operating outside law, manage to restore order by making things better[41] for society. In *Death Sentence* that principle is not fulfilled, because Nick Hume does not squarely fall into this category, as his redemptive arc is short-circuited by two facts: on one hand, he has been previously established as a good father. He has no redemption to prove since he was, already from the beginning, a good citizen. On the other hand, he gradually moves away from doing "what is right" (some notion of justice that will serve the community) toward the logic of "an eye for an eye" in which innocent people can be killed. In fact, Nick's family is brutalized after he killed the one gang member who murdered his son. For him, "the return of harm for harm and suffering is necessary to balance the scales of justice."[42]

Since Nick must shift from paternal figure to bloodthirsty avenger, the viewer requires a justification of his actions to accept his acts of revenge or, at least, generate empathy through narrative mechanisms. Working on how the construction of characters in film works, Murray Smith argues that there are three fundamental concepts: "recognition, alignment and allegiance"[43]; together, these elements form what Smith calls "structure of sympathy,"[44] giving the character tools to generate (or not) identification with the viewer. As the film progresses, Nick shifts from grieving father to (anti) hero who takes justice in his own hands to, finally, a kind of monster covered in blood. In the film's climax, Nick becomes a shadow of his former self, his expression gaunt and hardened. He becomes the embodiment of the state of exception, a specter of Jigsaw but without all the paraphernalia of the latter. Both are men trying to make justice suspending the rules that govern civil life and protect human life. Besides killing, many scenes depict Nick hurting and torturing some of the thugs as he does with Heco (Hector Atreyu Ruiz), whom is repeatedly punched by Nick at the face with a gun.

The idea of torture is anticipated in one key scene: after the killing of his son, Nick revises his house's garden shed. He looks for tools that will serve him as weapons for his revenge. At first, he does not know which one to grab, until he decides on a knife. His son Luke enters the shed, and Nick gets angry because his son touches the tools; the father continues his role as figure of authority, the one dictating the Law, while, ironically, preparing the suspension of all minimal rules of civility. Unlike Jigsaw, however, Nick's behavior is erratic, his personal life and personal appearance unraveling as his revenge progresses. *The difference lies in how both characters establish their own type of state of exception.* Jigsaw really believes in his own system of justice. Nick, in turn, knows that he is only after revenge. He wants to clean the streets of the people who killed his son, not so much eliminate all criminals. When Nick's friend asks him how is going through his pain, the former answers "you find compensations"; these compensations (basically, revenge) replace justice rather than being justice (as Jigsaw believes). Regarding feelings of revenge and resentment and state of exception, Ali Riza Taskale argues[45] that contemporary forms of modern state, intimately connected to states of exception (again, as Agamben argued, the state of exception is the norm, rather than an anomaly), are inextricably linked to forms of cruelty such as torture and displays of national prejudice and resentment, forms of vengeance against those considered as "less-than-humans." Through the investigation, Detective Wallis describes Joe as an animal, and later Helen calls him the same way; animal nature is usually defined in opposition to civilization so that animality is associated with impunity, misbehavior, the irrecoverable criminal. Indeed, in a series of in-depth interviews with victims of serious crimes, a common image of criminals as animalistic, savages, or beastly monsters prevailed among the points of view.[46] In *Saw*, the kidnapper wears an animal mask resembling a wild boar. The assimilation of a human being with an animal represents the human fear of what Dawn Keetley calls human "own savagery."[47] In *Death Sentence*, the animal nature becomes a projection upon those who violates the laws of civilization.

There are more differences between Jigsaw and Nick: for Taskale, "sovereignty is marked by action, the man of resentment for reaction."[48] Jigsaw has everything carefully prepared and all his plans go accordingly, his schemes right up to the point he looks omniscient.[49] Unlike Jigsaw, Nick's vengeance is abrupt, a reaction against the senseless murder of his son rather than a carefully prepared scenario. Contrary to the notion of the act of violence imbued with an "aura of righteousness"[50] so typical on the vigilante cycle, Nick is immediately tormented after killing Joe, his first victim. After the brutal attack on his family, however, Nick decides to take revenge to its final consequences. Although the last scenes have a tone of epic vengeance, one can hardly think of all this violence as "something virtuous"[51] but rather merely "vicious."[52] Nick's state of exception is one landscape framed by disorder, rushing and improvisation. Many sequences in the film—as when Nick, chased by the gang members, enters a parking lot and activates the alarms of all the cars—are filmed through sequential shots whose continuity involves the viewer in a fast paced rhythm. In the last major confrontation, Nick kills the gang members one by one in a rapid edition that privileges frenzy. Unlike the calm tone of *Saw*, *Death Sentence* presents an antihero who engages directly with violence rather than remain at the margins. This is mostly due to the fact that, for Jigsaw, the suspension of the law may be necessary for the common good, while Nick only wants to build a state of exception as a form of personal vengeance.

Since Nick's violence is fully disorganized, the borders separating his ethos from that of the gang of criminals are blurred. In the film's opening scene, the narration creates a warm and familiar environment for Nick through homemade video images in which the family is seen enjoying typical situations, such as opening Christmas gifts or Nick teaching his children how to play hockey or ride a bike. Nick, a risk analyst (who does not drink alcohol nor smoke), knows the fact that he has the perfect family. Upon arriving from work and tolerating a friendly quarrel between his two children, he kindly asks to end the discussion by arguing "be civilized for once before I kill somebody," unwillingly anticipating the murderous persona he will adopt later. This highlights how easily those moral values and human rights can collapse or become suspended. Nick is a paternal state in charge of caring for the citizens (his family). It is the paternal pride which becomes hurt when Nick is unable to help his loved ones, either his eldest son Brendan (Stuart Lafferty), killed at the service station or his wife (Kelly Preston), killed by the same gang at Nick's house. After the terrorist attacks performed upon his family—a terrorism punctuated by the senseless of the murders—Nick decides to suspend human life as a priority.

Bones Darley (John Goodman), father of the gang's leader and arms dealer, tells Nick "you've got a killing thing about you"; later, he says to him: "Go with God ... bag full of guns." Bones, as a father, is diametrically opposed to Nick. He does not care about his family. There is no law to suspend because he is chaos. Bones even turns a blind eye to an alleged internal attack (to his son) as long as the violent measures remain in the sphere of the private; that is, as long as Nick does not make him a participant/accomplice of the crime of his own son. The only one who can suspend law is Nick, *as he was law*.

The final step of Nick's metamorphosis into a full-blown antihero involves shaving his hair and adopting the persona of a gang member. His new appearance and clothing (black leather jacket) definitively places him on the other side of the law. Through some earlier scenes before Brendan's murder, Nick is depicted wearing a red jacket with the image of a wolf at the back. The image insinuates that Nick has always been, inside, a wolf. Man as the wolf to man. When he starts stalking Joe at the bar where the thug works, a woman taking the trash out spots Nick. She looks afraid of the man and keeps her guard up. Nick has become his distorted double, a thug himself who scares women at night. Also, the jacket codes him as member of some invisible gang of wolves, maybe all them mild mannered men waiting to explode into animality. After a bloody final confrontation, Billy tells Nick "Look at you ... you are like one of us." Both are bleeding out, sitting on a couch. Further, Billy mentions "Look what I made you," thus marking how his terrorist actions have transformed the paternal figure into state of exception. Terrorism made me do it, seems the final reflection the film has to offer.

After the final gore-filled battle between Nick and the gang, the former paternal figure returns to the site of the law, his home. Symbolically, Nick goes through the police "Do not cross" tapes that separate the crime scene from the rest of his house. The limits have been already transgressed. Nick returns to the living room where, miraculously, he did not die, but where he should have.

As mentioned, *Death Sentence* is part of the vigilante cycle, its violent conventions essentially "an excess of certain qualities and feelings beyond the necessity of the narrative."[53] This film provides first a brief family context to later fall into adrenaline-fueled action which goes hand in hand with excessive graphic violence. Despite the frantic pace of the sequences, *Death Sentence* ends the same way it began: with a technological image of the united family. Bleeding out, Nick sits at the couch in his house, watching old family tapes in his TV set. The film's climax suggests that the idea of the nuclear family is, today, little more than a frozen fantasy, but no longer current. Something that belongs to the past, before terrorism and the state of exception.

Conclusions: The Hypersensitized Image

At a fundamental level, graphic violence invites both empathy (we may feel the same pain in our body) and detachment (repulsion). Despite having been a fundamental piece in the beginnings of the subgenre known as torture porn, *Saw* does not contain as many gore images as viewers might think. The different scenes show as much as they suggest the horrors taking place within the torture chamber. The graphic descriptions of gore and torture go in crescendo as the franchise extends through time—in par with an increase in budget—each sequel depicting "more extravagant ways of destroying the human body."[54] More graphic violence is invested to satisfy a spectator built as "male adolescent."[55] Thus, as the franchise progresses, the identification comes from both, through a visual, spectatorial empathy with the victim being ritualistic tortured, or/and by the attractive strength of the gore on display.

This play between identification and emotional detachment (as the excess of cinematic blood may lead to numbness) parallels the investment viewers may have on the main antiheroes. It is known that the viewer answers to graphic violence in a way that "unites the intellectual and the visceral."[56] Although the excess of gore channeled through a codified system alleviate "the characters and the spectacle itself from ethical consideration,"[57] provoking "uneasy pleasure,"[58] spectators leave cinemas "knowing that evil lurks 'out there' and could pounce at any moment."[59] Both Jigsaw and Nick Hume have suspended human rights and turned other people into objects to be punishable. People may identify with his plight and his ideological ethos: the enthroning of a state of exception as the only way to punish evil people.

Facing the fallibility and passivity of the judicial system, both subjects apply their own state of exception through the suspension of the law itself, as the case may be, the suspension of legitimate rights for the victims of the bloodshed. The results of each experience are disparate: after liquidating the entire gang of criminals—in fact, this spiral of murders far exceeds its original idea that it was to take revenge on Joe, Brendan's killer—Nick ends up seriously injured, becoming a requiem for the inevitable: his imprisonment or death. Jigsaw, on the other hand, who has witnessed in complete silence the entire confinement of his victims posing as the corpse, retires triumphant, leaving his only alive victim, Adam, trapped again. Both antiheroes end the films alive and, seemingly, unpunished. Viewers never actually see Nick being punished by law, the last shot showing him resting at home. Viewers may infer he will die or become incarcerated, but this resolution remains a suggestion. The state of exception is, indeed, the norm and, as such, it survives.

As spectators, we understand the point of view and feel the fear or hate that both Nick and Jigsaw feel in the face of an unfair or immoral circumstance that puts them in dire situations. Murray Smith states that to "internally" understand the situation, viewers "do not need to experience the occurrent emotion of fear."[60] Also, the generation of parallel emotions between character and spectator is given when they share "basic cultural concerns and symbolic systems with a character."[61] Opening within a scenario of post 9/11 trauma, both films ask for deep identification. There is a tendency for the viewer to react to the horrific in the same way than the character does. There is another question, however, and is how long that identification can last. If the identification is permanent, viewers will be pushed to believe that the state of exception is the best of scenarios, the one governments should adopt to counter-attack terrorism.

At the end of both films, the antiheroes (or are they villains?) remain free of punishment. The bloodshed, however, demonizes them, turning their states of exception as monstrous landscapes of excessive violence (displayed in close shots) where the borders separating innocent people from those guilty (Tapp's throat is cut wide by Jigsaw, even when the cop only tries to save people) are labile. Agamben argues that anomy—lack of norms—dramatizes the irreducible ambiguity of juridical systems and, at the same time, show that what is at stake "is the very relation between law and life."[62] Law does (or, at least, it tries) separate right from wrong, the good people from the bad ones. The state of exception, however, suspends this logical norm; being considered morally "suspected" is enough to be turned victim.

Following Lacan, Charles Altman suggests about two levels of psychoanalytic identification postulated by psychoanalysis: primary identification—of the imaginary order—that is related to the stage of the mirror, and secondary identification, of the symbolic order, related to the oedipal stage.[63] Now, it may be argued that *Saw* and *Death Sentence* may be unpacked following this concept. While in the first instance we, as spectators, assimilate imaginary order as a form of access to identification by configuring two entities as identical (we put ourselves on Nick and Jigsaw's shoes as victims of an injustice), we demand justice and mostly accept their investiture as vigilantes. Then, when the "return to the Real" occurs,[64] viewers may be able to logically code both Nick and Jigsaw as ethical monsters who have taken things too far. This shift oblige us to reconsider in which side of the game we are on, because participating in one way or another, intellectually or emotionally, is inevitable.

Notes

1. Mary K. Bloodsworth-Lugo and Carmen Lugo-Lugo, *Projecting 9/11: Race, Gender and Citizenship in Recent Hollywood Films* (London: Rowman & Littlefield, 2015), 9.
2. *Ibid.*
3. Jason Ralph, *America's War on Terror: The State of the 9/11 Exception from Bush to Obama* (New York: Oxford Univesity Press, 2013), 4.
4. See Christopher Sharrett, "The Problem of *Saw*: 'Torture Porn' and the Conservatism of Contemporary Horror Films," *Cineaste: America's Leading Magazine on the Art and Politics of the Cinema* 35.1 (2009): 35.
5. Ward E. Jones and Samantha Vice, *Ethics at the Cinema* (New York: Oxford University Press, 2011), 3.
6. Jones and Vice, *Ethics at the Cinema*, 4.
7. *Ibid.*
8. Wheeler W. Dixon and Gwendolyn A. Foster, *21st-Century Hollywood: Movies in the Era of Transformation* (New Jersey: Rutgers Press, 2011), 115.
9. Rachel M. Stein, *Vengeful Citizens, Violent States: A Theory of War and Revenge* (Cambridge: Cambridge University Press, 2019), 7.
10. Stein, *Vengeful Citizens*, 8.
11. Paul Gormley. *The New Brutality Film: Race and Affect in Contemporary Hollywood Cinema* (Bristol: Anthone Rowe Ltd, 2005), 9.
12. Giorgio Agamben, *State of Exception* (Chicago: University of Chicago, 2005), 1.
13. Agamben, *State of Exception*, 2.
14. Steven G. Crowell, "Who Is the Political Actor? An Existential Phenomenological Approach," in *Phenomenology of the Political*, ed. Kevin Thompson and Lester Embree (Carbondale: Springer Science+Business Media, B.V., 2000), 18.
15. Agamben, *State of Exception*, 3.
16. *Ibid.*
17. Agamben, *State of Exception*, 4.

18. Alex Murray, "State of Exception," in *The Agamben Dictionary*, ed. Alex Murray and Jessica Whyte (Edinburgh: Edinburgh University Press, 2011), 186.
19. Agamben, *State of Exception*, 19.
20. Catherine Mills, *The Philosophy of Agamben* (Montreal: McGill-Queen's University Press, 2008), 68.
21. Agamben, *State of Exception*, 2.
22. Connal Parsley, "The Exceptional Image: Torture Photographs from Guantánamo Bay and Abu Ghraib as Foucault's Spectacle of Punishment," in *Law and the Visual: Transitions and Transformations*, ed. Desmond Manderson (Toronto University Press, 2016), 1.
23. Harvey O'Brien. *Action Movies: The Cinema of Striking Back*. (United States: Wallflower, 2012), 92.
24. Ibid.
25. Douglas M. Kellner, *Cinema Wars: Hollywood Films and Politics in the Bush-Cheney Era* (West Sussex: Wiley-Blackwell, 2010), 8.
26. Agamben, *State of Exception*, 67.
27. Hent De Vries, "Violence and Testimony: On Sacrificing Sacrifice," in *Violence, Identity and Self-Determination*, ed. H. De Vries and Samuel Weber (Stanford: Stanford University Press, 1997), 16.
28. Joseph Darda, *Empire of Defense: Race and the Cultural Politics of Permanent War* (Chicago: University of Chicago Press, 2019), 208.
29. Kimberly Jackson, *Technology, Monstrosity, and Reproduction in Twenty-First Century Horror* (New York: Palgrave Macmillan, 2013), 90.
30. Lucy Bond, *Frames of Memory After 9/11: Culture, Criticism, Politics, and Law* (Basingstoke: Palgrave Macmillan, 2015), 47.
31. Ibid.
32. Ibid.
33. Ibid.
34. Agamben, *State of Exception*, 23.
35. Sean Carter and Klaus Dodds, *International Politics and Film: Space, Vision, Power* (New York: Wallflower, 2014), 60.
36. O'Brien, *Action Movies*, 92.
37. Ibid.
38. Richard Attenborough, *The BFI Companion to Crime* (Berkeley: University of California Press, 1997), 100.
39. Drucilla Cornell, *Clint Eastwood and Issues of American Masculinity* (New York: Fordham University Press, 2009), 125.
40. Ibid.
41. Carter and Dodds, *International Politics and Film*, 61.
42. Stein, *Vengeful Citizens, Violent States*, 8.
43. Murray Smith, *Engaging Characters. Fiction, Emotion and the Cinema* (New York: Oxford University Press, 1995), 73.
44. Ibid.
45. Ali Riza Taskale, *Post-Politics in Context* (New York: Routledge, 2016), 58.
46. Esther Madriz, "Images of Criminals and Victims: A Study on Women's Fear and Social Control," *Gender and Society*, 11(3), 1997.
47. Dawn Keetley, "Frozen, The Grey, and the Possibilities of Posthumanist Horror," in *Animal Horror Cinema: Genre, History and Criticism*, ed. K. Gregersdotter, J. Höglund and N. Hallén (New York: Palgrave Macmillan, 2015), 190.
48. Taskale, *Post-Politics*, 58.
49. See Fernando Gabriel Pagnoni Berns and Amy Davis, "From Jigsaw to Phibes: God, Free Will and Foreknowledge in Conflict," in *To See the Saw Movies: Essays on Torture Porn and Post-9/11 Horror*, ed. James Aston and John Wallis (Jefferson, NC: McFarland, 2013).
50. Stein, *Vengeful Citizens, Violent States*, 8.
51. Ibid.
52. Ibid.
53. Martin Rubin, *Thrillers* (Cambridge: Cambridge University Press, 1999), 5.

54. Sharrett, "The Problem of *Saw*," 32.
55. *Ibid.*
56. James Williams, "His Life to Film: The Extreme Art of Jacques Nolot," *Studies in French Cinema* 9:2 (2009): 188.
57. Aaron Kerner, "Torture Porn: The American Sadistic Disposition in the Post-9/11 Horror Genre," in *Screening the Tortured Body. the Cinema as Scaffold*, ed. Mark de Valk (Winchester: Palgrave Macmillan, 2016), 32.
58. Kerner, "Torture Porn," 31.
59. Kerner, "Torture Porn," 32.
60. Smith, *Engaging Characters*, 79.
61. *Ibid.*
62. Agamben, *State of Exception*, 73.
63. Charles F. Altman, "Psychoanalysis and Cinema: The Imaginary Discourse," in *Movies and Methods Volume II: An Anthology*, ed. Bill Nichols (Berkeley: University of California Press, 1985), 520.
64. Altman, "Psychoanalysis and Cinema: The Imaginary Discourse," 524.

Works Cited

Agamben, Giorgio. *State of Exception*. Chicago: University of Chicago, 2005.
Altman, Charles F. "Psychoanalysis and Cinema: The Imaginary Discourse." *Movies and Methods Volume II: An Anthology*, edited by Bill Nichols, 517–531. Berkeley: University of California Press, 1985.
Attenborough, Richard. *The BFI Companion to Crime*. Berkeley: University of California Press, 1997.
Bloodsworth-Lugo, Mary K., and Carmen Lugo-Lugo. *Projecting 9/11: Race, Gender and Citizenship in Recent Hollywood Films*. London: Rowman & Littlefield, 2015.
Bond, Lucy. *Frames of Memory After 9/11: Culture, Criticism, Politics, and Law*. Basingstoke: Palgrave Macmillan, 2015.
Carter, Sean, and Klaus Dodds. *International Politics and Film: Space, Vision, Power*. New York: Wallflower, 2014.
Cornell, Drucilla. *Clint Eastwood and Issues of American Masculinity*. New York: Fordham University Press, 2009.
Crowell, Steven G. "Who Is the Political Actor? An Existential Phenomenological Approach." In *Phenomenology of the Political*, edited by Kevin Thompson and Lester Embree, 11–29. Carbondale: Springer, 2000.
Darda, Joseph. *Empire of Defense: Race and the Cultural Politics of Permanent War*. Chicago: University of Chicago Press, 2019.
De Vries, Hent. "Violence and Testimony: On Sacrificing Sacrifice." In *Violence, Identity and Self-Determination*, edited by H. De Vries and Samuel Weber, 14–43. Stanford: Stanford University Press, 1997.
Dixon, Wheeler W., and Gwendolyn A. Foster. *21st-Century Hollywood: Movies in the Era of Transformation*. New Brunswick, NJ: Rutgers University Press, 2011.
Gormley, Paul. *The New Brutality Film: Race and Affect in Contemporary Hollywood Cinema*. Bristol: Anthone Rowe, 2005.
Jackson, Kimberly. *Technology, Monstrosity, and Reproduction in Twenty-First Century Horror*. New York: Palgrave Macmillan, 2013.
Jones, Ward E., and Samantha Vice. *Ethics at the Cinema*. New York: Oxford University Press, 2011.
Keetley, Dawn. "*Frozen, The Grey*, and the Possibilities of Posthumanist Horror." In *Animal Horror Cinema: Genre, History and Criticism*, edited by K. Gregersdotter, J. Höglund and N. Hallén, 187–205. New York: Palgrave Macmillan, 2015.
Kellner, Douglas M. *Cinema Wars: Hollywood Films and Politics in the Bush-Cheney Era*. West Sussex: Wiley-Blackwell, 2010.

Kerner, Aaron. "Torture Porn: The American Sadistic Disposition in the Post-9/11 Horror Genre." In *Screening the Tortured Body: The Cinema as Scaffold*, edited by Mark de Valk, 25–49. Winchester: Palgrave Macmillan, 2016.

Madriz, Esther. "Images of Criminals and Victims: A Study on Women's Fear and Social Control." *Gender and Society*, 11.3 (1997): 342–356.

Murray, Alex. "State of Exception." In *The Agamben Dictionary*, edited by Alex Murray and Jessica Whyte, 185–186. Edinburgh: Edinburgh University Press, 2011.

O'Brien, Harvey. *Action Movies. the Cinema of Striking Back*. United States: Wallflower, 2012.

Pagnoni Berns, Fernando Gabriel, and Amy Davis. "From Jigsaw to Phibes: God, Free Will and Foreknowledge in Conflict." In *To See the Saw Movies: Essays on Torture Porn and Post-9/11 Horror*, edited by James Aston and John Wallis, 73–85. Jefferson, NC: McFarland, 2013.

Parsley, Connal. "The Exceptional Image: Torture Photographs from Guantánamo Bay and Abu Ghraib as Foucault's Spectacle of Punishment." In *Law and the Visual: Transitions and Transformations*, edited by Desmond Manderson, 229–248. Toronto University Press, 2016.

Ralph, Jason. *America's War on Terror: The State of the 9/11 Exception from Bush to Obama*. New York: Oxford University Press, 2013.

Rubin, Martin. *Thrillers*. Cambridge: Cambridge University Press, 1999.

Sharrett, Christopher. "The Problem of *Saw*: 'Torture Porn' and the Conservatism of Contemporary Horror Films." *Cineaste: America's LeadingMagazine on the Art and Politics of the Cinema* 35.1 (2009): 32–37.

Smith, Murray. *Engaging Characters: Fiction, Emotion and the Cinema*. New York: Oxford University Press, 1995.

Stein, Rachel M. *Vengeful Citizens, Violent States: A Theory of War and Revenge*. Cambridge: Cambridge University Press, 2019.

Taskale, Ali Riza. *Post-Politics in Context*. New York: Routledge, 2016.

Williams, James. "His Life to Film: The Extreme Art of Jacques Nolot." *Studies in French Cinema* 9.2 (2009): 177–90.

The Absent/Omnipresent Female Voice in *Dead Silence*

FERNANDO GABRIEL PAGNONI BERNS

James Wan's *Dead Silence* (2007), a film conceived while trying to emerge out of the shadow of his hit movie *Saw* (2004), represents the director's first misstep in his largely successful career to date. A box office flop, the film received poor reviews[1] on release. With the advantage of time, however, it is possible to re-evaluate *Dead Silence* for it acts as a blueprint for things to come, influencing all the horror films Wan (and his many imitators) will direct in the following years. Wan's approach to horror, one that privileges the subtle and a sense of atmospheric dread, finds its trademark in this unjustly neglected film. Like other of Wan's stories, *Dead Silence* evokes the horrors made by Universal Studios through the American golden age of horror (1931 to late 1940s) and, especially, the films produced by Val Lewton and directed by Jacques Tourneur, such as *Cat People* (1942). Even the logo of Universal Studios used in the film is an appropriation of the 1930s classical image in black and white with an old airplane model circling the globe (the appropriation also includes bad sound and an image with a scratched surface), a signpost indicating the love Wan has for classic cinema—a love that is shown for the first time in *Dead Silence*.

The imagery of creepy dolls, old crones wearing black veils over their faces, ghostly sheets revealing human forms behind, the bold use of color (especially red) scattered through the film, chiaroscuros hiding unseen horrors and the staging of innovative forms of "jump scares"—someone facing the camera obscuring what is taking place behind he/she, momentarily disappears from the frame to reveal something creepy in the background—are all auteur's trademarks that slowly develop through *Dead Silence*. Yet, the film lacks the academic recognition that it rightly deserves.

The movie also offers viewers a glimpse into Wan's interest in the gendered supernatural. While a film like *Insidious* (2010) revolves around male anxieties regarding fatherhood,[2] *The Conjuring* franchise is lead by Lorraine Warren (Vera Farmiga), a maternal heroine whose powers are vital for the safety of all those battling the forces of evil. Within Wan's corpus of films, *Dead Silence* is his most complex story in terms of gender. It is a "men's film" (arguably, the film can be read as a "buddy film") where women are either absent or silenced. Contradictorily, it is through this absence that the female voice is heavily emphasized.

With its creepy Victorian atmosphere, dilapidated landscapes and ghostly presences, *Dead Silence* is a Gothic film. This story of the supernatural is not only Wan's first venture into the Gothic but also his first engagement with one of the most important tropes of this particular form of fiction: the "Gothic image of a woman trapped in her own tower"[3] and her own narrative. As usual in the Gothic genre, the female's desire for empowerment is chastised with imprisonment and/or death at the end. Certainly, the wrathful ghost leading the film comes from the past to avenge the attempts made to silence her. This essay will argue that *Dead Silence* is predicated on the absent female voice, the latter, however, being the main foundation of the narrative as is a "dead silence" what speaks for the female ghost and is the film's main source of horror. Thus, the absence seems not so much a visual and auditory loss but a contradiction. Here, Wan moves past debates about the relationship or hierarchy between the male and female to find a site where these two seem to "meet" and to signify their contradiction most strikingly: first, through silence and, second, by the female voice being projected through male characters.

All About the (Absent) Woman

The film follows Jamie Ashen (Ryan Kwanten) who receives a mysterious, creepy ventriloquist doll as a gift sent by an anonymous party. Moments after receiving the doll (named Billy), Lisa (Laura Regan), Jamie's wife, is found brutally murdered, her jaw completely ripped apart and her tongue missing. The detective on the case, Lipton (Donnie Wahlberg), suspects Jamie, so the young man is obliged by the circumstances to prove his innocence. Returning to his childhood town of Raven's Fair, he faces the long-lost ghost story of Mary Shaw (Judith Roberts), a female ventriloquist who was murdered, apparently through vigilantism, after being suspected

Opposite: Promotional poster for James Wan's 2007 supernatural horror film *Dead Silence* (Universal). The film was a box-office flop for Wan but recently film scholars have been re-assessing the film in a positive light.

of the murder of an infant. After her death, it seems she has been taking revenge on the townspeople, many of whom are found, like Lisa, with their tongues missing. While investigating the legend and how it is connected to his wife's murder, Jamie could become the next victim.

As stated, the film can be read as one of the most "masculine" Hollywood filmic formulas; that of the buddy film. Even if antagonists at the beginning (a staple in many "buddie films"), Jamie and Detective Lipton unite forces later in their investigation of the murders, becoming uneasy partners. The "buddy film" is a "bromance" (an "intense masculine bond"[4]) which shows a close nonsexual relationship between men who work together, filled with "homosocial and homosexual subtexts."[5] Indeed, the detective seems to be obsessed with Jamie, going so far as following the young man in his trip to his native town (without nobody mentioning how strange is that Lipton has abandoned, albeit momentarily, his work as a cop in New York to travel thousands of miles to follow a weak case). Lipton even surreptitiously intrudes within Jamie's room in the hotel, a gesture that reveals desires of intimacy. Still, the "buddy film" negotiates and resolves "crises of masculine identity centered on questions of class, race and sexual orientation, by affirming dominant cultural and institutional apparati."[6] After attending an appointment in a dilapidated eerie theater, Lipton is killed by the ghost of Mary Shaw, thus leaving any tension between the two men unresolved. Still, the film narrates a story "between men": without any (alive) female lead, the narrative progresses with the investigation carried out by the couple of men.

In this scenario, women are (seemingly) relegated to the margins. Lisa has been killed in the opening, her role little more than a brief cameo. Mary Shaw is a ghost, her face never completely revealed to the audiences as it remains slightly covered by shadows, veils and curtains through the film. Wan arranges the *mise-en-scène* to avoid showing Mary Shaw in full even when the woman is performing at a well-lighted stage. In one of the film's flashbacks, the ventriloquist is shown for the first time to audiences. She is seen performing a show in a huge theater (the same both Jamie and Detective Lipton visit years later). The camera frames her from behind, her face obscured to viewers. In other shots, she is in front of the camera; her face, however, is cut by the frame, Billy, her ventriloquist doll being the center of the shot. When the eye of the camera finally centers her, her face remains half-obscured by shadows. Her only close-up takes place immediately before the flashback dissolves into the present. Being a ghost in the present and a ghost-like presence in the past, Mary Shaw lives at the margins of *Dead Silence*. The other only important female character, Ella Ashen (Amber Valletta), Jamie's stepmother, serves merely as the concerned companion of her husband and Jamie's father, Edward Ashen (Bob Gunton).

The marginal status of all these women will be revealed, at the end, as illusory. On the surface, however, the story is led by Jamie and Detective Lipton, as it is their inquisitive gaze what drives the narrative forward.

With women turned mute (Lisa) or invisible (Mary Shaw), the story is positively masculine. This is a heavy contradiction of the Gothic genre (to which *Dead Silence* is molded). Gothic fiction features "heroines preyed on by unspeakable terrors,"[7] a sign of social and spatial marginalization, as women were deemed, at the time when Gothic fiction was more fertile, inscrutable and frequently excluded from social life. The Gothic genre and style, "an extremely promiscuous and fertile aesthetic and affective category" is "characterized by stylistic excess, and by stories that thematize the transgression of boundaries and values. In its ability to express, evoke and produce fear and anxiety, the gothic mode figures the underside to the rational, the stable and the moral."[8] The Gothic heroine was an exploration on female selfhood, as the inquisitive female gaze denied the passivity and domestic nature associated with the feminine. Trapped within the domestic space, the Gothic heroine actively searched for an escape. The "Gaslight Gothic Melodrama," so popular in the 1940s, was predicated upon the idea of women slowly becoming mentally unhinged by actions of a patriarchal oppressive figure (usually, the husband) or a supernatural intervention, one of the other overlapping as seen in Alfred Hitchcock's *Rebecca* (1940), *Gaslight* (George Cuckor, 1944) or *Secret Beyond the Door* (Fritz Lang, 1947). In brief, the Gothic heroine looks for a place to inhabit within a patriarchal universe that denies woman any agency and voice. Still, *Dead Silence*, a Gothic text, recurrently suppresses the female voice.

Indeed, Wan's film has all the ingredients of a Gothic text. It has a spectral presence who simultaneously participates in the spheres of the corporeal (as reincarnated in a character within the film) and the incorporeal (as a ghost)[9] who is part of the main Gothic trope: the past haunting and shaping the present.[10] Mary Shaw and her vengeance is the communication between the past and the present, the dead and the living. The film also has murder, fear, and decaying buildings signifying the weakening of the rationale and the enthroning of disorder.[11] What the text lacks is a heroine, a female voice, a woman in distress.

The female voice, however, is the main architect of the film as it embodies the complexities of the narration. One is struck not only by the Gothic proportions of the film's plot but by the idea that *Dead Silence* is really all "about" the feminine. Ironically, the female subject is absent in this film—a bodiless absence that leaves spectators "to confront endlessly and on every level the specter of a femininity he supposedly finds intolerable."[12] Even male characters—if one can consider "male" Billy the dummy—might be imagined to constitute surrogate females rather than channels for male identification. It is the female voice what structures the film. Both Jamie and Lipton are just pawns, puppets moved by strings handled by a female specter who had come to the present to haunt and punish those who had harm her.

It may be argued, and rightly so, that the film, like many Gothic texts, demonizes female subjectivity and desire of agency. After all, the main monster of *Dead Silence* is a female ventriloquist who returns as a female ghost and reincarnates in a woman. Indeed, traditional Gothic demonizes and criminalizes female independence. As noted by Rita Antoni, "representations of strong women characters (and implicitly, feminism) often reach a surprisingly conservative conclusion instead of a subversive and radical one" in many Gothic texts[13] as women are turned into monsters that must be defeated so the status quo can resume. *Dead Silence* does not deny that Mary Shaw is the film's main monster. Still, the story explicitly explains that this specter is the creation of past crimes exerted upon the woman. Rather than a misogynistic tale that asks for the careful surveillance of women, Wan's film addresses how the figure of the monstrous feminine is, certainly, a patriarchal fantasy.

Male Throats, Female Voices

As the title credits roll, the film begins showing the images of female hands—those of Mary Shaw—opening a book and passing the pages. The scrapbook contains black and white photographs of Mary Shaw with her family and Billy, her favorite dummy. All the photographs, apparently (the editing cuts are abrupt, denying audiences a good look at what Mary is examining in the pages) illustrate Mary's life with her parents, as it seems she never married and never had kids (the legend of Mary Shaw explicitly mentions that she has not children "of her own"). Following the binary logic that "assigned intellectual reproduction to men and biological reproduction to women,"[14] Mary aches for reproduction. But it is not traditional maternal reproduction that Mary is looking for. Mary literally "fabricates" her children without male intervention. As the legend of Shaw says, "Mary had no children, only dolls," the latter replacing the former. Mary's scrapbook is filled with familiar photographs but, also, with drawings of dolls, as if the latter were part of her family. Immediately after closing her scrapbook, Mary starts sketching what would be her "perfect design" (as scribbled as a note in one of the pages), uniting studies on medicine (there are drawings of human parts and organs) with knowledge about puppetry. Mary Shaw thus unites the "essential" female trait (birth, the creation of human life, nurturing) with male characteristics as intellectuality. It is clear that Mary knows of medicine, art and carpentry, as she makes all her dolls herself (as depicted in the opening). She creates life using her skills and rationale rather than through her womb, thus disrupting gender expectations.

Kaja Silverman situates the maternal voice (related to creation and genesis) in "an anterior position to the paternal word, conferring upon it an original (if not originating) status."[15] Silverman, however, is quick to remark the problem with this conception, as the woman is inextricably linked with "the darkness and formlessness of the infant's earliest experiences, rather than with the form-giving illumination of the *logos*," this anteriority implying "primitiveness rather than privilege."[16] In other words, women created the infant from unformed cells, wateriness and fluidity while men are those who gave meaning and "exteriority" to the subjects. As stated, Mary denies the "primitiveness" attached to female birthing through intellectual labor, thus becoming, somehow, deviated from the normal and empowered at the same time. In *Dead Silence,* the maternal voice overpowers the patriarchal word, attesting to a quite remarkable shift of hierarchies and, in consequence, creating a topsy-turvy gendered scenario.

Further, the legend of Mary states that people should "hide" from the ventriloquist's eyes; if she sets her eyes on someone, that person (man or woman) will die. This is an inversion of "the insistent equation of woman with spectacle and man with vision"[17] as is Mary who has the scrutinizing gaze. The many close shots of Billy's eyes, a doll who is Mary's surrogate, emphasize the power of being seen. Even viewers become objects to be looked at, as the eyes filling the whole screen interrogate those watching the narrative unfold. In turn, Mary, as mentioned, remains obscured, blurred by lighting or veils. In one key scene, Jamie is trying to sleep in his hotel in Raven's Fair. Billy is propped against his room's window, the neon red sign outside casting eerie purple hues through the bedroom. The sound drops, announcing the presence of Mary Shaw. Jamie sees the female ghost sitting in the corner, her face slowly turning to see the man, a flowing curtain covering and discovering her face in turns, the light flickering on and off. It is Mary, the female blurred ghost, who scrutinizes Jamie, the (perfectly visible) film's male hero.

This shifting of gender categories is emphasized in the first scene after the credits titles. Jamie is trying to repair the kitchen sink, without any success. Lisa, sitting at the kitchen's table, makes fun of him. Home is imagined as a site for the recurrent enacting of normative heterosexual gender roles. Jamie is trying to perform properly "as a man," repairing what is broken in the house. His masculinity, however, is undermined when he is unable to undertake the repairs, resulting in the couple calling for food delivery. Lisa is the one who takes the initiative to call for food, subtly pushing Jamie's failed attempts at traditional roles at the margins. When the couple receives the doll at their door, it is Lisa who takes it from its box and starts to speak through it, while Jamie looks uninterested. That the doll represents a man, complete with tuxedo and topknot, genders the action. Through the film, those using the doll to speak are women, their female voices filtered through a male-like throat that allows them to speak man-like. Lisa actually uses the doll to scare Jamie (using a creepy voice and evoking Mary Shaw's legend), thus producing a new reverse of the gender expectations; Jamie is the one who is codified as the prototypical "scared woman" of classical horror cinema. When Lisa notes that Jamie is uncomfortable with the doll, she assures him (with a mocking edge in her voice) that she will not let the doll harm him in any way, furthering the reversal of the gender binary.

Lisa's empowerment is short lived, as only Mary has the power to see and speak with power as she, unlike Jamie's wife, is fully "deviant." Alone in the apartment, Lisa starts to experience supernatural occurrences. The ventriloquist doll shows signs of autonomous movement (it changes positions or opens its mouth without anybody touching it) and a deep silence obliterates all sound within the apartment. As viewers will learn as the film progresses, the supernatural entrance of the ghostly powers to the world of the living comes with a sudden and complete erasing of sound (the "dead silence" of the title). Nobody can hear anything, not even human words. Language, the first and most important social and cultural construction, is demolished to give voice to the spectral, to a new voice that blends together gender (the ghost is female) and the nonhuman, as the specter talks through dolls made of wood. Immediately after Jamie leaves the apartment, Lisa and her unborn child are killed by the ghost of Mary Shaw.

It can be argued that the specter's revenge also affects women. Like Mary Shaw, Lisa is reproductive, as she is pregnant with Jamie's baby. Still, Lisa' role is more traditional, as she follows common forms of motherhood linked to the "primitiveness" and conservatism. Unlike the wrathful ghost, Lisa is a wife and a mother, a sharp contrast with Mary's deviance. Lisa does not defy patriarchy since she is complementary to it through her reproductive role. As such, Lisa belongs to the patriarchal sphere and, thus, she becomes an eligible victim.

A surprising amount of negative effects accumulate around the human voice in *Dead Silence*, concentrating primarily around four disruptive images: the woman speaking through an item which works as a surrogate for a man (the man-like doll), the man who acts following the patterns traced by a woman (Jamie desists of fixing the kitchen sink and gets outside—under a heavy rain—to get Lisa Chinese food), the missing tongues (as the ghost takes with her the tool for speaking) and the supernatural silence that replaces the female, obliterated voice. It is through these interconnected terms, I suggest, that we can best grasp both the masculine identity for which the female voice poses a potential crisis, and the motive behind the displacement of patriarchal voice onto silence, the latter disrupting the (patriarchal) logos.

As Britta Sjogren sharply argues, women who are able to carry the narration—for example, through the resource of voice-over—are either elided or silenced at the end. Women in these films "'learn' in the course of the narrative, to 'hold their tongue' or suffer the consequences."[18] Indeed this is the case with many classic films in which women (for instance, the *femme fatale* of noir cinema) appear to speak only to be punished in the film climax, either with death or marriage, the latter a way to bind the female character within the space of domesticity. *Dead Silence* boldly stresses not Mary's access to a narrative extra-diegetic voice-over but her silence, barely showing her at all except to posit her as a cathartic medium through which patriarchy can exert oppression. The film does not emphasize the fact that Mary Shaw is a woman even when female ventriloquists were a rarity.[19] Mary was murdered by people of her town after a kid, who previously put in doubt Mary's ability as a ventriloquist, disappeared and was never found. Without anything concrete linking Mary with the disappearance, the murder seems especially unjustified, an act of misogyny carried out more due to Mary' disinterest in giving birth in a "normal" way than a reaction of vengeance. Mary is deviant long before the crime, both by her quality as a businesswoman and her non-nurturing nature. A flashback reveals that Mary knows how to perform before children and enchant them with her voice tricks, but also shows her lack of patience with kids' misbehavior. Mary looks especially annoyed at being interrupted in her performance for a kid. This lack of empathy with kids (exacerbated by her own lack of children) codifies Mary's femininity as a deviance from "proper" forms of womanhood.

Importantly, the ghostly Mary steals the possibility of others to speak, keeping the power of the said word only for herself. As mentioned, Shaw's ghostly attacks take place obliterating any sound and speech, stealing not just sound but voice. Even if taken to supernatural extremes, this ability to speak for others is an uncanny continuation of Mary in life. As both a ventriloquist and a woman, Mary achieved the ability to speak out in the public sphere through other mediums more than her throat. She speaks through her stomach (in ancient times, "people thought a ventriloquist's voice was generated in his stomach"[20]) and through a male dummy. At first, this seems a conservative shift, as Mary speaks from others in order to be heard. In fact, she needs a man (Billy) to be heard, to achieve the possibility of speaking in public. Still, Mary has had full agency since the beginning. Reviewing the box containing Billy the dummy, Jamie finds an old brochure mentioning "Mary Shaw & Billy." Rather than being part of the show, Mary *is* the whole show. It is clear the ventriloquist is a businesswoman who carries her career upon her shoulders. As such, she is obliged to speak out in a world of men. Still, she finds a male doppelgänger in her doll Billy. Only in death, now completely disembodied, she is able to take her voice to extremes, becoming, more than a narrative voice-over, the subject carrying the narrative. At its salient level, *Death Silence* is the story of a woman exerting vengeance and succeeding in doing so. As a woman, Mary has always been silenced by men, the most extreme case being her murder; the only survivor of the original massacre is, coincidentally, a man: Jamie's father. Now, as a ghost, she has the ability to shut down the voices of all those around her while only she can speak.

The film positions itself at a paradoxical juncture, as it presents itself as a "buddy film" but is actually constructed by an absent woman. When Jamie arrives at his father's mansion, he is greeted there by his stepmother, who uses the occasion to introduce herself to her stepson. Jamie gently pushes her aside and gets into the house, anxious to talk to his father. Jamie pays no attention to Ella, a mistake on his part, as the stepmother is the material reincarnation of Mary Shaw and the one behind Lisa's murder. Ella is not the only woman silenced by men; Marion Walker (Joan Heney), wife of the town's mortician, is the only character who wants to warn Jamie of the ghost haunting Raven's Fair. However, she is recurrently silenced by her husband Henry (Michael Fairman), who tells Jamie his wife is losing her mind and likes to spread weird gossip. Judith Baxter mentions "that women's speech is often relegated to non-prestigious genres (such as chatter or gossip)"[21] and, as such, is regarded as worthless. Ironically, Henry will tell Jamie all about Mary Shaw in a latter scene, his voice apparently "legitimate" by his condition as a man.

Lastly, the supernatural ability that the ghostly Mary has to imitate any voice (female or male) emphasizes the fact that she has the ability not only to speak even after her murder, but also the capacity to steal what is considered a man's right; to speak for everybody. In the film's climax, it is revealed that Jamie's father is dead and has been throughout the film. It is Ella/Mary who speaks for him and makes him move to simulate life. At the end, Mary has stolen the voices of all men in the film, including Jamie, who is killed at the climax. With this last act of murder, the film denies a comfortable return to the (patriarchal) status quo. It is Mary's voice that prevails at the end, revealing itself as the real master puppeteer all along.

Conclusions

Before the film credits, *Dead Silence* presents a title that says: "In the 6th century B.C, it was believed that the spirits of the dead would speak through the stomach region of the living." Thus, women and specters share the same marginal position; woman and spirits talk through the stomach. As a Gothic text, the film proposes ambiguity and the rupture of borders. Presented as a "men's film" where women are either absent, silenced or killed (here, analog terms), Mary Shaw is the architect of the story, as the film narrates her vengeance.

In the showdown taking place in the dilapidated theater, it is revealed that Mary, indeed, killed a kid years ago. This way, the film conservatively conflates together, once again, the feminine with the monstrous and the evil. This reactionary retreat into stale age-old prejudices, however, does not deprive the film of any of its potential as a "female text." The depiction of Mary as a woman capable of harming a child further separates her from the essential role of women as life-nurturers and life bearers.

In the same scene in the abandoned theater, audiences are shown Mary's spectral tongue: the appendage is a monstrous, over-long phallic thing covered with slime. Mary's monstrous tongue is the material manifestation of her voice, one that obliterates that of men and other women. Mary's voice is doubly monstrous because she is a child murderer and because she refuses to remain wordless, both in life and in death. The main difference lies in voice and embodiment. As a living woman, she has a body and a throat; she escapes patriarchal boundaries by projecting her voice and putting her male surrogate, Billy, in center stage. As a dead woman, as a vengeful specter, she is disembodied, her presence a blur not to be looked at. As such, she becomes the only site of enunciation, as everything goes as she has planned. She is monstrous not because of her killer nature, but because she drowns speech. Together with James Wan, she has been directing all the action in *Dead Silence*.

Notes

1. For example, Anna Smith invites viewers to "avoid this insipid attempt at reviving the killer doll horror" (https://www.empireonline.com/movies/reviews/dead-silence-review/), accessed April 1, 2020, while Mark Kermode calls the film "creaky" and filled with "over-familiarity" (https://www.theguardian.com/film/2007/jul/08/horror.markkermode/), accessed April 1, 2020.

2. Fernando Gabriel Pagnoni Berns and Canela Ailen Rodríguez Fontao, "New Paternal Anxieties in Contemporary Horror Cinema: Protecting the Family Against (Supernatural) External Attacks," in *Deconstructing Dads: Changing Images of Fathers in Popular Culture*, ed. Laura Tropp and Janice Kelly (Lanham, MD: Scarecrow Press, 2015), 165.

3. Gina Wisker, *Contemporary Women's Gothic Fiction: Carnival, Hauntings and Vampire Kisses* (New York: Palgrave Macmillan, 2016), 74.

4. Hilary Radner, "Grumpy Old Men: Bros Before Hos," in *Reading the Bromance: Homosocial Relationships in Film and Television*, ed. Michael DeAngelis (Detroit: Wayne State University Press, 2014), 56.

5. Annette Kuhn and Guy Westwell, *A Dictionary of Film Studies* (Oxford: Oxford University Press, 2012), 50.

6. Cynthia Fuchs, "The Buddy Politic," in *Screening the Male: Exploring Masculinities in Hollywood Cinema*, ed. Steven Cohan and Ina Rae Hark (New York: Routledge, 1996), 195.
7. Belinda Waller-Peterson, "The Convent as Coven: Gothic Implications of Women-Centered Illness and Healing Narratives in Toni Morrison's *Paradise*," in *Gothic Landscapes: Changing Eras, Changing Cultures, Changing Anxieties*, ed. Sharon Rose Yang and Kathleen Healey (New York: Palgrave Macmillan, 2016), 150.
8. Helen Hanson, *Hollywood Heroines: Women in Film Noir and the Female Gothic Film* (London: I.B. Tauris, 2007), 33–4.
9. Dani Cavallaro, *Gothic Vision: Three Centuries of Horror, Terror and Fear* (London: Continuum, 2002), 80.
10. Fred Botting, *Gothic* (New York: Routledge, 2014), 29.
11. Laura Hubner, *Fairytale and Gothic Horror: Uncanny Transformations in Film* (New York: Palgrave Macmillan, 2018), 58.
12. Britta Sjogren, *Into the Vortex: Female Voice and Paradox in Film* (Urbana: University of Illinois Press, 2006), 46.
13. Cited in Bethan Jones, "Buffy Vs. Bella: Gender, Relationships and the Modern Vampire," in *The Modern Vampire and Human Identity*, ed. Deborah Mutch (New York: Palgrave Macmillan, 2012), 54.
14. Valerie Rohy, *Impossible Women: Lesbian Figures and American Literature* (Ithaca: Cornell University Press, 2018), 160.
15. Kaja Silverman, *The Acoustic Mirror: The Female Voice in Psychoanalysis and Cinema. Theories of Representation and Difference* (Bloomington: Indiana University Press, 1988), 75.
16. Ibid.
17. Silverman, *The Acoustic Mirror*, 29.
18. Sjogren, *Into the Vortex*, 16.
19. Helen Davies, *Gender and Ventriloquism in Victorian and Neo-Victorian Fiction: Passionate Puppets* (New York: Palgrave Macmillan, 2012), 174.
20. Charles Hodgson, *Carnal Knowledge: A Navel Gazer's Dictionary of Anatomy, Etymology, and Trivia* (New York: St. Martin's Griffin, 2007), 160.
21. Judith Baxter, "Introduction," in *Speaking Out: The Female Voice in Public Contexts*, ed. Judith Baxter (New York: Palgrave Macmillan, 2006), xv.

Works Cited

Baxter, Judith. "Introduction." In *Speaking Out: The Female Voice in Public Contexts*, edited by Judith Baxter, xiii–xviii. New York: Palgrave Macmillan, 2006.
Botting, Fred. *Gothic*. New York: Routledge, 2014.
Cavallaro, Dani. *Gothic Vision: Three Centuries of Horror, Terror and Fear*. London: Continuum, 2002.
Davies, Helen. *Gender and Ventriloquism in Victorian and Neo-Victorian Fiction: Passionate Puppets*. New York: Palgrave Macmillan, 2012.
Fuchs, Cynthia. "The Buddy Politic." In *Screening the Male: Exploring Masculinities in Hollywood Cinema*, edited by Steven Cohan and Ina Rae Hark, 194–212. New York: Routledge, 1996.
Hanson, Hanson. *Hollywood Heroines: Women in Film Noir and the Female Gothic Film*. London: I.B. Tauris, 2007.
Hodgson, Charles. *Carnal Knowledge: A Navel Gazer's Dictionary of Anatomy, Etymology, and Trivia*. New York: St. Martin's Griffin, 2007.
Hubner, Laura. *Fairytale and Gothic Horror: Uncanny Transformations In Film*. New York: Palgrave Macmillan, 2018.
Jones, Bethan. "Buffy Vs. Bella: Gender, Relationships and the Modern Vampire." in *The Modern Vampire and Human Identity*, edited by Deborah Mutch, 37–54. New York: Palgrave Macmillan, 2012.
Kuhn, Annette, and Guy Westwell. *A Dictionary of Film Studies*. Oxford: Oxford University Press, 2012.

Pagnoni Berns, Fernando Gabriel, and Canela Ailen Rodríguez Fontao. "New Paternal Anxieties in Contemporary Horror Cinema: Protecting the Family Against (Supernatural) External Attacks." In *Deconstructing Dads: Changing Images of Fathers in Popular Culture*, edited by Laura Tropp and Janice Kelly, 165–184. Lanham, MD: Scarecrow Press, 2015.

Radner, Hilary. "Grumpy Old Men: Bros Before Hos." In *Reading the Bromance: Homosocial Relationships in Film and Television*, edited by Michael DeAngelis, 52–78. Detroit: Wayne State University Press, 2014.

Rohy, Valerie. *Impossible Women: Lesbian Figures and American Literature*. Ithaca: Cornell University Press, 2018.

Silverman, Kaja. *The Acoustic Mirror: The Female Voice in Psychoanalysis and Cinema (Theories of Representation and Difference)*. Bloomington: Indiana University Press, 1988.

Sjogren, Britta. *Into the Vortex: Female Voice and Paradox in Film*. Urbana: University of Illinois Press, 2006.

Waller-Peterson, Belinda. "The Convent as Coven: Gothic Implications of Women-Centered Illness and Healing Narratives in Toni Morrison's *Paradise*." In *Gothic Landscapes: Changing Eras, Changing Cultures, Changing Anxieties*, edited by Sharon Rose Yang and Kathleen Healey, 147–168. New York: Palgrave Macmillan, 2016.

Wisker, Gina. *Contemporary Women's Gothic Fiction: Carnival, Hauntings and Vampire Kisses*. New York: Palgrave Macmillan, 2016.

Wan and the Classical (New) Horror Film

James Wan's Dead Space
The Conjuring *Films, Siegfried Kracauer and the Revenge of Physical Reality*

JOSHUA SCHULZE

Horror has a unique relationship to *things*. In its quest to frighten us and keep us on edge, it works to make the frame itself volatile, and activates an unusual, even uneasy awareness of the *mise-en-scène*. The success of such awareness is largely dependent on a film's configuration of space and place. This has not escaped the attention of recent scholarship. Indeed, building on Carol Clover's famous notion of the "terrible place,"[1] Adam Lowenstein has developed the concept of "subtractive spectatorship" in the slasher genre, which provokes "a desire to subtract or erase human beings from the landscape, to leave it empty,"[2] while Karl Schoonover identifies "spaces replete with dark pockets of menacing vacancy"[3] as integral to the genre. In other words, horror has a singular relationship to what we might broadly categorize as "nonhuman" matter, or "dead" space in the frame, which warrants more exploration than it has so far yielded.

There are few filmmakers better suited to such a problem than James Wan, whose recent contributions to the genre, including *Insidious* (2010), *Insidious: Chapter 2* (2013), *The Conjuring* (2013), and *The Conjuring 2* (2016), exhibit something of a mastery of dead space. Wan's films navigate physical and architectural spaces with extraordinary grace and formal prowess, in a way that encourages the viewer to scan the frame for details that might otherwise escape their attention. While recent work has put the Gothic into conversation with eco-criticism,[4] approaches that negotiate how specific aspects of film form contribute to an ecological configuration of space remain few and far between. Thus, in its analysis, this essay will turn to film theory—the work of Siegfried Kracauer in particular—so as to retain an emphasis on Wan's filmmaking itself, in the spirit of this edited collection.

Focusing on both of Wan's *Conjuring* films, this essay will investigate to what ends the formal properties of the horror genre can suggest new ways of thinking about the world around us, or what is normally classified as "nonhuman." First, we will outline some prescient ideas from Kracauer's *Theory of Film: The Redemption of Physical Reality* (1960) in order to suggest their utility in contemporary discussions of horror and ecology, before moving into an analysis of *The Conjuring,* with the aim of extrapolating some of the ways in which its curious composition style results in a decentering of the human characters that can be read as ecologically progressive. Then, we will turn to some key moments from *The Conjuring 2* in order to explore how the presentation of nonhuman matter manipulates and is manipulated by the passage of time through Wan's use of the long take.

Re-Conjuring Kracauer

Because of his preoccupation with the camera's indexical qualities, the concepts in Kracauer's *Theory of Film* are often described in similar terms to those of André Bazin—Robert Stam, for example, argues that both Kracauer and Bazin "made the camera's putatively intrinsic realism the cornerstone of a democratic and egalitarian aesthetic."[5] Indeed, Kracauer famously characterized film as a medium "uniquely equipped to record and reveal physical reality and, hence, gravitates toward it."[6] In spite of this, throughout the book it is suggested that what we understand to constitute physical reality does not necessarily include the human at all. Near the end of *Theory of Film*, Kracauer invokes the notion that fragments of the material world, when captured by a camera, "inadvertently tell a story of their own, which for a transient moment makes one completely forget the manifest story."[7] In other words, the redemption of physical reality, as per the book's subtitle, often comes at a consequence of the narrative that is carried by the human actors on screen. One might go as far as to suggest that Kracauer's philosophy of the cinematic image actually favors a decentering of the human body, relying on a commonality between the filmmaker's subservience to the world around them, and the capacity of things to announce themselves to the camera as it is pointed toward t hem.

Can we really call such an attitude democratic and egalitarian? Bazin, for example, does laud *Bicycle Thieves* (Vittorio De Sica, 1948) for "not betraying the essence of things, in allowing them first of all to exist for their own sakes, freely; it is in loving them in their own singular individuality"[8]; but this depends on what we are willing to call a "thing," and

Bazin's commitment to humanism is more legible through his favoring of deep focus photography and long takes that democratize the space that the actors inhabit. While Jennifer Fay has recently argued that Bazin's humanism is "more capacious and creaturely than is typically acknowledged [and] very much aligned with critical theory's unending project to unmoor the human as the center of knowledge,"[9] it is my contention that Kracauer's later work can offer the field of film studies a great deal of insight during its current eco-critical turn.[10]

Scholars such as Schoonover and Fay have already read aspects of *Theory of Film* in ecological terms,[11] and yet, there is much more about our relationship to the world, and the horror genre in particular, that can be learned by (re)turning to Kracauer. For example, Johannes von Moltke describes Kracauer's vision as one that "entailed nothing short of a renewal of our capacity to experience the world, and thereby to reconstitute an integral sense of subjectivity, memory, and the freedom to act."[12] The emphasis on renewal and reconstitution highlights the enduring applicability of Kracauer's work, as the world, and our relationship to it, continues to evolve—for better or worse. Indeed, in the interest of exploring the utility of Kracauer at a time when the medium of cinema has been provocatively rebranded by Fay as "the aesthetic practice of the Anthropocene,"[13] we can begin to tease out the darker implications of his otherwise utopian vision of cinema as a connecting agent between humans and the world around them. What if the material reality that usurps the human story at hand does so with malevolence, or threat? Is there room for horror in Kracauer? In a strange sense, Kracauer's human-decentering vision of a perfect cinema foresaw the post-human turn in the humanities, and his love of material reality—and desire for cinema to bring us closer to it—to some degree anticipates the kind of thinking on which object-oriented ontology (OOO)[14] is founded. Yet, to make eco-critical use of Kracauer's horizontalized utopianism, and for physical reality to be properly redeemed, first, it may need to take its revenge.

The Conjuring: *Dead Space Comes Alive*

The Conjuring follows famed paranormal investigators Ed (Patrick Wilson) and Lorraine (Vera Farmiga) Warren as they come to the aid of the Perron family, who find their Rhode Island abode the unfortunate subject of supernatural occurrences. Far from a nuts-and-bolts haunted house story, the film is directed with stylistic flourish, and features a noticeable preoccupation with empty space. Wan deploys a variety of wide shots and sparse framing to accentuate the space surrounding the characters at any given moment, thereby increasing the sense of dread that something unsavory may be lurking close by. Not only that, but the film establishes, in its opening moments, the capacity for inanimate objects to be used as conduits by demonic entities. When Ed is quizzed on why he keeps these objects in a storage room, he responds: "sometimes it's better to keep the genie in the lamp." This expository dialogue thus informs the film's composition style when the audience are primed from the start to be aware of the possibility that seemingly innocuous *things* may in fact be under demonic control, which results in the film configuring an intriguing relationship to nonhuman matter.

Around a third of the way into the film, there is a moment involving a wardrobe that exemplifies *The Conjuring*'s horizontalizing attitude toward such matter. The oldest sister of the Perron family, Andrea (Shanley Caswell), is woken up in the night by the sound of her sister Cindy (Mackenzie Foy) banging her head against the aforementioned wardrobe. When she gets up to investigate, the camera pushes in along with her movement across the room, leaving the bed out of the frame for the time being. When Andrea gently stops her sister's head from hitting the wardrobe, she slowly walks her back toward the bed, while the camera accordingly pulls back to bring the bed into the frame again. Then, crucially, while Andrea tucks Cindy in, the decision to restore the original set-up with the wardrobe visible in the background, reaps its reward when its presence invokes a sense of unease in the suspecting audience, who wait for some kind of "activation"—and, indeed, the suspense pays off when the banging sound continues autonomously.

Normally, a wardrobe in the background of the frame, or any aspect of the décor for that matter, would not draw such attention to itself. Kracauer, on the one hand, would likely argue that nothing is stopping the viewer or a truly great film from drawing attention toward physical matter, but that for the majority of the time these kinds of things go unnoticed. He writes, "films in which the inanimate merely serves as a background to self-contained dialogue and the closed circuit of human relationships are essentially uncinematic."[15] In this moment alone, the wardrobe—an object of physical/material reality by all accounts—is elevated from passive matter to active agent through a combination of the visual import assigned to it by the film's framing, and our knowledge of the demonic presences lurking in the house. This is made clear by the fact that Cindy herself remains off-screen in bed while the wardrobe occupies nearly half of the image, indicating a hierarchy of agency that relegates the humans to passive subjects. Horror, in this mode, thus yields the capacity to upend our preconceived notions of subject/object binaries, and, in doing so, provokes an ecologically minded reconsideration of our relationship to the material world.

Promotional poster for James Wan's *The Conjuring* (Warner Bros., 2013).

The idea that matter, such as a wardrobe, can become an agent capable of affecting human subjects is indeed an unsettling one, but perhaps it is needed for us to attend to the devastating impact humans have had on the environment, which might well be framed as a consequence of such a hierarchical conceptualization of active/passive matter. In her book *Vibrant Matter: A Political Ecology of Things* (2009), Jane Bennett seeks to destabilize these binaries in an effort to horizontalize all matter, and move toward what she calls a "vital materialism."[16] She later describes her objective as being "to theorize a kind of geoaffect or material vitality, a theory born of a methodological commitment to avoid anthropocentrism and biocentrism—or perhaps it is more accurate to say that is born of an irrational love of matter."[17] In that respect, in order to achieve a love of matter, it may be that first we need to fear it. More insidiously, if matter were to use its agency for malevolent purposes, what would it mean for us to discover that even emptiness—the space between *things*—possesses the same ability?

To take an example from early on in the film, the father of the Perron family, Roger (Ron Livingston), is asleep at his desk in the middle of the night. The image is presented in a disorienting wide shot that covers two rooms in the house, keeping the static television on the left of the frame with Roger on the right. The lighting and asymmetrical positioning of the camera draw more attention to the television set than to Roger himself, and the general prevalence of décor renders the human subject difficult to locate in the frame. This pattern continues in the rest of the sequence, which has Roger at one point scanning the room from left to right after he hears a noise, and in both compositions the lamps are more noticeable than Roger himself. When he gets up to turn off the television, the image is comprised of various vertical structures of a similar color and tone, blending Roger in with the surroundings, and yet again refusing to regard him as visually more important. As he makes his way to the corridor, with the camera passing across the doorway and momentarily abandoning him, Roger is barely visible amongst the architecture of the house, and only the lamps really stand out in the frame. The sequence culminates when the door in the background begins to creak, and the film then cuts to a humanless shot of the door beginning to open by itself. In sum, this series of shots configures a disturbing attitude toward matter: that things, objects, and even space itself are more powerful than humans when they can be yielded by a demon or spirit. Roger is constantly decentered, even lost in the frame, and the audience are thus drawn to the physical structures of the house and a variety of otherwise inanimate objects more than they are to the human body, in a distorted interpretation of Kracauer's idea of what cinema ought to do.

If, in this sequence, it feels as though the empty space itself is malevolent, the expertise of Lorrain Warren around the halfway point of the film confirms this suspicion. Sitting Roger and his wife Carolyn (Lili Taylor) down to explain the situation, Ed and Lorraine inform them that the house is indeed haunted, and that—more pressingly—the demonic spirits have attached themselves to the Perron family itself. In a series of flashbacks from when the Warrens first stepped into the house, Lorraine narrates that she saw "the dark energy that haunts your house and your land [...] it was latched to your back." We see the same shots from before, with a dark presence now lurking in the background. Through Lorraine's clairvoyance, the space that we once perceived as empty—yet was coded by the film's framing as malevolent—is shown in retrospect to be occupied by demons. Thus, not only might inanimate objects themselves be weaponized as conduits by unsavory spirits, but also the very space between them is made accessible to them. This moment of exposition seems almost designed to encourage reviewing the film with the new knowledge in mind, activating not just awareness, but a fear of the emptiness surrounding the characters in Wan's signature sparse compositions. In a warped sense, then, this adheres to Kracauer's notion that cinema "aims at transforming the agitated witness into a conscious observer."[18] At the very least, it gives the term "dead space" an eerie resonance that it perhaps did not possess before.

The Conjuring 2: *Matter Takes Its Time*

If Wan's filmmaking in *The Conjuring* helped to recalibrate our emphasis on to the nonhuman matter that surrounds characters in the frame—redeeming it by showcasing its malice—in *The Conjuring 2* his use of the long take enables such matter to manipulate time itself. The film documents the famous Enfield poltergeist of 1977, with Ed and Lorraine Warren returning to offer their expertise to the family in need. While, interestingly, Wan adapts his style from the first film to accommodate the comparatively small architectural space of the Hodgson residence, there are several instances in which the durational qualities of the long take allow objects to negotiate their status within the image as it unfolds in time, often playing with or subverting the human elements that simultaneously occupy the same space. In doing so, they reiterate the material integrity of these objects, while, as in the first film, reemphasizing their power to upend the human story playing out, in a fashion that reworks and repurposes Kracauer's approach.

On one of the first nights that the Hodgson family begin to register the paranormal activity in their house, youngest son Billy (Benjamin Haigh) ventures downstairs to have a glass of water. When he makes his way back to his room, Billy passes the tipi tent at the landing of the stairs, before stubbing his toe on a toy fire truck that sounds its alarm. He responds by picking it up, turning it off, and wheeling it back into the entrance of the tent, from which it had (seemingly innocuously) escaped. When Billy returns on his way back to bed, the film cuts to a wide shot from within his room that keeps the tent at the end of the passage visible in the background. This sets up the long take that follows.

Lasting just under a minute, the shot is composed in a way that allows a simple lateral movement to either remove or re-introduce the tent from the camera's field of vision. First, as Billy enters the room and begins to climb on his bed on the left of the frame, the fire truck makes an acousmatic sound that stops him dead in his tracks. The camera then tracks right as Billy nervously peers around the door toward the tent, which responds with teasing, almost mocking silence. Then, Billy tries once more to climb into bed, but the suspicious goings-on have clearly unsettled him; he turns back for another look, the camera accommodating him with another tracking movement. Apparently satisfied, Billy dismisses the tent and returns to his bed—but this time the camera does not follow him, and remains locked on the object at the end of the passage for only the audience to see. For a few seconds, we are left alone with it. That is, until Billy re-enters the frame to catch yet another glimpse, before he eventually climbs into bed, and we wait for the inevitable: the fire truck wheels its way autonomously into Billy's room.

Given the toing and froing of the camera movement up to the point where it fixates on the tent, there is a strange sense of its being stuck, in its refusal (or inability) to follow what feels like the natural logic of Billy's movements. In the context of Wan's tendency to favor and point toward the unsettling agency of nonhuman things under the sway of a demonic presence, this short sequence proposes the idea that such objects have the power to dislodge the very focus of the camera, which normally privileges human movement. Further, by allowing the action to unfold in the space and time of a single shot, the film demonstrates the usurping of the human subject as a gradual process, or what Kracauer calls "reality as it evolves in time."[19] Material reality, in this case, encapsulates the dual effort of the tent and the truck, who conspire for the audience's attention and, over a passage of time, win it—even if we are made to dread the outcome.

Indeed, later on in the film Wan puts the long take to similarly fascinating use, when the police visit the Hodgson residence to investigate the occurrences. After scouting the house for evidence, the two constables (Annie Young and Eliot Joseph), the mother Peggy (Frances O'Connor) and neighbor Vic (Simon Delaney) arrive at the kitchen and walk around. The camera pans along with their movement as they circle the dining table. When a shuddering noise comes from the roof, the camera pulls back as the group approach it to reveal the entrance hall, where they continue to search for the source of the noise. With the kitchen still visible through the doorway, and the sound rattling its way through the walls, constable Heeps walks down the hall, the camera panning with her while Vic stands in the doorway to the kitchen. "Bring me a chair from the kitchen," she instructs to her colleague, who abides. Heeps stands on the chair to better hear through the walls, knocking against them with her torch. A presence knocks back. When she steps off the chair, and speculates with the others as to the cause of the sound, suddenly the chair begins to slide across the floor. It moves down in a straight line toward the doorway, before returning to its original spot at the table—leaving the group speechless.

Yet again, an allegedly inanimate object steals the scene from the human characters. Only this time, to add, it had first been used by one of them, and removed from its place with the other chairs. Crucially, Wan shoots everything in a single take, introducing us to the chair long before it will become the focal point of the scene. Indeed, allowing us to first encounter it as irrelevant, nonhuman matter, before then having it used as a tool, makes the final pay off—when it takes agency and returns to the kitchen—the result of a temporal progression that the audience are made to bear witness to. Thematically, the chair's movement encapsulates the film's broader themes about property ownership; initially, the terror caused in the Hodgson house is thought to be as a consequence of Bill

Wilkins, the previous owner who died in the living room, reclaiming his space from beyond the grave. In that sense, the chair's movement symbolizes a restoration of order and the tidy arrangement of the house back to what it was. In the context of my discussion, however, and in Wan's use of the long take, the chair's movement represents something ecologically significant.

When he outlines cinema's inherent affinity for "things normally unseen," Kracauer writes in particular about the medium's capacity to make cinematic things that "stubbornly escape our attention in everyday life."[20] In a turn of phrase that recalls Sigmund Freud's "Uncanny,"[21] but with a specific focus on film form, Kracauer describes the ways in which film can take familiar objects from everyday life and render them unfamiliar: cinema, he argues, can "alienate our environment by exposing it."[22] Accordingly, the scene with the chair in *The Conjuring 2* represents a vivid instance of an unassuming object taking agency, and changing its own status from passive to active matter in the space of a single shot. The human characters, who, like the audience, likely never paid it so much as a glance before, and used it so dispassionately to aid their investigation, are dumbfounded by their encounter with its agency when it slides across the room by itself. For a brief moment during its movement, Wan's camera fixates on the chair until it fills up a frame otherwise unobstructed by human presence. In other words, the audience, characters, and even camera are made passive subjects to an object's agency, momentarily upending the traditional binaries of human/nonhuman.

At one point in *Vibrant Matter*, Bennett argues that coming to terms with what we consider to be nonhuman, in various ways, can help to unsettle the vertical arrangement of status that shapes and informs the exploitative usage of *things* as exemplified by the constable's asking for the chair in the first place. Bennett writes, "encounters with lively matter can chasten my fantasies of human mastery, highlight the common materiality of all that is, expose a wider distribution of agency, and reshape the self and its interest."[23] The temporal progression of the chair scene encapsulates the range of human attitudes toward such matter, from total ignorance to exploitation, before an encounter with its liveliness emerges as the focal point. The human characters realize in a heartbeat the shortcomings of their assumed mastery and dominion, and are forced to acknowledge the common materiality and horizontal distribution of agency in all kinds of matter—even when it is inhabited by demons. For a transient moment at the end of an expertly orchestrated long take, the physical reality of the chair duly takes its revenge. At the very least, its doing so prompts us to reconsider our relationship to the things around us, if for no other reason than out of fear that they may do the same to us.

Conclusions

Both of James Wan's *Conjuring* films are amongst the highest grossing in the genre's history (*The Conjuring* grossed a total of $137,400,141 while the sequel reached $102,470,008). Undoubtedly due in part to the appeal of his singular filmmaking, his ability to orientate the audience within a particular space that he then mines for every ounce of tension and dread imaginable has not escaped the attention of critics. This edited collection's existence is evidence enough of his growing recognition. More specifically, this essay has foregrounded some overlooked tendencies of his filmmaking that carry with them the potential for ecologically progressive readings. The horror genre—especially entries involving a haunted house—has for a long time turned to the inanimate and the nonhuman to be used as vessels for the paranormal. At the same time, few filmmakers have been as tactful as Wan in their use of empty space and a sparse composition style to amplify our awareness of every object contained within the frame—so much so, as we have demonstrated, that the physical reality, and assumed-to-be-passive matter, yields the capacity to be redeemed. At a time when the humanities continues to revise such binaries as human/nonhuman, subject/object, and passive/active, filmmaking such as Wan's, and the work of theorists such as Kracauer, can help us to unlock what has gone so evidently wrong in our relationship to the world and its matter that surrounds us.

Notes

1. Carol Clover, *Men, Women and Chain Saws* (Princeton, NJ: Princeton University Press, 2015), 31.
2. Adam Lowenstein, "The *Giallo*/Slasher Landscape: *Ecologia del delitto*, Friday the 13th and Subtractive Spectatorship," in *Italian Horror Cinema*, ed. Stefano Baschiera and Russ Hunter (Edinburgh: Edinburgh University Press, 2016), 133.
3. Karl Schoonover, "What Do We Do with Vacant Space in Horror Films?," *Discourse: Journal for Theoretical Studies in Media and Culture* 40:3 (2018): 345.
4. For a useful overview, see the introduction to the inaugural issue of the *Gothic Nature* journal: Elizabeth Parker and Michelle Poland, "*Gothic Nature*: An Introduction," *Gothic Nature*. 1, 1–20 (2019), as well as *Ecogothic*, ed. Andrew Smith and William Hughes (Manchester: Manchester University Press, 2013) and *Ecogothic in Nineteenth-Century American Gothic*, ed. Dawn Keetley and Matthew Wynn Sivils (New York: Routledge, 2017).
5. Robert Stam, *Film Theory: An Introduction* (Oxford: Blackwell, 2000), 74.
6. Siegfried Kracauer, *Theory of Film: The Redemption of Physical Reality* (New York: Oxford University Press, 1960), 28.
7. Kracauer, *Theory*, 302.
8. André Bazin, *What Is Cinema?* Volume II. Trans. Hugh Gray (Berkeley: University of California Press, 1972), 69.
9. Jennifer Fay, "Seeing/Loving Animals: André Bazin's Posthumanism," *Journal of Visual Culture* 7:1 (2008): 42.
10. See Jennifer Peterson and Graig Uhlin, "In Focus: Film and Media Studies in the Anthropocene," *JCMS: Journal of Cinema and Media Studies* 58:2 (2009).

11. See Karl Schoonover, "Documentaries Without Documents: Ecocinema and Toxins," *NECSUS: European Journal of Media Studies* No. 4 (2013) and Jennifer Fay, *Inhospitable World: Cinema in the Time of the Anthropocene* (New York: Oxford University Press, 2018).
12. Johannes von Moltke, "Siegfried Kracauer: The Politics of Film Theory and Criticism," in *Thinking in the Dark: Cinema, Theory, Practice*, ed. Murray Pomerance and R. Barton Palmer (New Brunswick, NJ: Rutgers University Press, 2015), 52.
13. Fay, *Inhospitable World*, 4.
14. "OOO" Is a school of thought that contests that all objects exist independently of human perception. Notable works include Graham Harman, *Object-Oriented Ontology: A New Theory of Everything* (London: Penguin, 2018) and Timothy Morton's *The Ecological Thought* (Cambridge: Harvard University Press, 2010) and *Hyperobjects: Philosophy and Ecology After the End of the World* (Minneapolis: University of Minnesota Press, 2013).
15. Kracauer, *Theory of Film*, 46.
16. Jane Bennett, *Vibrant Matter: A Political Ecology of Things* (Durham: Duke University Press, 2009), Xvi.
17. Bennett, *Vibrant Matter*, 61.
18. Kracauer, *Theory of Film*, 58.
19. Kracauer, *Theory of Film*, 41.
20. Kracauer, *Theory of Film*, 53.
21. Sigmund Freud, "The "Uncanny," in *The Standard Edition of the Complete Psychological Works of Sigmund Freud, Volume XVII (1917–1919): An Infantile Neurosis and Other Works*, 217–256. Translated by James Strachey (London: The Hogarth Press, 1955).
22. Kracauer, *Theory of Film*, 55.
23. Bennett, *Vibrant Matter*, 122.

Works Cited

Bazin, André. *What Is Cinema? Volume II*, translated by Hugh Gray. Berkeley: University of California Press, 1972.
Bennett, Jane. *Vibrant Matter: A Political Ecology of Things*. Durham: Duke University Press, 2009.
Fay, Jennifer. *Inhospitable World: Cinema in the Time of the Anthropocene*. New York: Oxford University Press, 2018.
Fay, Jennifer. "Seeing/Loving Animals: André Bazin's Posthumanism." *Journal of Visual Culture* 7:1 (2008): 41–64.
Freud, Sigmund. "The "Uncanny." In *The Standard Edition of the Complete Psychological Works of Sigmund Freud, Volume XVII (1917–1919): An Infantile Neurosis and Other Works*, translated by James Strachey, 217–56. London: The Hogarth Press, 1955.
Keetley, Dawn, and Matthew Wynn Sivils (eds) *Ecogothic in Nineteenth-Century American Gothic*. New York: Routledge, 2017.
Kracauer, Siegfried. *Theory of Film: The Redemption of Physical Reality*. New York: Oxford University Press, 1965.
Lowenstein, Adam. "The Giallo/Slasher Landscape: *Ecologia del Delitto, Friday the 13th* and Subtractive Spectatorship." In *Italian Horror Cinema*, edited by Stefano Baschiera and Russ Hunter, 127–144. Edinburgh: Edinburgh University Press, 2016.
Parker, Elizabeth, and Michelle Poland. "Gothic Nature: An Introduction." *Gothic Nature*. 1 (2019): 1–20.
Peterson, Jennifer, and Graig Uhlin. "In Focus: Film and Media Studies in the Anthropocene." *JCMS: Journal of Cinema and Media Studies* 58:2 (2019): 142–46.
Schoonover, Karl. "Documentaries Without Documents: Ecocinema and Toxins." *NECSUS: European Journal of Media Studies* No. 4 (2013).
Schoonover, Karl. "What Do We Do with Vacant Space in Horror Films?" *Discourse: Journal for Theoretical Studies in Media and Culture* 40:3 (2018): 342–357.

Smith, Andrew, and William Hughes (eds) *Ecogothic*. Manchester: Manchester University Press, 2013.
Stam, Robert. *Film Theory: An Introduction.* Oxford: Blackwell, 2000.
von Moltke, Johannes. "Siegfried Kracauer: The Politics of Film Theory and Criticism." In *Thinking in the Dark: Cinema, Theory, Practice*, edited by Murray Pomerance and R. Barton Palmer, 42–53. New Brunswick, NJ: Rutgers University Press, 2015.

Chromatic Hauntings
The Uncanny Color Design of James Wan's Horror Films

Cody Parish

One of the most visually pervasive elements of director James Wan's horror films is indisputably his signature color design. A casual viewing of any one of his horror productions reveals Wan's affinity for red and black, one the filmmaker has publicly confirmed. "Red and black are my color palettes that I love," says Wan. "It [sic] really adds to the psychology of the film."[1] Wan grounds this palette in a desaturated aesthetic, lowering the contrast of the cinematography and applying blue filters to the picture to give his films a bleached look. This washed appearance allows the saturated blood reds and charcoal blacks of Wan's films to seize visual dominance over the *mise-en-scène*. While Wan's choice of a red and black palette is by no means novel, the director's stylized spatial orientation of red coloring throughout the *mise-en-scène* produces a meaningful affect beyond solely contributing to atmospheric tension, an affect that influences the viewing experience of his horror films. This affect contributes significantly to distinguishing Wan's brand from the existing cinematic horrorscape, as argued in this essay.

Despite the striking effect of Wan's signature color design, what little scholarly discussion exists on this horror auteur's films noticeably overlooks its significance. Interestingly, the only mention of Wan's red and black color palette appears not in the chapter devoted to color in Murray Leeder's recent treatment of the genre, *Horror Film: A Critical Introduction* (2018),[2] but rather in the final remarks of a discussion about sound design in Brigid Cherry's *Horror* (2009). Cherry notes in passing that Wan subdues red hues in *Dead Silence* (2007) only to punctuate the blood and gore of victims' wounds, generating emotional effects of shock, disgust and revulsion.[3] My own analysis of *Dead Silence* will contest Cherry's claim, proving that Wan aims for more than shock value with his spatial location of red coloring. Suffice it to say that Wan's color design has failed to capture the attention of film scholars until now, but this oversight likely stems from the fact that color analysis has been largely ignored within film studies due to the perceived subjectivity of its experience.

Some scholars have nevertheless posited frameworks with which color analysis can be validated. Sergei Eisenstein, Russian director and pioneer of montage, writes in *The Film Sense* ([1942] 1975) that absolute meanings for colors and their symbols do not exist. While there are "generally accepted" interpretations of color, he says one should derive a color's meaning in film based on "consistency in a definite tone-color key, running through the whole work," which must be "in strict harmony with the work's theme and idea."[4] John Belton builds on Eisenstein's methodology in his analysis of color in Alfred Hitchcock's *Marnie* (1964), stating that the viewer must take cues from the color's context, which "aris[es] from the association of a color with a character, event, object, or situation," in order to glean the specific meaning of that color and circumvent the pitfall of subjective interpretation.[5] It stands that a well-supported color analysis involves identifying consistency in the director's color design, positing specific meanings for colors that are grounded in textually evinced color patterns and associations taken from the film(s) as a whole. James Wan employs such a color design throughout his horror corpus, one of consistency and complexity that interplays with the Freudian conception of the uncanny and the return of the repressed.

The uncanny is an essential concept of psychoanalysis introduced by Sigmund Freud in his 1919 essay, "The Uncanny" ["Das Unheimliche"]. Freud defines the word *uncanny*, or *unheimlich* in German, in opposition to *canny*, or *heimlich*. *Unheimlich* translates to that which is "unhomely" or unfamiliar[6] while *heimlich* refers to what is "homely" or familiar.[7] Freud proceeds to explore a series of paradoxical definitions for *heimlich*, describing how the word signifies both "what is familiar and agreeable" and "what is concealed and kept out of sight."[8] Freud notes here that *canny* eventually assumes the meaning of its opposite; in other words, what is canny becomes uncanny, and what is uncanny becomes canny. With this paradoxical pair of definitions in mind, Freud lists another definition, which states *unheimlich* is something "that ought to have remained secret and hidden but has come to light."[9] Here Freud alludes to perhaps the defining trait of the uncanny—the return of the repressed. He claims that the uncanny entails the repression of something "familiar and old-established in the mind" that "has become alienated from it only through the process of repression."[10] What has been repressed from the past, Freud writes, produces anxiety, or an uncanny unease or fear, when it recurs in the present.[11]

The return of the repressed therefore operates always relationally with time, where something from the past recurs in the present. Moreover, repression functions, according to Freud, as the requisite condition to produce an uncanny effect.[12] Freud identifies death, dead bodies, and ghosts as among those stimuli that elicit the greatest feelings of uncanniness.[13] Going one step further, in his book-length study of the Freudian concept, Nicholas Royle claims that ghosts are "[t]he most striking example of the uncanny."[14] It is no wonder, then, that Wan's horror films evoke the uncanny often and effectively, for ghosts populate almost all of them, the uncanny effect of which Wan visually foregrounds through his signature color design.

Laying the foundation of Wan's color design is his bleached cinematography. Described by critics as "James Wan's aversion to bright color," the drained chromatography paints the *mise-en-scène* of Wan's films as antiquated, deteriorated, and bleak.[15] It is almost as if the narrative diegeses are worlds leeched of hope and life, in which death is either a foregone conclusion or the present reality. Such is the case in *Dead Silence*, for the community of Ravens Fair is all but a ghost town in the wake of Mary Shaw's vengeance. As I will discuss in detail later in this essay, Shaw successfully kills off the Ashen lineage by the time closing credits roll, the imminence of which is visually conveyed through the bleached cinematography. The cinemascape looks void of vitality, as if death has permeated the screen. Wan previously accomplished a similarly bleak affect with *Saw* (2004). The blue-tinged film captures the cold and emotionally calloused approach the Jigsaw killer takes to testing his victims in life-or-death scenarios. The killer's judgment to leave Adam to die in the abandoned industrial bathroom corroborates the clinically sterile affect the viewer may glean from Wan's cinematography, the meaning of which augments the presence of saturated blacks and reds.

Wan's charcoal blacks, oftentimes pronounced in his cinematography, work dialectically with red in order to produce meaning. To elaborate, Brian Price suggests "we perceive color relationally, such that the juxtaposition of two colors determines the colors we perceive."[16] Wan's color palette functions in this way, for the juxtaposition of red to black—of a bright color to a dark color—visually punctuates the presence of red in the *mise-en-scène*. Black therefore serves as a backdrop upon which stylized red hues starkly contrast. At the same time, black coloring develops the ominous atmosphere of each film by deepening shadows to obscure evil beings, ghosts, and/or entities. While black obscures the evil entity, red visually cues the viewer to its presence. To be sure, red can achieve this effect independently of black coloring, though these cases occur less frequently. Nevertheless, red typically interacts dialectically with black to function as the keynote signifier of the uncanny and bring to light what "ought to have remained secret or hidden." As a result, red is deserving of interpretation each time it appears onscreen.

Given that the color red carries numerous cultural connotations, the viewer can avoid subjective interpretation only by adhering to the rigorous methodology for color analysis previously laid out: that is, first, by identifying consistent patterns in Wan's color design throughout his horror films and, second, by positing specific meaning(s) for the stylized red coloring found therein based on its cinematic associations and narrative context. The viewer might begin by taking interpretative cues from Wan himself, for the director has publicly prescribed the meaning of red in his *Insidious* films, claiming that the color simply symbolizes evil.[17] If we understand evil to be a culturally specific religious interpretation of the supernatural and/or demonic, then red certainly represents evil, not just in *Insidious* (2011) but in each of Wan's horror films. After all, in Christian symbolism, red connotes impurity, the devil, demons, and the flames of Hell, each of which contributes to the themes of multiple Wan-directed horror films. It would be a mistake, however, to derive our understanding of red's meaning solely from Wan's authorial intent.[18]

It is my contention, then, that the red coloring in Wan's horror films operates in a complex manner (both deliberately by Wan's intent and of its own accord), signifying the evil, typically spectral and often maternal antagonist of each narrative. Moreover, red marks the presence or threat of this evil entity within human spaces both corporeal and structural. In the color analyses that follow, rather than provide a comprehensive catalog of each instance in which red appears, I will unpack only the most meaningful occurrences of spatially oriented red coloring in two of Wan's horror films: *Dead Silence* and *The Conjuring* (2013).[19] The former exemplifies Wan's stylized red and black color palette at its boldest while the latter, in comparison, presents that same palette in decisively minimalist fashion. Given the association red bears to the spectral antagonists of Wan's films, the color chromatically re-enacts the Freudian notion of the return of a repressed past each time it appears. This visual signification of the uncanny enhances the narrative themes of Wan's films, which, for *Dead Silence* and *The Conjuring*, concern reproduction as well as past and present violence, especially toward children. But not all red in Wan's horror films is meaningful and contributes to these themes, as my color analyses will demonstrate. While Wan often, though certainly not always, digitally brightens reds in postproduction that carry meaning, we can apply the methodology stated previously to distinguish with certainty color of significance from functional aesthetics. The resulting discussion should prove definitive in mapping the contours of Wan's signature color design, illuminating the ways in which this horror auteur has enriched the cinematic experience through formal elements of filmmaking.

Dead Silence: *Red in Extravagance*

Although *Dead Silence* is the most poorly reviewed of Wan's directorial efforts, earning a low score of 20 percent on *Rotten Tomatoes*,[20] it is nevertheless—at least in this author's opinion—his most intriguing horror film to date, which is in no small part due to its spectacular showcase of Wan's signature color design. The narrative concerns the murder of Jamie Ashen's wife on the night an unmarked package containing a mysterious ventriloquist dummy shows up on the couple's apartment doorstep. Jamie (Ryan Kwanten) returns to his hometown of Ravens Fair determined to find the owner of the doll and his wife's killer, exonerating himself in the process from culpability for her murder. Jamie learns that his wife's death is entangled in his family's hidden history of violence toward women and that he, like his wife and others from Ravens Fair, is being h(a)unted by the ghost of Mary Shaw.

More so than *Saw* and Wan's subsequent horror films, *Dead Silence* plays with aesthetic representations of time and space. The conflict of the film's plot revolves around the former, as the ghost of Mary Shaw (Judith Anna Roberts), a local ventriloquist, carries out violent retribution for being murdered by Jamie's ancestors and the other townspeople of Ravens Fair generations ago. After the authenticity of her ventriloquist act is publicly called into question by Jamie's great-uncle, Michael Ashen, who was a child at the time, Mary Shaw is suspected, but never charged and convicted, of killing the boy (in the present, Jamie confirms Shaw murdered his great-uncle when he uncovers the corpse-turned-marionette-puppet in Shaw's hidden doll room). Following Michael Ashen's murder, the Ashen family and other local townsmen take justice into their own hands, cornering Shaw in her private quarters above the theater stage where she performs; there they cut out her tongue, leaving her to bleed to death. Before her tongue is severed, however, Shaw curses the town and its citizens, vowing "to silence all those who silenced me."[21] As a personification of the return of the repressed, Mary Shaw returns from the grave in the form of a ghostly revenant to take her revenge, haunting and killing off each of the Ravens Fair lineages until all are dead. Thus, Jamie realizes that he and his immediate family are "paying for the sins of [his] fathers."[22]

When the past actions of the Ashens come back to haunt Jamie in the present, the two time periods meld together. For this reason, Wan fills the *mise-en-scène* of the film with vintage décor—antique grandfather clocks, old-fashioned stereo systems flanked by vinyl records, framed black and white photographs, and painted family portraits—to illustrate that Ravens Fair and its descendants are trapped by the past that haunts them. Since the past refuses to remain buried, Jamie, the Ashen family, and Ravens Fair cannot move forward with their lives, allowing Mary Shaw the time to kill them off one by one. Shaw assumes the role of evil incarnate in the film, and Wan employs his stylized red coloring to symbolize her presence, which also signals the return of Ravens Fair's violent past that Shaw represents as both deadly revenant and victim.

Recognizing the spaces where Mary Shaw is and is not, therefore, becomes an important task for viewers. Luckily, red-imbued objects, attire, décor, and structures in *Dead Silence* cue the audience to Shaw's presence or the threat thereof throughout the narrative. As one would expect of a ventriloquist, the most readily apparent space that Shaw occupies is that of her dolls. The film begins with a title card that reads, "In the 6th Century B.C. it was believed that the spirits of the dead would speak through the stomach region of the living." Subsequent text fades in on the screen that breaks down the etymology of the word *ventriloquist* into *venter*, or "belly," and *loqui*, meaning "to speak."[23] Just as a house may be occupied by an individual, a ventriloquist dummy may be occupied by a spirit. Hence, Mary Shaw's dummies function as the physical, anthropomorphic vessels through which she moves, speaks, and carries out her killings. Any space where her dolls can be found reveals the presence of Mary Shaw by extension. Her reach thus extends outside the limits of Ravens Fair, as we see when she kills Jamie's wife Lisa (Laura Regan) in their urban apartment located in an unnamed, distant city. Shaw's dummies, particularly her signature Billy doll, which she used in her stage performances, bear the familiar red markings that indicate her presence within the physical space of the doll, and thus the surrounding environment.

Similar to Jigsaw's Billie doll in *Saw*, Wan adorns Mary Shaw's Billy doll in the film proper with a bowtie and pocket square saturated in red coloring.[24] Wan also brightens the red lining of the Billy doll's travel case and, in doing so, highlights red in the frame for viewers to cue them to where Mary Shaw resides. Whereas the dummy often houses Shaw's spirit, the red lining recalls the permanent residence of the dummy and that of Shaw—the Guignol Theater.

In perhaps the most audacious use of stylized red coloring of his cinematic corpus, Wan presents the theater at which Shaw performed her ventriloquist act as a visual array of red. When Henry Walker (Michael Fairman), the Ravens Fair mortician, recalls his first and only experience as a young boy at Guignol, Wan tracks behind him as Walker enters the theater's interior, revealing a large auditorium and a main stage with vibrant red curtains laced with gold trim. Across the front of the stage ceiling hang red drapes to compliment the gold-painted decorative woodwork, these drapes similar to those suspended from each private viewing box flanking the stage. The wood running across the front of the stage and the front of the balcony is also painted red with gold panel designs. Large panels of red cloth patterned with gold diamonds adorn the walls of the auditorium, matching the theater's carpeting. And finally, the theater is furnished with rows of extravagant red seats with red upholstery, saving a special elevated chair on the stage with plush red upholstered cushions for Shaw. Even the host who introduces Mary Shaw in Henry's flashback wears a bright red suit.

Such a lavish color palette draws clear comparisons to the bold aesthetic of famous Italian horror director Dario Argento, for whom Wan has expressed admiration.[25] In *Suspiria* (1977), for example, Argento washes the coven where Suzie Bannion (Jessica Harper) stays in red lighting arguably to cast the entire space as dangerous or evil, but he achieves this affect only through sheer dominance of color. This lurid suffusion of red, as well as other primary colors throughout the film, produces a nightmarish visual assault on the senses that mirrors the violence done to the coven's victims, but otherwise loses specific meaning due to the frequency and expansive nature in which the color appears. Rather than replicate the intensity of Argento's aesthetic through lighting, Wan stylistically arranges the red structure, décor, attire, and props of the Guignol Theater, the color of which stands in stark contrast to Mary Shaw's solid black conservative dress. With her pale skin and old age, she becomes a figure of death.

That Mary Shaw personifies death complements the real-life historical origins of the Guignol Theater, which derives its name from the notorious *Theatre du Grand-Guignol* in Paris, France. Translating in English to "theatre of the large puppet show," the *Theatre du Grand-Guignol* flourished from 1897 to 1962 and was known for its frightening, brutally realistic displays of violence.[26] This homage to the Parisian theater predicates the Guignol Theater in Wan's film as a space of violence, its predominantly red interior visually associating with the blood of those killed within its walls—Michael Ashen, Mary Shaw, and Detective Lipton (Donnie Wahlberg). When coupled with its stylized connotations of evil, red defines the Guignol Theater as the house of evil incarnate and of death itself. Mary Shaw, then, is defined by the space where she lived for her career, in addition to her personal actions and character. The presence of virtually all red in *Dead Silence* is therefore just as much a marker of the Guignol Theater as it is of the evil spirit who inhabits it—the two inextricably intertwine.

Returning to the red-imbued attire on Shaw's Billy doll and the lining of its travel case, it is now clear that Wan visually connects these props to the red stage curtains of the Guignol Theater and to the performance of ventriloquism. Inherent in this connection to the stage and performance is violence and evil, which is made more explicit by the red sheets Shaw uses to conceal her failed puppet experiment on Jamie's great-uncle. Just as the ventriloquist must mask the secret of her performance, the crimson sheet masks Shaw's grisly attempt to create the perfect doll from a human being. The red sheet, however, gives away what it conceals via its color symbolism. For this reason, Wan refrains from dressing Jamie's new stepmother, Ella—Shaw's successful attempt at the perfect doll—and Jamie's father in red in order to prevent the viewer from visually linking either character to Mary Shaw.

Instead, Wan conspicuously places red candles throughout Edward Ashen's (Jamie's father) mansion, which signal that Jamie's childhood home is occupied by Mary Shaw and that the family's repressed history of violence has returned. The attentive viewer will recognize these candles from the film's opening sequence, when Wan first establishes a chain of associations between red and Shaw. Following the title cards to begin the film, the credits commence over a flashback after we see an extreme close-up of a match being struck and then a cut to another extreme close-up of a bright red candle being lit. The disembodied hand, completely bleached of color, belongs to Mary Shaw, drawing a connection between the color red, candles, and Shaw in the first moments of the film. When coupled with what we learn about red coloring as the narrative progresses, it becomes evident that the candles also recall the Guignol Theater and, by extension, the violence that characterizes it and the history of Ravens Fair. We know, then, that Edward's mansion is a site of violence, too, because red candles appear outside of Edward's and Ella's bedroom door and in their dining room during the dinner feeding scene. As if to confirm this visually, Wan graphically matches Edward's mansion with the Guignol Theater using a pair of tilts downward that capture the imposing size of each building while also hinting that the two spaces are both occupied by Mary Shaw, an imposing force.

With the red candles as the primary chromatic indicator that something is amiss in Edward's home, it is interesting that in the moment Jamie discovers his father is a dummy and that Ella (Amber Valletta) is Shaw's perfect doll, the gruesome wound down Edward's back is not saturated in red blood. Contrary to Cherry's previously mentioned assertion that the red hues of all wounds appear saturated in *Dead Silence*, the blood of Edward's wound is muted like most of Wan's cinematography. For Wan, it is not the aftermath of Shaw's retribution that matters, but what the red signifies holistically throughout the film—that Shaw's revenge is inevitable because her red-imbued signifiers mark virtually all spaces of the diegetic landscape. Lisa's wound, however, is an exception to this rule and bears significant weight when reading the film as a whole.

When Jamie arrives back at his apartment with Chinese takeout in the first act of the film, he finds Lisa's blood covering the floor and surrounding walls leading to the couple's bedroom. Jamie cautiously enters the room after being prompted by the uncanny, disembodied voice of his wife and by the sight of the white sheet that covers her propped body on their bed. Significantly, a splotch of blood stains the white sheet. Although not the most distinct red coloring of the film, its placement and meaning are nevertheless important because it symbolizes menstruation. The film grapples with themes of fertility and reproduction, placing children at its core. Children symbolize new life and a lineage continued. Mary Shaw is murdered for killing a child and threatening the Ashen lineage, one of many local families whose continuity ensures the future viability of Ravens Fair. She curses the town, once again posing a lethal threat to the children who inhabit its homes. As Jamie drives through the all-but-deserted town many years later, there are no women or children on the streets, signifying no signs of fertility. Ravens Fair is barren. The only living women directly attached to the town are Lisa Ashen and Marion Walker (Joan Heney), Henry's senile wife. Since Marion is past the age of childbearing, Lisa is the last hope for Ravens Fair, and, indeed, she is pregnant before her death.

Lisa hints at her pregnancy after Jamie leaves to pick up food by pushing a throw blanket under her shirt to mimic the physical signs of late-stage child-bearing. Mary Shaw confirms Lisa's pregnancy for the audience and for an unaware Jamie during their confrontation in her hidden doll room. The blood on the white sheet covering Lisa's corpse, then, represents the egg failing to be fertilized, or, to be precise, her child failing to come to term. Being propped in the couple's bed and wearing a death mask of sexual agony, Lisa's corpse symbolizes Shaw's attack on Ravens Fair's ability to reproduce at its very source. Returning to this moment with an understanding of how red functions throughout the rest of the film, we know that the color additionally indicates that the last hope for Ravens Fair's survival has been terminated. Mary Shaw, as representative of the town's repressed history of violence, as well as her own violence, has triumphantly returned, demonstrating the past has fully caught up with the present. Jamie is hopeless to stop Shaw from exacting her revenge, which is, as previously stated, reinforced by the film's muted cinematography, and through Ella, the ventriloquist's ghost turns Jamie into a dummy. Mary Shaw assumes the paradoxically conjoined roles of God and evil incarnate, delivering the ultimate judgment against Jamie for the sins of his fathers. With the people of Ravens Fair as her dolls, Mary Shaw becomes an omniscient puppet master with a ghost town for her stage.

Dead Silence exhibits Wan's signature color design in its full breadth, specifically the director's spatial orientation of red coloring. Wan saturates red hues throughout the film to denote Mary Shaw, the film's figure of evil, and red functions as a symbol of the return of Ravens Fair's repressed history of violence. Red also demarcates the human and nonhuman spaces Shaw occupies, including the Guignol Theater, Edward Ashen's mansion, Shaw's wooden dummies, and her human dummies like Edward and Ella. The Guignol Theater connects the color red with violence due to the historical nature of its name and the killings that have occurred within its walls. Having lived and performed in the Guignol Theater, Mary Shaw is spatially tied to it and its red connotation. Red acquires additional meaning once we learn of Lisa's pregnancy, for the isolated red coloring on the white sheet covering Lisa's corpse symbolizes menstruation and thus the loss of fertility and hope for the survival of the town of Ravens Fair. Wan defines this film's aesthetic by featuring saturated red coloring in virtually all spaces of the *mise-en-scène*. The subsequent horror films Wan directs, beginning with the first two *Insidious* films, demonstrate a visible process of red color reduction. In this act of stripping down his stylized palette, the meaning produced by Wan's isolation of red is in less danger of being obscured by pure inundation of the color's presence. With that said, *Dead Silence* serves as an extravagant display of Wan's aesthetic preferences in horror film—as his color design paradigm *par excellence*.

The Conjuring: *An Exercise in Color Minimalism*

In noticeable contrast to *Dead Silence*, Wan pares down his previously expansive spatial orientation of stylized red color to select attire and props in *The Conjuring*. The meaningful red items of this film continue to signify evil relating to the maternal antagonist, the presence or threat of that evil within human spaces both corporeal and structural, and the return of repressed violence from the past. Moreover, Wan's color design aesthetically reinforces similar narrative themes to *Dead Silence*, including the significance of reproduction and motherhood as they are tied to past violence against children.

Set in 1971 and inspired by ostensibly true events, the narrative of *The Conjuring* follows the supernatural phenomena that the Perron family experiences after moving from New Jersey into their new home in Rhode Island. Most of the phenomena occur to Carolyn (Lili Taylor), the mother of the family, including inexplicable bruising on her body and unsettling interactions with the ghost of a young boy named Rory. Carolyn seeks the help of renowned paranormal investigators, Ed (Patrick Wilson) and Lorraine (Vera Farmiga) Warren, who gained real-life fame and notoriety for handling the Amityville Horror case. The Warrens discover that both the property and Carolyn are haunted by the ghost of an accused witch from the mid–1800s named Bathsheba, the evil maternal antagonist of this film.

Having sacrificed her week-old infant to Satan, Bathsheba cursed her land and all its future tenants before hanging herself from a tree in the backyard. Since her suicide, Bathsheba's spirit has killed many people on the property out of revenge for "stealing" her land, among the dead a maid, a mother and child (Rory), and a young boy. Lorraine eventually discovers Bathsheba's *modus operandi*, declaring, "She possessed the mother to kill the child."[27] In other words, Bathsheba occupies the corporeal space of the mother in order to perpetuate a cycle of violence against children, marking a distinct shift away from the killing methods of Mary Shaw from *Dead Silence*, who moves through predominantly structural human spaces. With Bathsheba targeting Carolyn and her family as her next victims, Wan's stylized red attire and props allude to the historically rooted maternal threat posed against children in the film and specifically signal not only the threat Bathsheba poses to Carolyn but also the threat Carolyn poses toward her own children once she is possessed by Bathsheba.[28]

During their university lecture, the Warrens outline the three stages of demonic activity: infestation, oppression, and possession. Carolyn experiences each stage, during which the appearance of red objects makes explicit the danger looming over Carolyn and her family the longer they stay in their new home. From the first night the Perrons move in, Carolyn bears the familiar red color that anticipates her eventual possession. She dresses in a red sweater, the crimson hue of which stands out visually against the otherwise neutral brown, beige, and cream color tones of the costuming, aged home, and décor. We learn from a flashback scene further into the film that Carolyn wore this sweater on the drive up from New Jersey just prior to the events of the narrative. In fact, Carolyn wears the red sweater in a family photograph taken along the coast at an impromptu pit-stop. That she wore the sweater before she arrived at the house indicates that Carolyn was predestined to be Bathsheba's target.

Carolyn's red sweater appears again on her and her husband Roger's (Ron Livingston) bed the night of the move-in. As the couple prepares to "christen" the house, the red color of Carolyn's sweater functions as a reminder to the viewer that she has been marked for possession by Bathsheba and as a cue to the witch's presence in the bedroom. Moreover, the sweater's location on the bed in the *mise-en-scène* foreshadows the bruises Carolyn finds on her shin and shoulder blade the next morning, these being the first signs of Bathsheba's feeding process. With Carolyn visually marked for possession, it becomes apparent at this point in the film that there is an association between red, Carolyn, and the threat of filicide she poses to her children. This association is further established through three objects related to childhood: a red and white pin-striped music box, a red blindfold, and a red rubber ball with black and grey spots.

Carolyn's youngest daughter, April (Kyla Deaver), discovers the music box on move-in day beneath the tree from which Bathsheba hung herself. The toy originally belonged to Rory, the young child of the previous tenant who was murdered by his mother while she was possessed by Bathsheba. Because Rory's death came about as a result of Bathsheba's actions through his mother, his spiritual presence in the house signals Bathsheba's presence by extension. The red stripes on Rory's music box visually associate with Bathsheba both directly via color and indirectly due to the object's attachment to Rory as Bathsheba's victim. That this music box is found on the Perrons' yard reinforces that Bathsheba remains a lingering presence on the property. With April in possession of the toy, she is now entangled in Bathsheba's cycle of maternal violence that killed Rory.

This cycle of maternal violence plays out figuratively when Carolyn plays a game of "hide and clap" with April, during which Wan makes visual use of Rory's music box and a red blindfold. A derivative version of hide-and-seek, the goal of "hide and clap" is for the blindfolded seeker to find one of the hidden players, using the sound of their claps as guidance. The scene occurs the morning after move-in day. With the older daughters off to school, Carolyn notices April talking to an invisible friend in her room. From Carolyn's point of view, Wan internally frames April in the doorway to her room with the red blindfold hanging above an ironing board in the background of the *mise-en-scène*; the blindfold confirms Rory's presence in April's bedroom. After attempting and failing to see Rory in the mirror of the music box, Carolyn agrees to play "hide and clap" with April. With the red blindfold secured around Carolyn's eyes, in addition to having handled the red-striped music box, Wan foreshadows that the ensuing game between Carolyn and her daughter will lead Carolyn to an encounter with Rory, a proxy for Bathsheba, seeing as Carolyn is visually marked as Bathsheba's next target for possession.

Indeed, as Carolyn proceeds to play "hide and clap" with April around the house, she experiences her first supernatural encounter with Rory's ghost. Carolyn slowly navigates the rooms of the house in search of April, occasionally calling for her to clap. When Carolyn follows the sound of the claps into the room of her eldest daughter Andrea (Shanley Caswell), Wan reveals in a bit of unnerving dramatic irony that it is Rory's claps—not April's—that have lured Carolyn here. With victory seemingly in hand, Carolyn pulls off the red blindfold only to discover that April is in another room of the house altogether. Although Rory ostensibly means Carolyn no harm, masking his actions as playful mischief with giggles, he toys with her from this scene forward in a manner suggestive of the violent tango between mother and child that characterizes the central conflict of the film. That Rory only terrorizes Carolyn and is friendly with her daughters reaffirms that the boy's ghost is carrying out Bathsheba's agenda, which consists of oppressing and weakening Carolyn for Bathsheba to possess her body.

Rory terrorizes Carolyn again the following evening, but this time in the house's cellar. In what appears to be Rory's attempt at continuing the "hide and clap" game from the previous day, and thus continuing the mother-child tango, he once again uses his clapping to lure Carolyn out to the second-floor stairwell. As Carolyn checks her daughters' bedrooms, believing them to be up past their bedtime, Rory knocks all the framed photographs of the children and family off the stairwell wall as an explicit threat to the Perrons that Bathsheba means to kill, or "knock off," their family. It is significant that April and Christine (Joey King) are the only children clearly pictured wearing red clothing. The girls' red attire visually marks them for the viewer as Carolyn's victims in the final act of the film. When Carolyn follows Rory's noises to the top of the cellar stairwell, he knocks her down the steps. Hurt and visibly frightened, Carolyn bolts back up the cellar steps when Rory tosses his red rubber ball out from behind the derelict furniture left by the previous tenants. She is unable, however, to open the locked door, and Rory continues to harass her with his presence and clapping.

Here Rory's red rubber ball figuratively represents the return of the repressed. Carolyn found the ball in the cellar the previous morning before playing with April, but she tossed it to Roger, who left it behind the old furniture. That Rory's ball was left down in the boarded-up basement, the very site where we later learn the boy was murdered by his possessed mother, links the ball to Bathsheba and to the property's history of violence, all of which the landlords tried to repress and forget. When Rory tosses it back out onto the open cellar floor, the red ball symbolically represents the return of Bathsheba, who refuses to be repressed any longer. As if on cue, above in the upstairs of the house, Bathsheba makes her terrifying debut, pouncing on Andrea from atop her armoire. Hanging conspicuously on Andrea's wall above the fireplace mantel is a large painting of a white cat with a red collar atop a bright red cushion, a portent of Bathsheba's sudden, cat-like ambush from the wardrobe.

If Rory's red ball signals Bathsheba's return, it also functions as a reminder of the increasing maternal threat Carolyn presents to her children the more Bathsheba weakens her for possession. And this second encounter with Rory certainly weakens Carolyn, for she sustains psychological and physical trauma as a result of Rory's game. The violence that characterizes Rory's relationship with Carolyn starkly contrasts the love emanating from Carolyn's interactions with April. The two distinctly opposed relationships between mother and child represent the clashing portrayals of motherhood in the film. The moments leading to the cellar scene, in particular, depict this conflict between motherhood paradigms, at least insofar as Carolyn attempts to care for and protect her children while Rory re-enacts the violence that ultimately defined his relationship with his own mother. Since Rory was killed by his mother in the cellar, his red ball establishes the cellar as a space in which maternal violence against children has been carried out in the past and will again by film's end. This violence manifests in Carolyn's symbolic birthing of Bathsheba in the cellar during the film's exorcism scene.

Arguably the most significant red color placement in *The Conjuring*, the birthing of Bathsheba brings to the forefront the abjection of motherhood signified by the blood of childbirth. Earlier in the film, Bathsheba first renders Carolyn abject through symbolic insemination, possessing Carolyn by vomiting blood into her mouth. Carol J. Clover discusses the trend of possession via oral transmission of fluids in her monograph, *Men, Women, and Chain Saws* [1992] (2015). Clover claims that women, by nature of having female anatomy, are "naturally enterable."[29] The throat, she says, associates with the vagina, allowing for penetration through the mouth. Clover argues that such oral penetration occurs in films like *Prince of Darkness* (John Carpenter, 1987), where possession is shared via vomiting into the mouths of other characters.[30] Carolyn, too, is "naturally enterable," a point made implicit by having given birth to five children. Bathsheba enters Carolyn in a scene staged to resemble rape. Pinning Carolyn's arms to the bed, Bathsheba "mounts" her sleeping, prone body. Carolyn awakens suddenly, gasping for air in a moment reminiscent of the Freudian primal scene. Carolyn appears in the throes of either intense pleasure or pain, arching her back and staring into her assailant's eyes. Bathsheba then vomits into Carolyn's mouth, inseminating her with abject blood, which surfaces again when Carolyn gives birth to Bathsheba through a white sheet in the cellar.

As a subterranean space, the cellar of the Perrons' house serves as a symbolic womb for the murders Bathsheba commits through possessing mothers. The cellar is, therefore, an image of what Barbara Creed calls "intra-uterine iconography" in her formative study on the representation of women in horror cinema, *The Monstrous-Feminine* (1993).[31] The womb, according to Creed, is the site of abjection in horror cinema because it often gives rise to monstrous offspring.[32] The cellar is certainly the site of monstrous offspring in Wan's film, as Carolyn births Bathsheba in a display of ultimate abjection. Having taken Christine and April back to the house without warning, a possessed Carolyn is stopped from stabbing Christine in the cellar by the Warrens, Roger, Ed's technical assistant, and a police officer. They manage to wrestle the scissors from Carolyn's hands, tie her to a chair, and muzzle her with a white sheet. As Ed begins the exorcism by reciting Latin scripture from the Bible, Carolyn reacts violently, coughing blood that saturates the white sheet from inside. The bloody sheet recalls Carolyn's abject insemination and explicitly symbolizes Bathsheba's contaminating presence in Carolyn's body. Ed proceeds to command Bathsheba to show herself, at which point the soiled sheet rips, and Bathsheba's grotesque face appears crowning through the blood-soaked hole. The red color of the blood thus accrues additional significance, symbolizing at once the successful return of the repressed past, the abject birthing blood that begets maternity, the inherent violence of childbirth, and ultimately the violence Carolyn—while possessed by Bathsheba—will now attempt to inflict upon April. Transmogrified into a monstrous-feminine figure, Carolyn/Bathsheba breaks her bonds and attempts to kill April in the crawl space underneath the house. Only through the combination of Roger's and Lorraine's appeals to Carolyn as a mother and the stylized grace of God (produced cinematically via the use of a key light illuminating Carolyn's face) does Carolyn overcome Bathsheba's will, expelling the contaminated blood, and Bathsheba with it, out of her body and onto the dirt floor.

The Conjuring is a film which, like *Dead Silence*, places reproduction at its core. Carolyn and Lorraine treat childbirth as a "God-given gift" while Bathsheba views it as a means of "elevat[ing] her status in the eyes of Satan."[33] Barbara Creed claims that the womb and childbirth in horror cinema present a "loss of boundaries,"[34] in which what is inside is brought to the fore, bearing signifiers of abjection like blood.[35] When Carolyn symbolically births Bathsheba, the boundary between the past and the present blurs. Bathsheba personifies the return of the repressed violent past, which then exists through Carolyn as an external manifestation in the present, if only until the temporal boundaries are re-established once Bathsheba is exorcised. Wan's stylized location of red coloring throughout the film, therefore, conveys not only the presence or threat of evil in spaces both structural and corporeal, but also the blurring of the boundaries between past and present, a liminal zone constructed through the red blood of childbirth that gives way to a history of violence perpetrated against children by their mothers.

Conclusions: Visual Games, Chromatic Hauntings

As the previous color analyses have made clear, James Wan's stylized red and black palette assists in bringing to light what should have been kept hidden in the director's horror narratives. The color design traced throughout these two case studies defines the visual aesthetic of Wan's other directorial horror features—*Saw* (2004), *Insidious* (2011), *Insidious: Chapter 2*

(2013), and *The Conjuring 2* (2016)—as well as horror films Wan has produced, such as *Lights Out* (2016), with remarkably consistent results despite thematic differences. What Wan has achieved, then, is a sustained and complex color design that seeks not just to visually stimulate but to truly augment the viewing experience by providing red signifiers for the audience to recognize, interpret, and follow. It is as if Wan, like Belton says of Hitchcock in *Marnie*, deploys red in his films to create a "game of detection" with his audience.[36] Vera Dika describes a similar game, or "play of expectations,"[37] that occurs with the audiences of stalker films in her book, *Games of Terror: Halloween, Friday the 13th, and the Films of the Stalker Cycle* (1990). She explains that the predictable formula of stalker films like *Halloween* (1978) allows conventions of the subgenre to function as cues by which participating viewers can try to guess what will happen next.[38] Wan's color design creates a similar game for his audiences, where spatially oriented red cues direct the attention of viewers to the presence of evil, allude to the antagonist's violent past that has been repressed, and foreshadow future plot developments, all while augmenting narrative themes. In doing so, these visual cues shape the spectatorship of Wan's horror films. Paul Coates claims that the most interesting color designs "unharness" the rainbow, guiding "spectatorial attention to colours functioning not as automatic, indifferent adjuncts of a realistic tracing of the surfaces of things, but as keynote signifiers" of meaning.[39] With the ubiquity of color in contemporary film and television, it is significant when directors utilize it as a conduit of meaning rather than simply to mimic realism. Wan's stylized implementation of color certainly achieves such a feat. The result is a chromatic haunting, one in which Wan's color design serves as a unique tool for viewers to grapple with and ultimately unpack the meaning of his horror films.

Notes

1. "Horror 101: The Exclusive Seminar," *Insidious*, directed by James Wan (2010; Culver City, CA: SONY Pictures Home Entertainment, 2011), DVD.
2. Murray Leeder, *Horror Film: A Critical Introduction* (New York: Bloomsbury Academic, 2018).
3. Brigid Cherry, *Horror* (New York: Routledge, 2009), 73.
4. Sergei Eisenstein, *The Film Sense*, trans. and ed. Jay Leyda, Revised (New York: Harcourt Brace Jovanovich, 1975), 152–53.
5. John Belton, "Color and Meaning in *Marnie*," in *Color and the Moving Image: History, Theory, Aesthetics, Archive*, ed. Simon Brown, Sarah Street, and Liz Watkins (New York: Routledge, 2013), 189.
6. Sigmund Freud, "The Uncanny," in *The Standard Edition of the Complete Psychological Works of Sigmund Freud, Volume XVII (1917–1919): An Infantile Neurosis and Other Works*, trans. James Strachey, Reprint (London: Hogarth Press and the Institute of Psychoanalysis, 1957), 219.
7. Ibid., 220.

8. *Ibid.*, 224–25.
9. *Ibid.*, 225.
10. *Ibid.*, 241.
11. *Ibid.*
12. *Ibid.*, 242.
13. *Ibid.*, 241.
14. Nicholas Royle, *The Uncanny* (New York: Routledge, 2003), 51.
15. Nick Pinkerton, "*Insidious*: The *Saw* Duo Take Us Through a Haunted House," *Village Voice*, March 30, 2011, accessed October 8, 2019, https://www.villagevoice.com/.
16. Brian Price, introduction to *Color, the Film Reader*, ed. Angela Dalle Vacche and Brian Price (New York: Routledge, 2006), 5.
17. "Horror 101," *Insidious*.
18. We cannot assume that Wan is aware of the various connotations and meanings that we argue his color design communicates. Based on his comments in the interview for the special features of *Insidious*, it can only be said with certainty that Wan recognizes red as representative of evil. The deliberate and consistent specificity of Wan's spatial orientation of red coloring throughout his horror films does suggest, however, that the director is aware to a moderate extent that his color palette operates in ways more complex than just to denote evil, one of which perhaps being that the color also signals a threat to a subject interacting with red colored objects, attire, décor, or structures.
19. Restricting my analyses to the essential cases of red coloring in each film also mitigates the potential for tedious prose.
20. "Dead Silence," *Rotten Tomatoes*, Fandango, accessed October 8, 2019, https://www.rottentomatoes.com/m/dead_silence/.
21. *Dead Silence*, directed by James Wan, Unrated (2007; Universal City, CA: Universal Studios Home Entertainment, 2007), DVD.
22. *Ibid.*
23. *Ibid.*
24. Wan initially increases contrast on the Billy doll's red lips during the opening title sequence before desaturating the coloring for the remainder of the film. Being the gates of the mouth to the tongue and body, these red lips highlight the importance of the mouth as the site of entrance for Shaw into the physical vessel, nonhuman and human, and as the tool with which Shaw performs her ventriloquist act to lure her victims to their deaths.
25. James Wan, interview by Brad Brevet, ComingSoon.net, Mandatory, March 14, 2007, accessed October 9, 2019, https://www.comingsoon.net/.
26. Mel Gordon, *Theatre of Fear and Horror: The Grisly Spectacle of the Grand Guignol of Paris, 1897–1962*, Expanded (Port Townsend, WA: Feral House, 2016), 18.
27. *The Conjuring*, directed by James Wan (2013; Burbank, CA: Warner Home Video, 2013), DVD.
28. I do not discuss here the red trim and cloth rose on the cursed Annabelle doll's dress, nor her red hair bows or red crayon drawings because Annabelle does not directly associate with Carolyn and the main story arc. With that said, Bathsheba does use Annabelle as a conduit to attack the Warren's daughter, Judy. In a conceptual graphic match to Lorraine brushing Judy's hair in an earlier scene, Bathsheba brushes the hair of the Annabelle doll, mocking the earlier scene of idealized motherhood. Bathsheba then throws the rocking chair, a signifier of comfort and the maternal, at Judy, who is saved by Ed and Lorraine at the last second. That the rocking chair shatters against the wall is indicative of Bathsheba's views of traditional maternal values. Whereas the red on Annabelle generally represents that she is a nonhuman space occupied by evil, it additionally represents the maternal threat of violence toward children in this one scene.
29. Carol J. Clover, *Men, Women, and Chain Saws: Gender in the Modern Horror Film*, Updated (Princeton, NJ: Princeton University, 2015), 80.
30. *Ibid.*, 79.
31. Barbara Creed, *The Monstrous-Feminine: Film, Feminism, Psychoanalysis* (New York: Routledge, 1993), 50.
32. *Ibid.*, 49.

33. *The Conjuring*, James Wan.
34. Barbara Creed, *The Monstrous-Feminine*, 58.
35. Ibid., 49.
36. John Belton, "Color and Meaning in *Marnie*," in *Color*, 194.
37. Vera Dika, *Games of Terror: Halloween, Friday the 13th, and the Films of the Stalker Cycle* (Cranbury, NJ: Fairleigh Dickinson University Press, 1990), 54.
38. Ibid.
39. Paul Coates, *Cinema and Colour: The Saturated Image* (London: Palgrave Macmillan, 2010), 6.

Works Cited

Belton, John. "Color and Meaning in *Marnie*." In *Color and the Moving Image: History, Theory, Aesthetics, Archive*, edited by Simon Brown, Sarah Street, and Liz Watkins, 189–95. New York: Routledge, 2013.
Cherry, Brigid. *Horror*. New York: Routledge, 2009.
Clover, Carol J. *Men, Women, and Chain Saws: Gender in the Modern Horror Film*. Updated ed. Princeton, NJ: Princeton University, 2015.
Coates, Paul. *Cinema and Colour: The Saturated Image*. London: Palgrave Macmillan, 2010.
Creed, Barbara. *The Monstrous-Feminine: Film, Feminism, Psychoanalysis*. New York: Routledge, 1993.
"Dead Silence." *Rotten Tomatoes*. Fandango, https://www.rottentomatoes.com/m/dead_silence/ accessed October 8, 2019.
Dika, Vera. *Games of Terror: Halloween, Friday the 13th, and the Films of the Stalker Cycle*. Cranbury, N.J.: Fairleigh Dickinson University Press, 1990.
Eisenstein, Sergei. *The Film Sense*, translated and edited by Jay Leyda. Revised ed. New York: Harcourt Brace Jovanovich, 1975.
Freud, Sigmund. "The Uncanny." In *The Standard Edition of the Complete Psychological Works of Sigmund Freud, Volume XVII (1917–1919): An Infantile Neurosis and Other Works*, translated by James Strachey, 217–56. Reprint, London: Hogarth Press and the Institute of Psychoanalysis, 1957.
Gordon, Mel. *Theatre of Fear and Horror: The Grisly Spectacle of the Grand Guignol of Paris, 1897–1962*. Expanded ed. Port Townsend, WA: Feral House, 2016.
Leeder, Murray. *Horror Film: A Critical Introduction*. New York: Bloomsbury Academic, 2018.
Pinkerton, Nick. "*Insidious*: The *Saw* Duo Take Us Through a Haunted House." *Village Voice*, March 30, 2011. https://www.villagevoice.com/, accessed October 8, 2019.
Price, Brian. Introduction to *Color, the Film Reader*, edited by Angela Dalle Vacche and Brian Price, 1–9. New York: Routledge, 2006.
Royle, Nicholas. *The Uncanny*. New York: Routledge, 2003.
Wan, James, dir. "Horror 101: The Exclusive Seminar." *Insidious*. 2010; Culver City, CA: SONY Pictures Home Entertainment, 2011. DVD.
———. Interview by Brad Brevet. ComingSoon.net. Mandatory, March 14, 2007. Accessed October 9, 2019. https://www.comingsoon.net/.

Suburban Gothic and Cosmic Horror in *Insidious*

ELISABETE CRISTINA SIMÕES LOPES

> We sleep ... among the shadows of another world.[1]

Introduction

Insidious (2010) had been an embryo gestating, for a long time, in the minds of James Wan and Leigh Whannell. Inspired by classic horror films from the 1980s such as *Poltergeist* (Tobe Hooper, 1982) or *Nightmare on Elm Street* (Wes Craven, 1984), the talented duo decided to invest their creative effort in a supernatural story with original contours, thus drifting away from the explicit violence and gore that characterized the previous films. In so doing, Wan and Whannell successfully depart from traditional gothic tropes, such as the iconic haunted house, hence reshaping them, with the purpose of creating a truly original narrative anchored upon supernatural events. Director Wan has stated that "One of the things Leigh Whannel and I wanted to do ... as much as we love the tropes, the conventions in some ways, of the haunted house sub-genre, we also wanted to break a lot of them as well. We wanted to subvert a lot of them [...]."[2]

Indeed, *Insidious* bears echoes of the cosmic horror and cosmic indifference theorized by H.P. Lovecraft (1890–1937) in his seminal essay "Supernatural in Horror in Literature" (1927), and later adopted by writers that chose to tread the path of the Gothic genre, inscribed in the sub-genre of weird fiction, such is the case of the contemporary writer Thomas Ligotti (1953–).[3] The author is known for his philosophical doctrines whose premises, despite relying on Lovecraft's cosmic indifferentism, take it further into the abysses of nihilism where a pessimist view concerning humanity prevails. In many of his horror tales, human existence is paralleled to a nightmare, and the notion of agency and free will are based on pure illusion. Gilles Menengaldo, wraps up Lovecraft's theory of cosmic horror, as he observes, "Beyond the veil of reality, there is something threatening, coming from outer space or another space-time continuum or already there ... which makes our world nightmarish."[4]

The ongoing dialogue between *Insidious* and cosmic horror lends Wan's cinematic diegesis that power of subversion concerning conventional Gothic tropes, thus ascribing a touch of originality to the director's suburban horror film. The fact that Wan introduces cosmic horror into the domain of the domestic space creates a new form of haunting, as forces that emanate from a parallel realm interact dangerously with the Lamberts, hence destabilizing the family dynamics by provoking the emergence of the uncanny and instilling uncertainty as to what is and is not in fact real.

The Suburban Gothic in Insidious

In *Suburban Gothic and American Popular Culture* (2009), Bernice Murphy classifies the Suburban Gothic as a sub-genre within the wide scope of the Gothic tradition. The author stresses that, normally, the source of horror comes from within the domestic space and does not originate in the outside, a fact which establishes a deep connection between this subgenre and the haunted house horror film:

> In the Suburban Gothic, one is almost always in more danger from the people in the house next door, or one's own family, than from external threats. Horror here invariably begins at home, or at least very near to it, and in that sense the sub-genre continues the uneasy fascination with the connection between living environment and psychology which helped reinvigorate the haunted house story in the mid-twentieth century.[5]

Reinforcing this connection of the haunted house motif with the Gothic, Anne Williams underlines in *Art of Darkness: A Poetics of Gothic* (1995), that "the nightmarish haunted house as a Gothic setting puts into play the anxieties, tensions and imbalances inherent in family structures."[6]

In *Insidious*, Wan and Whannel revisit this suburban nightmare by portraying a family in crisis that is forced to deal with skeletons coming out of the paternal figure's closet. As Kimberley Jackson's remarks, in *Gender and the Nuclear Family in the Twenty-First-Century Horror* (2016), many of the contemporary horror films are centered upon familial ineptitude to sort out problems combined with the character of the guilty father:

> In general, the family violence portrayed in twenty-first-century horror presents the father as a guilty figure. His guilt stems from some form of weakness,

whether his failure is moral, economic, professional or personal. He does not necessarily wish to put his family in harm's way, but his actions nonetheless lead them there, and he is unable to fight the malevolent forces that menace his kin, whether because he is disabled or killed or because he lacks the knowledge required to undo the family curse.[7]

Jackson's point of view ties in with the dilemma that affects the Lamberts. As the drama builds up in the Lambert's household by virtue of the haunting, the female character, Renai (Rose Byrne), feels alone and somehow helpless, calling to mind the damsel in distress depicted in so many Gothic narratives. On the other hand, Josh (Patrick Wilson), Renai's husband, seems unable to overcome the problems related to the haunting as they cannot be tackled from a rational point of view. Wan and Whannel's narrative will be essentially anchored upon the paths the couple thread in order to overcome their unusual family crisis brought about by the strange events that seem to manifest in their house. In this respect, Elisabeth Bronfen, in *Women in Hollywood: The Imaginary Geography of Cinema* (2004), argues that this masculine frustration that the male character feels for not being the full master in the house can be held accountable for the sudden presence of uncanny events in the domestic space.[8] In the case of *Insidious*, Josh, the family's paternal figure, is one of the main targets of the haunting, together with his son, Dalton, and his particular position makes him vulnerable and tense, which makes it difficult for him to cope with his complicated familiar context. Therefore, it is Renai, Josh's wife and Dalton's mother that, to a certain extent, will have to behave as if she were indeed a true Gothic heroine. As Kimberley Jackson contends, in many contemporary horror films, the key to the resolution of the haunting or curse that afflicts the family resides in the effort carried out by female characters,[9] a fact that holds true in the case of James Wan's film.

In this way, we can say that Wan and Whannel set out to explore a Gothic visual narrative, focusing upon the motif of the family in crisis, whose ordeal is caused by a haunting whose tentacles reside in the secrets of the past.

The Haunting

This Suburban Gothic horror story conceived by Leigh Whannel and James Wan starts with the Lambert family moving to a new house. The viewer is invited into the lives of the Lamberts as they are settling in. From the onset we can feel Renai's tension as she tries to balance the role as a mother with her professional career as a songwriter. In truth, she is not happy with the fact that Josh is never available to help her with daily ordinary tasks such as organizing the home, taking the children to school, or picking them up.

Josh is a schoolteacher who seems rather alienated in relation to his family. Most times, he uses the excuse that he has tests to grade at school when, in truth, he appears to be avoiding the domestic sphere. In addition, he is portrayed as the owner of a narcissistic personality. There is a scene where the camera is fixed on the image of Josh applying anti-ageing cream, while he is talking to his wife, in the couple's bedroom.

The familial tension will reach a climax when Renai starts complaining about weird things that are going on in the house. Josh, proclaiming to be the voice of reason, dismisses his wife's worries and ascribes them to the stress she is undergoing. Given the circumstances, the romantic atmosphere between the couple slowly deteriorates.

One particular scene in *Insidious* features Josh at school, where he appears to be mulling over his life and his problems. Discreetly, the camera moves to give the viewer a glimpse of the blackboard, where he can see a chalk-made drawing of Billy-the-Puppet, the charismatic and eerie doll that appears cycling in the *Saw* franchise. The puppet, besides of representing Wan and Whannel's trademark, also hints at an impending challenge. It is at this moment that the viewer is offered some clues about Josh being the key to the puzzle behind the strange occurrences that start to take place in the family house. The surfacing of the puppet means that Josh has been targeted, like the characters in *Saw*, and therefore he ought to go through a certain kind of test.

One evening, everything changes in the household, by virtue of an accident that occurs in the home's attic. Josh and Renai's son, Dalton (Ty Simpkins), while trying to reach out for the light switch, falls off a deteriorated wooden ladder. This tragic occurrence marks the start of the tragedy for the Lamberts. The next morning, Josh is unable to wake up his son, and, as a result, the family rushes to the hospital. There, they are told that their son is in a kind of mysterious coma. The doctor stresses that he has never seen anything that might resemble Dalton's condition. They take their son back home. Dalton's bedroom does not resemble a child's room anymore: it has the appearance of a wardroom. He becomes connected to a heart monitor and is doomed to be, from then on, intravenously fed. In the Lamberts' household, Renai struggles to adjust herself to the new additional routine that consists of monitoring her son's health. To make matters worse, Renai still has to deal with occasional eruptions of the supernatural that highly destabilize her and the rest of the family. Consequently, she convinces Josh that their house is haunted and that they need to go somewhere else. Overshadowed by these tragic events, the couple decides to move to another house. But whatever is going on, follows them to the new house and Renai decides to call a psychic named Elise Rainer (Lin Shaye). Elise's diagnosis is quite different from the one given by the doctors, and she informs the parents: "Your son isn't in a coma. [...]. His physical body is here but his spiritual body is not. And the reason these disturbances followed you to a new home is because it's not the house that is haunted, it's your son."[10]

Elise explains that Dalton is now an empty vessel, and the creatures from beyond can smell his vulnerable condition and therefore might feel tempted to get inside his body. Moreover, she informs the Lamberts that there are dead souls who crave for another opportunity to live, and alongside them, there are more sinister creatures that have an insidious agenda. She then warns the family that demons constitute the most dangerous threat to their son.

Startled, the family understands that Josh's illness is endowed with preternatural undertones and they realize that the "cure" will probably require a solution that goes well beyond the remedies offered by the traditional medicine. Suddenly, they must come to terms with the fact that their son has been abducted by an entity that does not belong to their world. Therefore, Dalton appears enveloped by a web unknown circumstances, events that turn him into the victim of a supernatural threat. At this point, it is important to revisit Bernice Murphy's views regarding the Suburban Gothic, as the author believes that the child plays a crucial role within this type o narrative highlights, "The child or teenager under threat is a common plot trope."[11] This evidence contributes to root *Insidious* within this subgenre, as Dalton becomes the focus of some phenomenon which appears to have supernatural contours. In practical terms, the child is not only immersed in an unnatural coma, but he has also turned the family's domestic environment into something uncanny and permeable to ghosts and other types of entities. Anthony Vidler, in *Architecture of the Uncanny* (1992), concurs with Murphy when he remarks "the house provided and especially favored site for uncanny disturbances: its apparent domesticity, its residue of family history and nostalgia, its role as the last and most intimate shelter of private comfort sharpened by contrast the terror of invasion by alien spirits."[12]

Given the dismal prognostic given by Elise, and despite his initial resistance, Josh eventually accepts the psychic's suggestion of doing a séance. The fact that triggers Josh's acceptance is related to some drawings done by Dalton that he suddenly sees hanging in the boy's bedroom that are suggestive of the haunting that plagues their household. This séance will take Elise into the Further, where she thinks Dalton might be. Next, it will be Josh's turn to venture into that parallel dimension, because Elise tells him that he has handed in his gift of astral projection over to his son. The experienced psychic defines astral projectors as travelers, explaining

"…there are people with the ability to leave their physical body and travel to different places in astral form. Dalton, he is a very accomplished astral projector."[13]

Emotionally pressured by the unusual circumstances, Josh's mother, Lorraine (Barbara Hershey), ends up by confessing that she had resorted to Elise's help when Josh was a child. Apparently, Josh was being preyed upon by a veiled woman in black he had come across in one of his astral journeys. With time, and with Elise's help, he had managed to sublimate those nightmarish child memories, but now, they would have to be brought to light. Interestingly, these events all concur to prove Barry Curtis's contention that "[t]he encounter with a haunted house often stages a generational conflict."[14] Also illustrating this generational conflict we have the scene in which Lorraine is telling Josh and Renai about the dream she had in which she saw the demon-like creature lingering besides Dalton's bed. Suddenly, both the viewer and the characters are caught by surprise when the creature appears just next to Josh. Curiously, the black and red colors of the demon coincide with the colors of the clothes which both Lorraine and her son are wearing, thus suggesting that the core of the haunting is definitely linked to family matters.

That is the reason Elise advises Josh to go into the Further to seek his son. Hypnotized, Josh travels toward the eerie place Elise calls the Further, in search of his son. The Further is described by Elise as "a world far beyond our own, yet it's all around us. A place without time as we know it. It's a dark realm, filled with the tortuous souls of the dead, a place not meant for the living."[15]

The Further as a Projection of Cosmic Horror

The Further informs a parallel realm, where restless souls wander. According to Elise's point of view, some of them covet what humans have in their reality and, as result, they become hunters. This alternative dimension echoes H.P. Lovecraft's ideas, to the extent that it can be considered an expression of the cosmic horror and an emanation of what the author deems the "cosmos-at-large,"[16] meaning the great slice of the universe that remains unknown to human beings. This paragraph that opens H.P. Lovecraft's horror tale "The Call of Cthulhu" (1928) can be said to summarize the premises that sustain the writer's theory regarding cosmic horror:

> The most merciful thing in the world I think, it is the inability of the human mind to correlate all its contents. We live on placid island of ignorance in the midst of black seas of infinity, and it was not meant that we should voyage far. The sciences … have hitherto harmed us little; but some day the piecing

together of dissociated knowledge will open up such terrifying vistas of reality, and of our frightful position therein, that we shall either go mad from the revelation or flee from the deadly light into the peace and safety of a new dark age.[17]

It means that the human being is widely ignorant concerning the occult mechanisms that lie beyond human reality and that make it look the way people "thinks" they know it. However, reality as humans know it is something deceptive. In Lovecraft's perspective, the revelation of the secrets that lie within the shadow of reality would cause madness, and that is why the author states that given the horrors that lurk behind that illusion, humans would prefer to remain unaware of it, in the "safety of a new dark age."

Actually, a clear reference to Cthulhu mythos is introduced in *Insidious*, in the *mise-en-scène* of the séance held at the Lambert's house. In H.P. Lovecraft's "The Call of Cthulhu," Cthulhu is depicted as "a monster of vaguely anthropoid outline, but an octopus-like head whose face was a mass of feelers, a scaly, rubbery-looking body, prodigious claws in hind and fore feet."[18] In Lovecraft's tale, Cthulhu is said to reside in the accursed city of R'lyeh, under water, where he lies dreaming.

Interestingly, to immerse herself into the Further, Elise puts on a gas mask, a clear allusion to the Lovecraftian Cthulhu mythos. In this fashion, she disguises herself as a replica of Cthulhu in order to travel to the parallel cosmic dimension which symbolically alludes to the hidden realm of the Lovecraftian Old Gods.

This transition between dimensions entails the concept of frontier: a frontier that divides the Lambert's domestic reality from their other alien reality. Roger Salomon emphasizes the existence of frontiers as a landmark of the horror narrative: "Horror narrative involves thresholds—a narrative in which two worlds, settings, environments impinge, where crossing (and the resulting experience of horror) is the basic action."[19] Therefore, there are thresholds and doorways that lead to other dimensions which, ultimately, inform the very source of horror. Yet, in Wan's film, the concept of frontier is somehow subverted, because the séance will lead to the Further, a parallel world accessed through the mind that offers a reality that overlaps with the domestic reality of the Lambert family. Having these circumstances as background, the only thing that resembles a frontier is Dalton, whose body remains in a coma, to the extent that his soul is out there while the body remains at home.[20]

The impending notion that reality-as-we-know-it might have a breach and become something else, with its frontiers suddenly destabilized, is likewise present in Ligotti's tales, such as "Dream of a Manikin" (1995). Similar occurrences take place in Lovecraftian fiction, such as in the novella *The Shadow Over Innsmouth* (1936) or in "Pickman's Model" (1927), where there is this underlying idea that the world as we know it might crumble due to some knowledge that a given character acquires or by virtue of the discovery of something new. In general, this acquired knowledge or discovery does not bring bliss to the protagonists of both H.P. Lovecraft and Thomas Ligotti's horror stories.

Marko Lukić and Tijana Parezanović, drawing on Michel Foucault's article "Of Other Spaces: Utopias and Heterotopias" (1984), contend that in James Wan's *Insidious*, the haunted hostile space assumes the configuration of a heterotopia. Having into account the Gothic undertones that are implicit in *Insidious*, the authors consider the Further to be a dark heterotopia.[21] In Foucauldian terms, the concept of heterotopia refers both to something real and imagined, physical and mental, something susceptible of disturbing time and space as we know it. Furthermore, the whole concept comprises a space of Otherness that co-exists and is juxtaposed to our own reality. In this regard, Michel Foucault argues that the metaphor that better translates the emergence of the heterotopia is provided by the mirror. By looking at the mirror we acknowledge our reflection; however, we likewise see ourselves in the mirror, meaning our reflection is somewhere else, in an unachievable place.[22] Thus, this sense of double location generates in the subject an uncanny feeling that is at the root of anxiety and disorientation.[23] Along these lines, it can be prefigured as a sort of doppelgänger of our reality. In fact, there is a scene in *Insidious* that features Josh in the Further, trying to reach home and his domestic reality, and he catches a glimpse of his face in a window. This scene plainly illustrates this duplicity that is inherent in mirrors.

As a heterotopian space, the Further constitutes a projection of the "cosmos-at-large" theorized by H.P. Lovecraft, a dimension that escapes the common human being's knowledge and that lies beyond the usual awareness and perception. In many Lovecraft's tales, the dream is precisely the vehicle that provides the way of acceding to these parallel realms.[24] In fact, Lovecraft's character of the dreamer is highly reminiscent of the astral traveler that both father and son incarnate in Wan's film. In a tale called "The Silver Key" (1929), the narrator observes, "There are twists of time and space, of vision and reality, which only a dreamer can divine."[25] The narrators in Lovecraft's universe have access to unknown dimensions that co-exist with our reality. The author extends this notion in the tale "Beyond the Wall of Sleep" (1919), when the narrator observes:

> From my experience I cannot doubt but that man, when lost to terrestrial consciousness, is indeed sojourning in another and incorporeal life of far different nature from the life we know; and of which only the slightest and most indistinct memories linger after waking.[26]

In Thomas Ligotti's tale, "Miss Plarr" (1991), the topic of astral projection is likewise present. It tells the story of a young boy whose mother gets sick and needs to hire a caretaker to help in the daily chores and also to look after her son. In an interesting twist, the narrator finds out that this mysterious lady is also a kind of interdimensional traveller, as she seems to dislocate between the narrator's world and her own world.[27] Likewise in Ligotti's tale, entitled "In the Shadow of Another World" (1991), the protagonist's discovery of an oneiric alternate reality where darkness prevails recalls Josh's immersion in the Further.

In effect, this dark heterotopia that engulfs the Lambert's mansion can be said to be an expression of the "shadow of another world" in Ligottian terms. What Josh truly finds when he steps into the Further is a replica of his former house located in another dimension. However, this replica displays a distorted reality, as the domestic space of the Lambert's family has become unhomely and profaned by the presence of the demon who has captured Dalton and by the presence of hostile ghosts that seek a doorway to the realm of the living. In the light of Foucault's metaphor of the mirror, we can say that this heterotopian space that consubstantiates the Further works as a kind of dystopian double for the Lambert's household; they both co-exist, and interact with each other, thus forming a Gothic symbiosis that translates itself into the haunting of the Lambert's domestic space.

Therefore, by playing with ambiguity, Wan invites the viewer to question what is real and what constitutes the supernatural, because the Further features a parallel world, meaning a different type of reality that, although possessing an oneiric nature, surfaces as a well-defined autonomous reality in *Insidious*. In this sense, the Further appears as a sort of adulterated mirror-land of the Lambert's first house. This once familiar place will be duplicated in the Further with certain nuances that render it unfamiliar, thus awakening an uncanny feeling liable of being experienced by the characters and spectators alike.

Speaking of the volatility of space and time, it is likewise relevant the role of the grandfather's clock in the Lambert's domestic space. The clock signals the passing of linear time. Thus, it is also a symbol for the human configuration of time, since in the Further time and space seem to collapse. Inside the "home" in the Further, Josh comes across a family that seems to date back to the 1950s and he sees paintings on the walls that seem to date back to Elizabethan times, all of these elements pointing to a fusion of time and space.

In the same vein, the ghosts Renai sees wandering around the house also seem to belong to the distant past. For example, the little boy that she sees dancing next to the record player is depicted in sepia tones, as if it had been detached from a photograph from the Victorian epoch. In this light, the ghosts there are seen both by Josh's wife and the paranormal investigators that accompany Elise Rainer, lingering by the clock, almost seem to parody the construction of human time, for they stand as symbols of atemporality. Barry Curtis highlights that the phenomenon of the haunting bears strong connection with temporal and spatial anomalies. The author remarks, "'Haunting' has always been associated with place and it mobilizes the distinction between place and space by introducing unregulated and irrational spatial supplements."[28]

On the other hand, the imposing grandfather's clock at the Lambert's house bears strong resemblance with the clock in Edgar Allan Poe's "The Masque of the Red Death" (1842) that signals the passing of time as an inevitable journey toward death. In addition, it likewise indicates the intrusion of the supernatural in the diegesis as something that does not obey the rules of linear time. This intrusion, in Poe's tale, is incarnated by a personification of death. As Iolanda Brito unveils, "It is the very phantasmagorical strike of the clock that announces hesitation and mystery and that foreshadows the arrival of the moment of interpenetration of two worlds, the physical and the supernatural."[29] So, in "The Masque of the Red Death" the grandfather's clock is also invested with uncanny properties liable to predict the colliding of human reality with a supernatural realm.

Among the nuances and subversions mentioned by Wan is precisely the process that entails possession, which in turn is depicted in *Insidious* as if it were a parasitic infection. The dead restless souls, hungry for life, try to find a human vessel to make them alive again. This *mise-en-scène* of the possession as a disease is quite interesting because we can talk about paranormal parasites that come from the Further to steal the body and souls of the living. That is why, that when Dalton's soul is imprisoned in the Further, he appears to be in a coma.[30] In this way, the ghost appears consubstantiated in Wan's film as a viral threat, a parasite and a disease. Sharing a similar point of view, Jack Morgan, in *Biology of Horror* (2002) asserts that "[h]orror monstrosities typically carry primarily the threat to pollute and infect […]."[31] These ideas are in tandem with the Gothic literary tradition and recall once more Poe's "The Masque of the Red Death." In the tale, Prince Prospero gathers a group of noble people to take refuge in an abbey from a terrible plague called the red death. In a predictable way, death manages to intrude during a masked ball and, in the end, takes everyone with it. When comparing Poe's story with *Insidious*, we are liable to find some parallels: the importance of the time factor symbolized by the clock; the intrusion of a malefic character in the domestic space of the castle, whose objective is to kill all Prospero's guests; the trope of the disease, and finally, the marked prevalence of the colors red and black. As a matter of fact, in Poe's horror tale, there is a sort of forbidden room within the abbey, in which no soul dares venture, which is decorated in these tones:

The seventh apartment was closely shrouded in black velvet tapestries that hang all over the ceiling and down the walls falling in heavy folds upon a carpet of the same material and hue. But in this chamber only the colour of the windows failed to correspond to the decorations. The panes here were scarlet—a deep blood color [...]. It was in this apartment also, that there stood against the western wall, a gigantic clock of ebony.[32]

In *Insidious*, the lipstick-face demon[33] that is trying to take hold of Dalton, in the Further, is red and black, hence echoing the forbidden room in "The Masque of the Red Death," thus being symbolically reminiscent of blood, violence and death.[34]

Actually, prior to the séance, Elise sets out a preliminary investigation of the Lambert's house with the aim of finding evidence of a potential paranormal manifestation. It is precisely in Dalton's room that she will come across a creature that she describes as having a black body, hair that looks like horns, a blood-red face and hooves for feet.[35] At that moment, the Lamberts realize that their son faces one of the most dangerous supernatural creatures, a demon.

The red door, that marks the entrance to the dominion of this demon, also bears a direct allusion to Poe's tale because it indicates that Josh is on the verge of immersing himself into a secret and dangerous space, liable of contaminating him. Manifestations of this red door abound in contemporary horror films and TV series alike. In general, the red door signals a portal to something evil and dangerous. Much like it happens in Trey Edward Shults' *It Comes at Night* (2017), the red door, once opened, invites the disease in. In *Insidious*, the disease consubstantiates itself in a kind of infection provoked by ghosts and other malevolent entities, such as the demon, also referred to by Dalton as "the man with fire on his face."[36] The portrayal of this demon vividly evokes the intruder in Prince Prospero's abbey, which is described by the narrator in an eerie fashion: "His vesture was dabbed in blood—and his broad brow, with all the features of the face, was besprinkled with the scarlet horror."[37]

In a symbolic dimension, the color red can be said to represent the wound in the domestic realm, the secret fragility in the familial structure that everyone is trying to hide or disguise. Only by venturing toward the Further, and only by trespassing that red door, can the wound be healed. That is the mission Elise confides to Josh: he needs to rescue his son from the realms of darkness; he needs to come face to face with the events he repressed during his childhood. In *Insidious*, the domestic bliss is put at stake by a Gothic overturn; it becomes afflicted by a supernatural parasite which wants to claim the soul of one member of the family. The supernatural horror is then turned into a kind of disease susceptible of infecting all the members of the family. In the same respect, the masked figure in Poe's tale can be said to embody a personification of a lethal plague, an aspect that once more connects horror with supernatural-based infection disease and parasitism. The trope of disease is also alluded in another classic of the Gothic tradition, *The King in Yellow and Other Stories* (1895) by Robert W. Chambers. The character of King in Yellow configurates a sort of lethal character that brings uneasiness and disease in the form of madness to those who cross his path.

This cinematic translation of possession into a potential physical and psychological disease, in which the ghost is treated as a parasitic entity, as an infestation, lends a twist of originality to the universe of horror films that have the house and the family as its focus. Jeffrey S. Sartin notes, with reference to parasitism in horror cinema, that "some creatures are scary because they hide within our bodies."[38]

In this sense, the astral traveller is in a highly vulnerable position, as he may be infected with the disease that lurks in those parallel dimensions he dares visit. Like the mysterious city of Carcosa, mentioned in "An Inhabitant of Carcosa" (1886), a short horror tale by Ambrose Bierce, the Further embodies a mysterious location which is impossible to track down in a geographical level.

The Red-Faced Demon as the Master of Puppets

In Thomas Ligotti's tales, mannequins and puppets embody the unawareness of the human being. Human beings think they control their actions, but, within the dismal universe, they are at the mercy of darker omnipotent forces. Matt Cardin notes that Ligotti's characters "move as shadow-puppets move, badly and lit blurringly, through two-dimensional landscapes cast by dirty lights, tracked under malevolent, spiteful, star-lacked skies."[39] Under this premise, the reality—as—humans—know—it is just a disguise to keep on making them live because, once revealed, the truth would be unbearable. Those characters that in Ligotti's tales get to have a glimpse of what really lies behind human reality, plunge deep into madness, remain in a state of shock, or eventually die. For instance, in "Dream of a Manikin" (1995) there is a psychiatrist who, after delving into the odd fantasy one of his female patients (who believes to be a mannequin), finds out that he is also a mannequin, devoid of life. The reality where his adventures take place is a mere dream-world engendered by the malevolent mind of a female demon. When the story reaches its denouement, the psychiatrist is deeply shaken as he sees all his certainties collapse.

Dolls, puppets and mannequins that spring up all over in many of Ligotti's tales operate as a metaphor for the human being as powerless,

Robert W. Chambers' *The King in Yellow and Other Stories* (Dover Books, 2004).

as an object under the control of alien forces. By transforming humans into puppets, Thomas Ligotti can be said to take Lovecraft's cosmic horror to an extreme. As Stefan Dziemianowicz observes, "All of Ligotti's stories have a psychological focus, especially the paranoia characters feel once they sense that reality is being manipulated by forces beyond them."[40]

In a Ligottian fashion, the red-faced demon plays the role of the puppet-master in *Insidious*.[41] He is in a dark room, behind the red door, sharpening his long claws while pedaling a device that is also connected to marionettes that dance to the sound of the music "Tip Toe Through the Tulips."[42] The song, whose apparently innocent lyrics invite someone to walk through the tulips under the moonlight, evokes a certain dissonance because its lyrics seem to parody Josh and Dalton's difficult situation inside the Further. As a result, the ambience becomes fertile ground for the emergence of the uncanny.

The presence of the puppet or doll is also at stake in *Insidious* when it comes to Dalton. While constituting a mere flesh and blood body, devoid of soul, Josh's son can likewise be considered something inhuman, and susceptible of being likened to a marionette; instead of being controlled by wires, he is connected to electronic devices instead. As Jessica Balanzategui notes, "Dalton's coma raises fears about the child as less-than-human and unformed subject through invoking his uncanny mutation from an innocent, helpless child into an abject, indefinable 'thing.'"[43] The author also considers the ghosts that wander around Josh and Renai's home, as being endowed with doll-like qualities due to the way their movements appear choreographed in Wan's visual diegesis. Balanzategui argues that these ghosts are depicted as "uncanny images of frozen time in their stiff, doll-like aspect and aberrant movement."[44]

James Trafford is quite elucidative regarding the mad realities crafted by Ligotti's imagination, where "Life is played out as an inescapable puppet show, an endless dream in which the puppets are generally unaware that they are trapped within a mesmeric dance of whose mechanisms they know nothing and over which they have no control (...)."[45] In *Insidious* the fear arises when the viewer realizes that the Lamberts might be a family of dolls, controlled by supernatural forces, as if it were an episode of *The Twilight Zone* (1959–1964).

This is illustrated when Josh, once immersed in the Further, comes across a semi-animate family, in a living room. There is something artificial enveloping this entire scene, as the members of the family are all doll-like, forming a sort of tableau vivant. This strange smiley family portrait is characterized by David Christopher as a parody of the family togetherness. The author observes that they are:

[a] mockery of the myth of 1950s bourgeois domestic bliss in a series of graphic tableaux. A father, daughter, and mother dressed in antiquated habiliment and coated in horrific make-up parody an eerie 1950s domestic scene. These idealized families are now frozen in "a place without time as we know it" and are depicted as horrific ideological misrepresentations of family life.[46]

Therefore, within the dismal universe conceived by Ligotti, the autonomy of the self is something delusional and humanity seems to be controlled by mysterious, unnamable entities or forces.[47] A similar feeling strikes the viewer when he realizes that Josh has indeed access to another reality (the Further) that, although portrayed in dreamy undertones, is not less real than the conventional domestic one. In truth, it is dangerously real because the root of the disease that afflicts his son resides in there. Inside that parallel dimension consubstantiated in the Further, Josh is shown that otherworldly beings are liable of interfering with their own private space, hence causing havoc.

As aforementioned, when in the classroom, Josh fails to notice the drawing of Billy the Puppet in the blackboard, a symbolic reference that underlies the message that he is about be submitted to a kind of test, just like it happens with the characters within the tradition inaugurated by *Saw*. Actually, both the puppet and the lipstick-face demon share similar characteristics: the hair color is identical, and both have a painted face.

Within a figurative framework, Billy the Puppet can be said to stand as a symbol for human alienation, hinting at the fact that humans are liable to be instrumentalized by invisible forces. Along the same lines, the demon that haunts the Lamberts in *Insidious*, can be said to represent the fallacy of human free will, as he impersonates the supernatural entity that appears to be pulling the strings of his marionettes that, within a symbolic framework, operate as human surrogates. Within the metaphorical language of Wan's visual narrative, this demonic creature incarnates the monster that lurks in the shadows with the malevolent intention of possessing Dalton's body. As Judith Halbertsam observes, the monster stands for "the disruption of categories, the destruction of boundaries, and the presence of impurities,"[48] an aspect which endows it with undeniable subversive potential. In fact, this monstrous demon is not only subversive, but also transgressive, as it trespasses the frontier of the Lambert's home and pollutes it with its presence, thus causing a haunting that resembles a kind of sickness or infection.

In a surprisingly twist of events, *Insidious II* will focus upon the mystery of the veiled woman that haunted Josh in his childhood. This time, Josh will become the embodiment of evil as he becomes possessed by the parasitic ghost. Interestingly, when they discover that the spirit is not a woman but a man, a serial killer named Parker Crane, Josh is transformed into a queer monster.[49] According to Gustavo Subero, the queer monster disrupts normative sexuality because it entails sexual ambivalence, and by doing so shakes the pillars that sustain hegemonic heterosexuality.[50] The author adds, "most monsters are depicted as rather androgynous figures."[51] In this sense, the monster seems to fully embrace the subversive role of parodying the vulnerable happiness of heterosexual families, the Lambert's in particular.

Conclusions

Insidious proves to be more than a suburban horror film. It throws the characters toward the tentacles of the Great Cthulhu and rejoices in their immersion in the cosmic horror of the Further, where a Ligottian demon dwells, surrounded by dolls which he controls. Therefore, in an original way, Wan plays with textual reference and past films to recreate an original diegesis where no conception of reality is stable, and dark heterotopias are liable to surface. Unaware of the threats that lurk in their domestic space, the family featured in *Insidious* finds itself at the mercy of unknown cosmic forces that seem to play with their lives as if they were marionettes.

Anchored upon Lovecraft's cosmic horror, Wan invites the viewer to scrutinize the life of a family, whose sick son cannot be cured by medicine or science. As a consequence, only by defying the unknown and walking into the parallel universe of the Further can Josh bring his son back. In this light, Josh resembles a character taken from the pages of Lovecraft or Ligotti's fiction, who must come to terms with the fact that there are nightmarish realities that overlap with his, hence making him doubt which is the valid reality. By stepping into uncanny territory, and by immersing himself within the mysterious space unveiled by the Further, Josh's certainties crumble to the ground as he must tackle a threat whose origins are rooted in the supernatural.

In the end of *Insidious*, Elise notes that something is different with Josh and decides to take an instantaneous picture of him. When this happens, Josh feels extremely angry and asphyxiates the clairvoyant. In a flashback, Wan shows the viewer what triggered Elise's appalment: the photograph no longer showed Josh, but the "parasite" of the veiled hag in black instead. Consequently, Josh's autonomy is compromised as he becomes infected by a parasitical ghost. In this way, he becomes a human marionette, controlled by unknown forces, an image that recalls Thomas Ligotti vivid premise that human beings are puppets unaware of their sad condition.

This turn of events ties in with the canons professed by H.P. Lovecraft and Thomas Ligotti's fiction, according to which there is no experience with the unknown that will not leave characters permanently affected, changed.

In Josh's case, this is quite evident because the picture shows that, in a spiritual level, there has been a replacement. By venturing into the Further, Josh has become infected by a paranormal parasite and clearly this event will produce an impact upon his family.

Wan refuses to reward the viewer of *Insidious* with a comfortable closure. In the end, what the viewer sees is Josh approaching Renai from behind, as she turns around and screams. The denouement of *Insidious* is left open, although it suggests that Josh is indeed possessed by the veiled woman. In so doing, the visual diegesis perspires with suspense and leaves the viewer waiting for the sequel.

Josh's soul is left wandering in the Further, hence being locked in a duplicated reality that has its roots in the unknown "cosmos-at-large," ultimately being lost in the shadow of another world.

NOTES

1. H.P. Lovecraft, *The Call of Cthulhu and Other Weird Stories* (London: Penguin, 1999), 372.
2. Alan B. Orange, "James Wan and Leigh Whannell Talk *Insidious*," *Movieweb*, last modified March 30, 2011, https://movieweb.com/exclusive-james-wan-and-leigh-whannell-talk-insidious/. It is noteworthy to observe that Wan and Whannel are the famous creators of the *Saw* franchise and fathers of the so-called torture-porn cinema, alongside directors such as Eli Roth.
3. H.P. Lovecraft reinforces this belief rooted in the cosmic horror philosophy in a letter, in which he asserts, "Now all my tales are based on the fundamental premise that common human laws and interests and emotions have no validity or significance in the vast cosmos-at-large." H.P. Lovecraft, *The Call of Cthulhu and Other Weird Stories* (London, New York: Penguin, 1999), xvi.
4. Gilles Menengaldo, "H.P. Lovecraft on Screen: A Challenge for Filmmakers (Allusions, Transpositions, Rewritings)," *Brumal* VII, No.1 (2019): 58.
5. Bernice Murphy, *The Suburban Gothic in American Popular Culture* (New York: Palgrave, Macmillan, 2009), 2.
6. Anne Williams, *Art of Darkness: A Poetics of Gothic* (Chicago: University of Chicago Press, 1995), 46.
7. Kimberley Jackson, *Gender and the Nuclear Family in the Twenty-First-Century Horror* (New York: Palgrave Macmillan, 2016), 3.
8. Elisabeth Bronfen, *Women in Hollywood: The Imaginary Geography of Cinema* (New York: Columbia University Press, 2004), 23.
9. Jackson, *Gender and the Nuclear Family*, 3.
10. *Insidious*, directed by James Wan (2010, USA, Canada, UK: Universal Pictures, 2011), DVD, 102 Min.
11. Murphy, *The Suburban Gothic*, 9.
12. Vidler, Anthony, *The Architectural Uncanny: Essays in the Modern Unhomely* (Cambridge, MA: MIT Press, 1992), 17.
13. *Insidious*, directed by James Wan.
14. Barry Curtis, *Dark Places: The Haunted House in Film* (London: Reaktion Books, 2009), 15.
15. *Insidious*, directed by James Wan.
16. H.P. Lovecraft, *The Call of Cthulhu*, 139.
17. H.P. Lovecraft, *The Call of Cthulhu*, Introduction, Xvi.

18. Lovecraft, *The Call of Cthulhu*, 148. James Wan openly acknowledged the influence of H.P. Lovecraft's fiction in his last film, *Aquaman* (2018). It is then no coincidence that a book by Lovecraft, "The Dunwich Horror" (1929), appears on the coffee table of one of the characters. Interestingly, this is one of the most paradigmatic stories that forms part of the Cthulhu mythos.

19. Roger B. Salomon, *Mazes of the Serpent: An Anatomy of Horror Narrative* (Ithaca: Cornell University Press, 2002), 9.

20. Balanzategui, Jessica, "It's Not the House That's Haunted: It's Your Son. the Child's Body as Abject Fissure in *Insidious*," in *Fairy-Tales, Folklore and Femininity: Making Sense of the (Un)Sexed Body Across Time and Space*, ed. Loyola Mclean, Lisa Stafford and Mark Weeks (Oxford: Interdisciplinary-Press, 2014), 184.

21. Marko Lukić and Tijana Parezanović, "Challenging the House: Domesticity and the Intrusion of Dark Heterotopias," *Komunikacija I Cultura Online* 7 (2016): 29..

22. Michel Foucault, "Of Other Spaces: Utopias and Heterotopias," Translated by Jay Miskowiec. *Architecture /Mouvement/ Continuité*, 1984, p.4, https://web.mit.edu/allanmc/www/foucault1.pdf

23. Lukić and Parezanović, "Challenging the House," 28.

24. Addressing the role dreams play among horror films, David Christopher, who weaves an analysis of *Insidious* based on previous cinematic references, highlights the similarities that are likely to be observed between the "the nightmarish labyrinth" of The Further and "the dreamscapes in the Elm Street films." David Christopher, "*Insidious* and the Return of the Negligent Parent: The Elm Street Kids Come of Age," *The Word Hoard* 3 (2015): 57.

25. H.P. Lovecraft, *The Complete Fiction Omnibus* (Corvallis: Pulp-Lit Productions, 2016), 77.

26. H.P. Lovecraft, *The Dream Cycle of H. P. Lovecraft: Dreams of Terror and Death* (New York: Random House Publishing, 1995), 15.

27. The character of Miss Plarr, described in Ligotti's tale, with her black medusean hair evokes the veiled woman that haunted Josh in his troubled childhood, as this passage remarks, "within the frame of that window was Miss Plarr, her entire form shaded into a silhouette as black as the blackness of her hair, which was all piled up into the wild shape of some night-blossom." Ligotti, *Songs of a Dead Dreamer and Grimscribe*, 428–29.

28. Barry Curtis, *Dark Places*, 13.

29. Iolanda Brito, "The Masque of the Red Death-Castle of Alterity," *Revista Anglosaxonica III*, no.1 (2010): 29.

30. In *Insidious II*, when Josh is possessed by the veiled ghost, he also manifests symptoms of a disease, as his teeth start falling off.

31. Jack Morgan, *Biology of Horror* (Carbondale: Illinois University Press, 2002), 100.

32. Edgar A. Poe, *The Collected Tales and Poems* (Hertfordshire: Wordsworth Editions, 2004), 248.

33. Due to the double-colored face, the Satan-like creature from *Insidious* became known as "the Lipstick-demon."

34. Actually, the colors red and black seem to constitute a type of "bloody" signature of Whanell and Wan's horror cinematography. As aforementioned, Billy the Puppet is also characterized with these tones. If black hints at death, grieve and the emptiness of a cosmic void, red, in turn, symbolizes violence, and blood. In the particular case of *Insidious*, black is intimately related to the darkness that fills the cosmic space, The Further, where Josh and his son venture. It is also the color of the dress of the ghostly creature that haunts Josh. On the other hand, red appears in this context intimately connected to family, mainly standing for blood ties.

35. Interestingly, in H.P. Lovecraft's tales, similar creatures that have hooves for feet appear. For example, in "Pickman's Model" or in "The Whisperer in the Darkness."

36. *Insidious*, dir. by James Wan.

37. Edgar Allan Poe, *The Collected Tales and Poems*, 250.

38. Jeffrey S. Sartin, "Contagious Horror: Infectious Themes in Fiction and Film," *Clinical Medicine and Research* 17, Number 1–2 (2019): 43.

39. Matt Cardin, "Liminal Terror and Collective Identity in Thomas Ligotti's "'The Shadow

at the Bottom of the World,'" in *The Thomas Ligotti Reader: Essays and Explorations*, ed. Darrell Schweitzer (Holicong: Wildside Press, 2003), 115.

40. Stefan R. Dziemianowicz, "Nothing Is What It Seems to Be: Thomas Ligotti's Assault on Certainty," in *The Thomas Ligotti Reader: Essays and Explorations*, ed. Darrel Schweitzer (Holicong: Wildside Press, 2003), 44.

41. A similar space to the one Josh encounters in the Further emerges in the tale "Dr. Voke and Mr. Veech" (1995), in which Ligotti describes a loft filled with life-size dolls suspended by wires, whose floor is covered with dismembered dolls and puppets.

42. "Tip Toe Through the Tulips" is a song written by Al Dubin (lyrics) and Joe Burke (music). It was published in 1929. The song is performed by Tiny Tim, who has a quite strident voice that lends a creepy atmosphere to the scenes in which it is played in James Wan's film. The scene in which the demon sharpens the claws to the sound of this theme is quite disturbing, since Josh is facing a difficult situation by trying to save his son, while the demon, being aware that he is in control, remains ironically watching the scene.

43. Balanzategui, "It's Not the House That's Haunted,"182.

44. Balanzategui, "It's Not the House That's Haunted,"183.

45. James Trafford, "The Shadow of a Puppet Dance: Metzinger, Ligotti and the Illusion of Selfhood," *Collapse* 4 (2008): 202.

46. David Christopher, "*Insidious* and the Return of the Negligent Parent: The Elm Street Kids Come of Age," 57.

47. By being the director of *Insidious*, James Wan is also, to a certain degree appropriating the role of the puppet master, in a filmic reality engendered by his creativity.

48. Judith Halberstam, *Skin Shows: Gothic Horror and the Technology of Monsters* (Durham: Duke University Press, 1995), 27.

49. The doll motif is also featured in the second part of *Insidious*, as the serial killer Parker Crane collects the bodies of his female victims in a somber basement. Parker is himself a sort of toy in the eyes of his mother. She is not a fulfilled woman, as she wanted to have a girl instead of a boy. Consequently, she makes her son's life a hell by trying to turn him into a girl. This dysfunctional upbringing becomes the root that explains Parker Crane's evil nature and his hate for women.

50. Gustavo Subero, *Embodiments of Evil: Gender and Sexuality in Latin American Horror Cinema* (London: Palgrave Macmillan, 2006), 47.

51. Gustavo Subero, *Embodiments of Evil*, 47.

WORKS CITED

Balanzategui, Jessica. "It's Not the House That's Haunted: It's Your Son. the Child's Body as Abjectt Fissure in *Insidious*." In *Fairy-Tales, Folklore and Femininity: Making Sense of the (Un)Sexed Body Across Time and Space*, edited by Loyola Mclean, Lisa Stafford and Mark Weeks, 181–192. Oxford: Interdisciplinary-Press, 2014.
Brito, Iolanda. "The Masque of the Red Death-Castle of Alterity." *Revista Anglosaxonica*, Série III, no.1 (2010):19–34.
Bronfen, Elisabeth. *Home in Hollywood: The Imaginary Geography of Cinema*. New York: Columbia University Press, 2004.
Cardin, Matt. "Liminal Terror and Collective Identity in Thomas Ligotti's 'The Shadow at the Bottom of the World.'" In *The Thomas Ligotti Reader: Essays and Explorations*, edited by Darrell Schweitzer, 85–115. Holicong: Wildside Press, 1986.
Christopher, David. "*Insidious* and the Return of the Negligent Parent: The Elm Street Kids Come of Age." *The Word Hoard* 3 (2015): 55–66.
Curtis, Barry. *Dark Places: The Haunted House in Film*. London: Reaktion Books, 2009.
Dziemianowicz, Stefan R. "Nothing Is What It Seems to Be: Thomas Ligotti's Assault on Certainty." In *The Thomas Ligotti Reader: Essays and Explorations*, edited by Darrel Schweitzer, 38–52. Holicong: Wildside Press, 2003.
Foucault, Michel. "Of Other Spaces: Utopias and Heterotopias," translated by Jay Miskowiec.

Architecture/Mouvement/Continuité (1984): 1–9, https://web.mit.edu/allanmc/www/foucault1.pdf, accessed May 15, 2020.

Halberstam, Judith. *Skin Shows: Gothic Horror and the Technology of Monsters*. Durham: Duke University Press, 1995.

Jackson, Kimberley. *Gender and the Nuclear Family in the Twenty-First-Century Horror*. New York: Palgrave, Macmillan, 2016.

Ligotti, Thomas. *Songs of a Dead Dreamer and Grimscribe*. New York: Penguin, 2015.

Lovecraft, H.P. *The Call of Chtulhu and Other Weird Stories*. New York: Penguin, 1999.

_____. *The Complete Fiction of H.P. Lovecraft*. Chartwell Books, 2016.

_____. *The Complete Fiction Omnibus*. Corvallis: Pulp-Lit Productions, 2016.

_____. *The Dream Cycle of H.P. Lovecraft: Dreams of Terror and Death*. New York: Random House, 1995.

Lukić, M. & Parezanović, T. "Challenging the House Domesticity and the Intrusion of Dark Heterotopias." *Komunikacija I Cultura Online* 7 (2016): 22–37.

Menegaldo, Gilles. "H.P. Lovecraft on Screen: A Challenge for Filmmakers (Allusions, Transpositions, Rewritings)." *Brumal* VII, no.1 (2019): 55–79.

Morgan, Jack. *Biology of Horror*. Carbondale: Illinois University Press, 2002.

Murphy, Berenice M. *The Suburban Gothic in American Popular Culture*. New York: Palgrave, Macmillan, 2009.

Orange, B. Alan. "Exclusive: James Wan and Leigh Whannell Talk *Insidious*." *Movieweb*, March 30, 2011. https://movieweb.com/exclusive-james-wan-and-leigh-whannell-talk-insidious/, accessed June 30, 2019.

Poe, Edgar Allan. *The Collected Tales and Poems*. Hertfordshire: Wordsworth Editions, 2004.

Salomon, Roger B. *Mazes of the Serpent: An Anatomy of Horror Narrative*. Ithaca: Cornell University Press, 2002.

Sartin, Jeffrey S. "Contagious Horror: Infectious Themes in Fiction and Film." *Clinical Medicine and Research* 17, no. 1–2 (2019): 41–46.

Subero, Gustavo. *Embodiments of Evil: Gender and Sexuality in Latin American Horror Cinema*. London: Palgrave Macmillan, 2006.

Trafford, James. "The Shadow of a Puppet Dance: Metzinger, Ligotti and the Illusion of Selfhood." *Collapse* 4, edited by Robin Mackay. Falmouth: Urbanomic, 2008, 185–206.

Vidler, Anthony. *The Architectural Uncanny: Essays in the Modern Unhomely*. Cambridge, MA: MIT Press, 1992.

Williams, Anne. *Art of Darkness: The Poetics of Gothic*. Chicago: University of Chicago Press, 1995.

"Do you want to play hide and clap?"

The Jump Scares of James Wan's Supernatural Horror Films

Brandon R. Grafius

Introduction

On a dreary, rainy night in New York City, a police sergeant and his partner are investigating a complaint of strange noises emanating from a house's basement. They enter the dimly lit house to hear the family's story. "Ever change a lightbulb around here?" the sergeant asks. The father responds in halting, broken English, "No matter how many times we get new, they burn out in a few hours." Even candles will not burn, so the police officers lead the family down a narrow hallway in the flickering half-light, slowly making their way toward the basement stairs. The hallway is claustrophobic, and the tension builds as the family's young son points out a crucifix that recently tumbled off the wall and broke. Both characters and audience are waiting for something horrifying to burst out.

The terrifying reveal comes as the group approaches the end of the hallway. The silence is punctuated with a loud shriek, and the audience's reaction of shock is mirrored by the shock on the face of the sergeant as he nervously recoils. The camera cuts to reveal the source of the shriek: a housecat, angry at having been disturbed. If the film is having its intended effect, the audience will laugh as their tension is released, then settle back into their seats while the narrative continues. This tension is punctuated by the sergeant's (supposedly) humorous quip: "What the hell's wrong with it?" his partner asks. The sergeant dryly replies, "It's a cat." With the suspense effectively dispelled, the police can continue to explore the basement, and the plot moves forward.

The scene described above is from Scott Derickson's 2014 horror film *Deliver Us from Evil*,[1] but horror fans will undoubtedly recognize similar scenes from dozens of other films. (Ridley Scott's 1979 *Alien* might be the biggest offender in the category of cat-induced fake jump scares, with at least three scattered throughout the film.) The jump scare has become a staple of horror films, an easy way for filmmakers to build tension, then offer audiences a cathartic release before moving on with the real plot. As many film critics have observed, jump scares are the fart jokes of horror films: a lazy way to achieve a quick, reliable effect.[2] If the audience responds as they are supposed to, the jump scare produces a combination of a frightened jolt followed by nervous laughter.

Robert Baird, in his exploration of the films of Val Lewton from the 1940s, identifies three main elements of what he refers to as a startle effect: "(1) a character presence, (2) an implied off-screen threat, and (3) a disturbing intrusion into the character's immediate space."[3] These three elements (character, threat, and off-screen space) have served as the foundational elements of countless jump scares throughout cinematic history. Baird notes that these scares are frequently denigrated by critics and scholars, who frequently view the jump scare as "mindless and a 'hallmark of B-movies and exploitation fare.'"[4]

But in his supernatural horror films, James Wan has demonstrated that not all jump scares are created equal. While films such as *The Conjuring* (2013, and its 2016 sequel) and the first two Wan-directed *Insidious* films (2010; 2013) are known as understated, relatively slow-paced ghost stories, jump scares are an important part of their effectiveness. Wan's films frequently employ a different approach to jump scares. Recounting a conversation with Wan after Wan's first read-through of a rough draft of *The Conjuring*, co-screenwriters Chad and Carey Hayes remember the director saying, "I love all these scares, there's just too many of them." They responded with disbelief, countering that a horror movie should have scares. But Wan convinced them that the scares needed more time to be built up, more space to breathe.[5]

From a technical perspective, Wan's jump scares often involve a continuous, unbroken shot, rather than the more common technique of creating surprise through editing. From a narrative perspective, Wan employs jump scares using objects, locations, and motifs that have been previously established, such that they emerge as an outgrowth of the story, rather than an interruption to the plot. This means that the audience's tension is not diffused in the same way as in traditional jump scares, which serve as a way to interrupt and break the film's mounting suspense. Instead, the scares of Wan's films do not break into catharsis, as they have emerged from the context of the film's story itself. And finally, Wan is aware of audience expectations regarding jump scares. Through this awareness, Wan is able to subvert the standard formulae of jump scares, frequently providing scares that either come from a different area of the screen than expected, or even setting up situations where jump scares are expected, but never materialize.

This essay will provide close readings of several of Wan's most effective jump scares, organized by increasing order of complexity: (1) the "false" jump scare of the child's walker in *Insidious: Chapter 2*; (2) the "hide-and-clap" sequences from *The Conjuring*; and (3) the multiple scares and false scares involving the music box, also in *The Conjuring*.[6] Through a detailed examination of these scenes, this essay will demonstrate how Wan's ability to establish jump scares, incorporate them into the narrative, and subvert traditional formulae all contribute to the effectiveness of these scares as individual moments, as well as the films as a whole.

The Child's Walker (Insidious: Chapter 2)

While not as highly regarded as the first *Insidious* film (or first two *Conjuring* film installments), *Insidious: Chapter 2* (hereafter *I2*) was still considered a successful entry into the franchise and did reasonably well with fans.[7] Subsequent discussions will involve scares which include elaborate set-ups; in contrast, the establishment of this scare is straightforward, but still serves to enhance its effectiveness. This example serves primarily to demonstrate some of the filmic techniques Wan will use in creating jump scares.

As the sequence begins, we see Renai (Rose Byrne) sitting at the kitchen table. Renai works from home as a musician while also trying to raise the family's toddler, Cali. The camera begins in a medium close-up, observing Renai from the front, at a 45° angle to the left. As she hears distant music and looks up in surprise the camera pivots, shifting to regard her from an angle 45° to her right side. Now, the frame is split between her face, and the house's front door, some distance down the hallway. Still continuing the same shot, the camera slowly glides down the hall toward the front door; this movement is interrupted by a reverse shot of Renai's face, moving back toward her, before returning to a shot in which the camera continues down the hallway. Another reverse shot, with the eerily plaintive piano music still continuing, and this time Renai stands up from the table, walking toward the camera (and the partially open door behind it). Returning to the previous perspective, the camera follows her down the hall for a brief moment, then abruptly makes a perpendicular cut in order to look straight on at the door to the family's music room, revealed to be slightly ajar. Renai enters the frame from the left. She pauses for several seconds; the camera subtly moves toward her. At this point, horror audiences are primed for a jump scare—we are certain that Renai will be assaulted by some enemy (or an ornery cat), accompanied by a loud burst of music. Instead, Renai opens the doors silently, then stands for a moment in front of an empty room. The grand piano which occupies the center of the room is silent; in front of the piano is Cali's empty walker, its garish pink and green design causing it to stand out from the room's stately dark coloring. Renai notices that the antique radio has been left on and switches it off, but then glances back at the piano as if not entirely convinced that the radio was the source of the music.

Now, the walker has been established as an item of importance, one which has been linked to a sense of impending dread in the audience's mind, which Wan will subsequently make use of. Renai goes upstairs to check on the sleeping Cali but hears music again. This time, she returns directly to the music room, and the music stops as she enters. The radio is still turned off. She shuts the keyboard cover firmly and looks around nervously for other possible sources of the noise. While she is distracted, she stumbles into Cali's walker—finally, we have the scene's jump scare. Rather than employing the soundtrack to induce a quick fright, Wan chooses to stay with diegetic sounds, though ones that seem to be enhanced beyond what would be their natural volume. Renai's stumble into the walker is accompanied by a loud thud and an immediate quick cut to the walker itself, then followed by the loud, carnivalesque noises of the now-activated walker.

While relatively simple in structure, this scene embodies several of the characteristics that makes Wan such an effective scare-manufacturer. First, the pace of the scene slows down significantly, to where the audience is expecting something of consequence. Secondly, Wan allows the camera to linger over particular objects: the door, the piano and the walker. Wan establishes each of these elements early in the scene before using them for the scene's concluding scare. And finally, Wan eschews several opportunities for obvious scares—the opening of the door, Renai's closing of the keyboard cover—in order to extend the tension further.

Wan makes further use of this walker later on in the film. As Renai is receiving a disturbing phone call from the police department, she paces around the house, from the front hallway and into the living, where the walker is now resting. She idly kicks it as she walks by. Renai leaves the living room as her phone call is concluding, but the walker emerges, lights blinking, seemingly under its own power. This leads into one of the film's more frightening scenes, as Renai finds the ghost of an elderly woman singing quietly to herself; after the woman disappears, the song re-appears emanating from Cali's baby monitor. The effectiveness of this scene is greatly

Promotional poster for James Wan's *Insidious Chapter 2* (Blumhouse Productions, 2013).

increased by the re-appearance of the walker, previously established as an object of dread.

Hide and Clap in *The* Conjuring

When I saw *The Conjuring* in a packed theater, this scene was the one that made the audience explode. Its impact has been dulled somewhat through increased familiarity—the scene has entered popular culture to the point where even many people who have not seen *The Conjuring* have heard about this scene. But in the theater that evening, shortly after the film's release, the audience's response to it was electric. As this analysis will show, the jump-scare itself is masterfully crafted, but its effectiveness is also due to the care with which Wan sets up the scare, many scenes in advance.

The game of "hide and clap" is first introduced as the Perron family is moving into their new farmhouse. (The "moving in" scene is a staple of haunted house films, from *The Amityville Horror* [1979] to *Darkness* [2002], and calls attention to the first *Hellraiser* [1987] film's connection to the haunted house genre.) The four older daughters play a variation on hide-and-seek, in which one of the participants is blindfolded while the others hide. The seeker, stumbling through the unfamiliar house without the aid of sight, can ask for three "claps" from the other participants as her only aid to locate them. This scene serves to establish the relationship between the siblings, to demonstrate the sort of chaos that constantly exists in the Perrons' seven-member household, and to give the viewers a sense of the house's geography; throughout the game, the camera glides and swoops down the house's hallways, moving more quickly and with a greater sense of freedom than the famous hallway tracking shots of Kubrick's *The Shining* (1980).[8] This scene ends with one of the sister's being discovered hiding in the closet, where a playful tussle leads to the discovery of a boarded-up and previously unknown cellar.

For the Perron family's first nights in their new house, ominous signs begin to mount. The clocks stop each morning at 3:07, and the family dog is killed by an unknown cause. And in the middle of the second night, young Cindy sleepwalks into older sibling Andrea's room, and methodically bangs her head against the antique wardrobe left in the room by the house's previous owners. It is within this mounting atmosphere of discomfort that the second game of hide-and-clap is played.

This time, the game is between young April and her mother; the older siblings are away at school. While the audience is still in a state of tension from unfulfilled jump-scare of the music box (discussed below), April blindfolds her mother and hides. Time is again elongated. April runs into

"Do you want to play hide and clap?" (Grafius) 199

the hallway, while the camera lingers on the blindfolded Carolyn, slowly counting to ten as she spins around with outstretched arms. The second clap, heard in the distance, leads Carolyn into Andrea's bedroom. As Carolyn stands facing the camera, the wardrobe looms in the background, and its doors slowly creak open. Carolyn, unaware of the dread that the audience is experiencing, smiles and turns toward the dresser before announcing, "I know where you're hiding—give me the third clap!" A pair of hands extends from behind the hanging clothes, and slowly clap together twice. Carolyn, still smiling, walks slowly toward the wardrobe, playfully saying, "I'm gonna get you!" as she rummages through the clothes. Finding nothing, she takes her blindfold off, her smile replaced by an expression of concern; the audience steels itself, expecting a jump scare as the camera alternates between a close-up of Carolyn's face and a reverse-shot of hanging clothes. Instead, April enters the room, laughing because she has fooled her mom. Carolyn is unsettled, certain she heard something in the wardrobe. Since we saw the emerging hands, we know she is right, but the expected jump scare still has not materialized. We will need to wait for this for the next hide-and-clap scene, the culmination of this sequence.

After several other scenes of escalating fright, a nighttime noise leads Carolyn to the house's main floor to investigate. She finds the closet door, leading to the newly discovered cellar, open. She stands cautiously at the head of the cellar stairs and announces her intention to lock the door, but as she turns to leave the door slams in her face, sending her sprawling backwards down the stairs. As she gathers herself in the cellar, a child's ball comes bouncing from behind some of the discarded furniture, and a faint sound of laughter is heard. Carolyn scrambles up the stairs as the basement's only lightbulb bursts, leaving her in pitch darkness. Thankfully, her husband left a box of matches at the top of the stairs on his previous expedition into the cellar; Carolyn lights one of the matches, huddled at the top of the stairs, and looks around anxiously. She is first shown in the center of the screen, the lit match forming an orange halo around her as she leans into the darkness, panting. A reverse shot from over her shoulder peers into the darkness as well, revealing nothing. The shot reverses again, returning to a medium shot of Carolyn, and holds steady as the match goes out and Carolyn hurries to light another. This is followed by another reverse shot, but this time from a much closer perspective, almost on top of Carolyn's shoulder. With this second reverse shot, the audience begins to suspect that we are being presented with an unattributed point-of-view shot; this suspicion is confirmed when a voice whispers to Carolyn, "Hey, want to play hide and clap?" The camera returns to a frontal view of Carolyn, and holds for several seconds, her face continuing to flicker in the match's wavering light. The silence is broken by a pair of hands emerging from the darkness, also over Carolyn's shoulder, giving two loud claps. These claps are followed by a jolting string queue and a quick cut to the outside of the cellar door, but the jump scare has already happened.

Figure 1: Shot breakdown of the Hide and Clap scare

Shot	Framing	Duration (frames)[9]
Scramble up the stairs	Darkness	353[10]
Lighting the first match	Medium, frontal view	148
Reverse shot (over shoulder)	Medium-close	106
Lighting the second match	Medium-close, frontal view	163
Reverse shot #2, with voice (over shoulder)	Close	77
Waiting for the clap	Medium-close, frontal view	82

This sequence demonstrates Wan's expertise at crafting scares, patiently establishing the themes, motifs, and locations that will be used well in advance of their payoff. As in the scene analyzed from *I2*, Wan stretches out time; while the entire sequence from the bursting bulb through to the clapping hands takes approximately 40 seconds, the lack of movement and building anticipation causes it to seem much longer. The expertise of Wan's pacing is further demonstrated by the length between the disembodied voice inviting Carolyn to play and the appearance of the clapping hands; the approximately four second interval is enough time for the audience to begin to register the previous associations with hide and clap and begin to build an expectation, just as the clapping hands appear on-screen. Wan's subtle camera placement also does an outstanding job of preparing the audience for this jump, by using the implied point-of-view of the reverse shots (with the second growing ominously closer) to suggest a presence behind Carolyn. It is from exactly this direction that the clapping hands appear.

This elaborate sequence, starting when the Perron family moves into the house, demonstrates the deliberateness with which Wan crafts his jump scares. The hide and clap scare is so effective because the motif has been built up through three distinct scenes, each leading the audience to this culminating scare like a trail of breadcrumbs. Wan has effectively woven this scare into the narrative, providing it with a full backstory and development.

An equally elaborate series of scares is found in another motif from *The Conjuring*, one which sometimes overlaps with hide and clap. The next section examines April's haunted music box.

The Conjuring's *Haunted Music Box*

Soon after the film's "Annabelle" prologue, *The Conjuring* introduces viewers to the haunted music box. The first scene of the Perron family is a delightful long take which follows them as they move in, during which the camera swoops beneath a couch being carried through the front door and veers from room to room. As the camera moves onto the back porch we hear young April call out, "Look what I found!" from the other side of the yard. After a short, slow zoom across the yard, the camera cuts to April, leaning against the crooked tree which will become such a key image for the film, admiring an old music box as the camera moves closer. She opens up it, the frame slowly closing in on her as she listens to the slightly off-key tune and gazes into the mirror affixed to the box's lid. When the short refrain comes to a stop, April looks over her shoulder, somewhat surprised, then shrugs and runs back to the house. It is a brief scene, easy to overlook, but it serves to establish the music box as a motif that will be present throughout the film. Immediately afterwards is the first hide-and-clap sequence, described above.

Several key elements have already been introduced. First, April's expression and glance over her shoulder indicates that she saw something, and leads the viewer to wonder what it might have been. But more subtly, and even more importantly, this scene establishes the musical theme. The theme is simple and short, and April's over-the-shoulder glance comes after the tune has come to a stop. So the audience is also provided with details regarding *when* to expect something; Wan will put this to expert use in several additional scenes.

In the three music box scenes to follow, a consistent pattern emerges.[11] Each scene begins with an establishing shot, in which the character picks up the music box and winds it. The scene then proceeds in a series of frontal shots of the character, usually in medium shot, focusing on their face as they hold the music box. The reverse shot features the music box's mirror as the primary object of focus; this is usually a medium-close shot, framed from over the character's shoulder. This shot-reverse-shot pattern repeats roughly three times before the scene concludes, in all three cases either with a false or actual scare. Part of the scenes' effectiveness is the way in which this pattern is established, then altered slightly, to simultaneously build anticipation and keep the audience off-balance.

After the music box's brief introduction, April shows it to her mom in an early scene. After sending the older children off to school, Carolyn goes upstairs to check on April. She hears the girl engaged in a conversation, but when she opens the door April is sitting alone, holding onto a stuffed bear. The music box is resting on the table in front of her. "Who are you talking to?" Carolyn asks. "Rory," April responds. "He's my new friend. Want to see him?" April hands the music box to her mother. "When the music stops," she says, "you see him in the mirror standing behind you." This short phrase activates the two salient features from the previous scene with April and the music box; April has revealed that it is "Rory" whom she saw in the mirror, and she reminds the audience that this vision will appear when the music stops. The audience knows what to expect, and when to expect it. All that remains is the anticipation.

But Wan is too canny for things to proceed in such a predictable manner. Carolyn picks up the music box and turns the key to start the music; we see the spiral pattern spinning around on the mirror, and an eerie clown peaking his head up from the box itself as the music begins. The shots alternate between Carolyn's POV as she looks at the music box, and a reverse shot showing Carolyn's reaction to the experience. This sequence repeats three times, with each shot lasting approximately three and a half seconds. Each time we return to Carolyn's face, she seems slightly more concerned. The tension builds as the music stops during the third sequence of shot-reverse-shot, leaving only silence as Carolyn looks into the music box's mirror. Her face becomes even more tense as the camera returns to her in close-up. A final POV leads the audience back to the music box. This time, the camera only settles on the music box for two seconds, before April's loud "boo!" causes Carolyn to jump and the audience to laugh at the frustration of expectations. After all of this set-up, we are only rewarded with a half-hearted, fake jump-scare. But because the scare had been established through the film's narrative, the audience is not allowed to completely relax. The meeting with Rory has only been delayed. This scene, also, leads into the next hide-and-clap sequence, this one between April and her mother.

The music box returns roughly a half-hour later, after Ed and Lorraine Warren have been called to the house. Lorraine speaks with April about what she has seen, and April tells her that Rory is always sad, "because he thinks something bad happened to him." April then hands the music box to Lorraine. Lorraine turns it over in her hands for a while before turning the key. The familiar music starts up. A similar shot-reverse-shot sequence ensues, although the camera begins with Lorraine in a medium shot, slightly to her left, growing closer each time the camera returns to this angle. Similarly, the reverse-shot begins as a view of the music box's mirror from over Lorraine's shoulder, but grows steadily closer each time. As the music plays, the sequence of three shot-reverse-shots echoes Carolyn's experience with the music box. On the third reverse-shot, the camera is close enough to the music box mirror that it seems indistinguishable from a POV shot, and the shot holds significantly longer than the preceding shots.

Looking directly into the mirror, the visible field of the frame swirls around with the spiral pattern, although there is no indication that Lorraine is moving it. The mirror moves back and forth between a view of April's room and the latticed door in a circular pattern. While the music is still playing, the mirror's journey reveals a ghostly boy standing behind the latticed door. The next time the mirror loops around, he is gone. As the music stops, Lorraine looks over her shoulder; nothing is there.

Through the setup of the first two sequences with the music box, the audience was primed to expect a jump scare at this moment, waiting until the precise instant when the music stopped. Instead, Wan presents a much subtler scare, one without any accompanying sound effect queue. The result is a disquieting dread, rather than the sudden jolt that the scene led audiences to expect. By substituting one type of horror for another, Wan continues to keep the audience off-balance, subverting expectations and refusing to offer the expected catharsis of the jump-scare.

Later in the film, Cindy goes missing in the middle of the night. Ed sweeps the room with a UV light and finds a large quantity of fingerprints on one panel at the back of the wardrobe; the same wardrobe that Cindy was banging her head against earlier in the film, and from which the ghostly hands emerged during Carolyn and April's game of hide-and-clap. Removing this panel reveals a hole in the wall, with Cindy hiding within. As Ed announces that he's found her, we see April watching from the doorway, holding her music box. "That's where Rory goes to hide," she announces. Ed finds a small, dusty shelf with some children's toys in the space behind the wardrobe. The dust has been disturbed in one small, hexagonal patch. April's music box fits it perfectly.

The music box is not done figuring into this extended sequence. As Lorraine explores the crawlspace, the floorboards give way, sending her tumbling into the basement. Taking stock of her surroundings, she sees the music box has fallen down with her as well. She picks it up and turns the key, scanning the basement for apparitions in the music box's mirror. In an echo of the previous two scenes with the music box, this is shown in a shot-reverse-shot pattern as well, though Lorraine's agitated state causes her to move the music box much more quickly. The camera frequently follows Lorraine's field of vision, turning away from the music box to scan the basement and returning to it again. The pattern is interrupted by the sounds of a woman sobbing, and when the camera returns to the reverse-shot the mirror shows a crying woman, holding a bloody knife. Now when the camera reverses, viewing Lorraine from behind the music box, this woman is featured prominently in the background. The ghostly woman slowly turns her head toward Lorraine. Lorraine looks back into the music box in the reverse-shot, and the woman is gone. Returning to the frontal view of Lorraine, the camera watches as she looks over her shoulder to see if the woman is still there. A close-up of Lorraine's face, turning slowly back to a shot of the music box's mirror; however, rather than lingering on the mirror, the ghostly woman appears behind it, accompanied by a startling musical queue. The music box has finally led to a jump scare, though not in the manner the audience has been led to expect. Instead of locating the ghost's appearance behind the character, viewed through the mirror, the ghost appears directly behind the music box, defying audience expectations again.

From the first scene, Wan has established that the jump scare involving the music box will occur (1) as the music stops, and (2) from within the mirror. This scene allows for the possibility of both of those criteria, but fulfills neither of them. Instead, the jump scare happens long after the music has stopped playing, and it comes from the opposite direction. By establishing clear expectations, then subverting them, Wan is able to both build anticipation and also maintain the element of shock.

Figure 2: Music Box 1

Shot	*Framing*	*Duration (frames)*
Establishing shot (winding the box)	Medium-close	167
Music box	Medium-close (over the shoulder)	119
Reverse shot	Close	101
Music box	Close (beside the face)	82
Reverse shot	Close	57
Music box	Close (beside the face)	89
Reverse shot	Close	65
Music box	Close (beside the face)	46

Figure 3: Music Box 2

Shot	*Framing*	*Duration (frames)*
Establishing shot (winding the box)	Medium-close	146
Music box	Medium-close (over the shoulder)	108
Reverse shot	Medium	110

Shot	Framing	Duration (frames)
Music box	Medium-close (over the shoulder)	142
Reverse shot	Medium	140
Music box (ghostly figure appears in mirror)	Close	287
Reverse shot		--- (not present)
Music box	Medium close (over shoulder, Lorraine turning)	124
Reverse shot	Close (Lorraine turning back)	111

Figure 4: Music Box 3

Shot	Framing	Duration (frames)
Establishing shot (picking up the box)		149
Music box	Medium (side-view)	159
Reverse shot		--- (not present)
Music box	Medium-close (over shoulder)	164
Reverse shot	Close	145
Music box (ghost in mirror)	Close	159
Reverse shot (ghost in background)	Medium	206
Music box	Close, Lorraine turning	57
Reverse shot	Medium	102
Music box	Close, ghost jump scare	90

But Wan is not done with the music box yet.

The final scare, sometimes known as "the stinger," has become somewhat of a cliché in horror films. One might think of *The Woman in Black* (2012), ending on a slow shot of the titular figure, head bowed as the camera slowly pans closer. The camera holds on a close-up, when her eyes suddenly pop open, accompanied by a sudden musical queue, her gaze looking out into the audience just before the credits start to roll. A similar scare concludes the 2012 film *Sinister*. Countless examples could be added to this list.

For the conclusion of *The Conjuring*, Wan returns to the music box. As Ed and Lorraine return home, having successfully freed the Perron family from their ghostly and demonic tormentors, we see Ed place the music box in their artifacts room.[12] As Ed leaves the room, closing the door behind him, the camera lingers and returns to the music box. The camera pauses on an intertitle featuring a quote from Ed about demonic powers; once we have been given the chance to read, the camera continues its slow motion across the artifacts room. But now the haunting music box song has started to play. The camera settles on the music box, open and playing, and closes in on the mirror. The audience is led to expect a final jump scare, both from the structure of previous music box scenes and from the frequency of this ending in modern horror films. The song finishes playing, and the motion of the mirror slows down. For almost four seconds, the camera holds on this image in silence, anticipation building yet again. This time, a single drumbeat breaks the silence and ushers in a sharp cut to the end credits. Once again, the music box has served as the launching pad for a jump scare that does not materialize.

The music box is Wan's most elaborate set of sequences to date, with only Bill's chair in *The Conjuring 2* coming close. The music box first appears at roughly the fifteen-minute mark of the film, then reappears at roughly half-hour intervals, ensuring that the viewers are easily able to recall each encounter and carry over their expectations. And in the way it weaves around the hide and clap scenes, utilizes the wardrobe from Cindy's room, and draws in multiple characters, it becomes a major piece in the architecture of Wan's film.

Conclusions

A detailed analysis of these three scenes makes clear that Wan has become adept at inducing scares while also moving the plot forward, making the audience jump while also deepening his films' thematic resonances. The jump scares in these films are a far cry from a cat jumping out from the shadows, or any other number of clichéd scenes that have become the stock-in-trade of many horror films.

In an examination of the baby walker of *I2*, Wan's technical expertise becomes apparent. With the hide and clap game, it becomes apparent that Wan has the patience and vision to establish a jump scare several scenes in advance, then develop a motif that will be used to great effect due to the audience's previous exposure. And with the haunted music box, Wan demonstrates his adeptness at re-using the same visual motifs and editing patterns to construct a series of scares that builds anticipation, confounds audience expectations, and adds thematic richness to the work as a whole. This is the stuff that great nightmares are made of.

Notes

1. The only scholarly treatment I have been able to locate of *Deliver Us from Evil* is found in chapter 12 of Steve Wiggins' monograph, *Nightmares with the Bible: The Good Book and Cinematic Demons* (Horror and Scripture; Lanham, MD: Lexington Books/Fortress Academic, 2020). Thanks to Dr. Wiggins for allowing me to reference this manuscript when it was in-progress.

2. For example, the *HuffPost* article by Julian Sancton, "Horror Movie Trailers Should Be Banned," Sancton compares the affects of comedy and horror, before remarking, "but the jump scare is the equivalent of a fart joke. A movie—let alone a trailer—should really only be allowed one or two before it becomes the horror-flick equivalent of *The Klumps*." https://www.huffpost.com/entry/horror-movie-trailers_b_1237495, accessed July 1, 2019.

3. Robert Baird, "The Startle Effect: Implications for Spectator Cognition and Media Theory," *Film Quarterly* 53.3 (2000): 12–24, quote from 15. These startles are sometimes referred to as "buses," after a famous jump-scare in *The Cat People*. See also Murray Smith's discussion of the effect these scares have on audiences in *Film, Art, and the Third Culture: A Naturalized Aesthetics of Film* (New York: Oxford University Press, 2017), 92–105.

4. Baird, "The Startle Effect," 15.

5. This conversation is recounted in a supplement on the Blu-Ray release of *The Conjuring*, a short featurette entitled "Scaring the @$*% Out of You."

6. There are many other examples in Wan's supernatural horror films; with more space, this article could profitably examine the intruder in the infant's bedroom in *Insidious*, or the multiple uses of Bill's chair in *The Conjuring 2*, among others.

7. As of the time of this writing, there is little scholarly literature written on the *Insidious* films. Julio Angel Olivares Merino has looked at the combination of how Wan's camera work and Joseph Bishara's score combine to provide a sense of Lovecraftian cosmic terror in the first *Insidious* in his article "El sentido de lo abisal en *Insidious*: James Wan y Joseph Bishara. Sintaxis y s'intesis del horror," *Brumal: Research Journal on the Fantastic*, 6.2 (2018): 283–305; a feminist reading (offering a rather negative assessment of the films from a thematic perspective) is found in Maja Pandzic, "Female 'Madness' as the Driving Force Behind the Monstrous in the *Insidious* Films," *Outskirts* 35 (2016): 1–20.

8. A more detailed description of Kubrick's famous tracking shots can be found in Paul Sunderland, "The Autonomous Camera in Stanley Kubrick's *The Shining*," *Sydney Studies in English* 39 (2013): 58–85. Kenneth Johnson explores the "wandering camera" as a means of instilling dread in several films, including *The Shining*, in Kenneth Johnson, "The Point of View of the Wandering Camera," *Cinema Studies* 32.2 (1993): 49–56.

9. With most "films" now being shown in digital format, the term "frame" is often not precisely accurate. For this study, "frame" actually refers to the number of "steps" using a Blu-Ray remote. However, this works out to 24 steps per second, equivalent to the standard frame rate of 24 frames per second.

10. The exact duration of this shot is difficult to determine, since well over half of it occurs in darkness, after the light bulb has burst. For the sake of this chart, I have included all frames in darkness in the "scramble up the stairs" sequence. The next shot begins as the match is lit.

11. See figs. 2–4 for a shot-by-shot breakdown of each scene..

12. This was the room in which Ed and Lorraine kept all of the objects that had become conduits for spiritual forces, both in *The Conjuring* universe and in real-life. For a while, the real-life room had been transformed into "Ed and Lorraine's Museum of the Occult," and was open to the public. As of the writing of this article, it had been closed due to "zoning

regulations," and the New England Society for Psychic Research was seeking a new home for it. "The Warren's Occult Museum," http://www.warrens.net/occult-museum-tours/. Accessed June 26, 2019.

WORKS CITED

Baird, Robert. "The Startle Effect: Implications for Spectator Cognition and Media Theory." *Film Quarterly* 53.3 (2000): 12–24.
Johnson, Kenneth. "The Point of View of the Wandering Camera." *Cinema Studies* 32.2 (1993): 49–56.
Merino, Julio Angel Olivares. "El sentido de lo abisal en *Insidious*: James Wan Y Joseph Bishara. Sintaxis y s'intesis del horror." *Brumal: Research Journal on the Fantastic*, 6.2 (2018): 283–305.
Pandzic, Maja. "Female 'Madness' as the Driving Force Behind the Monstrous in the *Insidious* Films." *Outskirts* 35 (2016): 1–20.
Sancton, Julian. "Horror Movie Trailers Should Be Banned." *HuffPost*, 27 January 2012. https://www.huffpost.com/entry/horror-movie-trailers_b_1237495, accessed July 1, 2019.
Smith, Murray. *Film, Art, and the Third Culture: A Naturalized Aesthetics of Film*. New York: Oxford University Press, 2017.
Sunderland, Paul. "The Autonomous Camera in Stanley Kubrick's *The Shining*." *Sydney Studies in English* 39.1 (2013): 58–85.
"The Warren's Occult Museum." *Warrens.net*. http://www.warrens.net/occult-museum-tours/, accessed June 26, 2019.
Wiggins, Steve. *Nightmares with the Bible: The Good Book and Cinematic Demons. Horror and Scripture*. Lanham, MD: Lexington Books/Fortress Academic, 2020.

About the Contributors

Emiliano **Aguilar** has an MA from the Universidad de Buenos Aires (UBA)—Facultad de Filosofía y Letras (Argentina). He has essays in *The Bible Onscreen in the New Millennium* (Wickham Clayton, ed., 2020), *The Man in the High Castle and Philosophy* (Bruce Krajewski and Joshua Heter, eds., 2017), *Giant Creatures in Our World* (Camille Mustachio and Jason Barr, eds., 2017) and *Gender, Sexuality and Queerness in American Horror Story* (Harriet Earle, ed., 2019), among others.

Shastri **Akella** is a Ph.D. candidate at the University of Massachusetts (Amherst) where he previously earned an MFA in writing. His academic writing has appeared in *Childhood in Stephen King's Fiction and Films* (2019) and *Making Strangers* (2018), *Supernatural Studies* and *World Literature Today*, among other places. His fiction and essays are available on Guernica, Electric Literature, The Rumpus, The Common, Bridge 8, and Danse Macabre, among other places.

Matthew **Edwards** is the author and editor of numerous books, including *Twisted Visions* (2017), *The Rwandan Genocide on Film* (2018), and *Murder Movie Makers* (2020). His work has appeared in *Titan Books*, *88 Films*, *Cinema Retro*, *Late Tackle*, *Venue*, *Headpress* and *Naked*. He has also written extensively on Hong Kong Cinema for *Screen Power* (Jackie Chan's official magazine) and *Jade Screen*.

Brandon R. **Grafius** is an associate professor of biblical studies at Ecumenical Theological Seminary in Detroit. He has published widely in academic journals and edited volumes. His monographs include *Reading the Bible with Horror*, nominated for the Grawemeyer Prize in Religion, and a handbook on *The Witch* from the Devil's Advocates series. He is coeditor, with John W. Morehead, of *Theology and Horror* as well as the forthcoming *Oxford Handbook of Biblical Monsters*.

Luis A. **Grande Branger** was born and raised in Caracas, Venezuela. He is a communication scholar with over a decade of experience. He has a master's degree in liberal studies from the University of Miami and a master's degree in communication from the University of Puerto Rico. He is a doctoral fellow at Drexel University where he is completing his studies in communication, culture and media.

Elisabete Cristina Simões **Lopes** is an English professor at the Polytechnic Institute of Setúbal, and a researcher at the University of Lisbon Centre for English Studies. She holds a master's degree in English studies and a Ph.D. in North American literature, both with a focus on the Gothic and horror. Her research interests also include women's studies (in relation to the Gothic and horror), and weird fiction.

About the Contributors

Adam **Lovasz** is an Australian-born philosopher and a Ph.D. student in the Ethics and Political Philosophy Program at Eötvös Loránd University, Budapest. His interests include continental philosophy, embodiment, phenomenology, posthumanism and speculative realism. He is the author or co-author of numerous books, including the first Hungarian-language textbook on speculative realism and new realism, and is also co-founder (with Mark Horvath) of Absentology.

Fernando Gabriel **Pagnoni Berns** (Ph.D. in arts) works as a professor at the Universidad de Buenos Aires (UBA)—Facultad de Filosofía y Letras (Argentina), where he teaches courses on international horror film. He is the author of a book about the Spanish horror TV series *Historias para no Dormir* (Universidad de Cádiz, 2020), editor of a volume on the Frankenstein bicentennial, and a contributing author to numerous collections of essays on film and popular culture.

Cody **Parish** is an educator and the coordinator of the Redwine Honors Program at Midwestern State University in Wichita Falls, Texas. He holds a master's degree in English from Illinois State University, with a focus on literary and cultural studies. His research spans horror cinema, literature, and culture, as well as best practices for community building in honors programs and colleges. His work also examines nostalgia and trauma in contemporary American horror films.

Joshua **Schulze** is a doctoral student in the Department of Film, Television, and Media at the University of Michigan, having previously studied at the University of Warwick. His research interests revolve around cinema's relationship with space and place, and the materiality and environmental impact of film culture. To date, his work has appeared in the *Quarterly Review of Film and Video,* the *Journal of Popular Film and Television,* and *Horror Studies.*

Rebecca **Wynne-Walsh** is a Ph.D. candidate at the Manchester Centre for Gothic Studies at Manchester Metropolitan University. She received a M. Phil. in international history from Trinity College Dublin. Her Ph.D. project focuses on Basque Gothic cinema (1990–2020) and other areas of interest include film studies, cinema history, horror cinema, Gothic studies, cultural studies, Hispanic studies, regional and transnational identities, postcolonialism, trauma studies and folklore studies.

Index

Agamben, Giorgio 11, 112–115, 119, 122
American Horror Story (TV series) 54
The Amityville Horror (film) 23, 198
anarchy 11, 48–49
Annabelle (film) 2, 6
Annabelle Comes Home (film) 2
Annabelle: Creation (film) 11, 53–54, 58–60, 64, 66
anthropocene 46, 145
antihero 118–122
Aquaman (film) 7–8, 10–12, 24, 34, 39, 40, 43–45, 49, 71–73, 79, 82, 84–85, 190n18
Argento, Dario 3, 8, 161
Atlantis 40, 42–43, 47, 71, 76–77, 81–83, 85
auteur theory 2–4, 6, 9–10, 17–18, 20–21, 29, 31, 158

Barthes, Roland 74
Batman vs. Superman (film) 71, 75
Bazin, André 144–145
Billy the Puppet 116, 131, 135, 176, 187
black communities 85
bromance 130
Buddha 65–66
buddy film 128, 130, 136
Bush, George 109, 114–115

Cahiers du Cinéma 2
The Call of Cthulhu (H.P. Lovecraft's novella) 42, 178–179
car culture 94, 96–97, 101–102, 104
Chambers, Robert W 184
Cheney, Dick 114
Clover, Carol 143, 168
Cold War 59, 109
color design 155–158, 163–164, 169–170, 171n18
The Conjuring (film) 1, 2–8, 10, 12, 23, 128, 143–144–146, 139, 152, 158, 164, 168–170, 194–195, 198, 200–201, 206–207
The Conjuring 2 (film) 11–12, 53, 56, 143–144, 149, 151, 206–207n6
Creed, Barbara 168 169

DC Comics 39, 71, 76

Dead Silence (film) 4, 6, 8, 10–12, 127–128, 130–137, 155, 157–165, 169
Death Sentence (film) 4, 6, 8, 11, 93–94, 98, 101–102, 104–105, 107n11, 110, 112–113, 117–119, 121, 123
Deleuze, Gilles 11, 53, 62
demonologist 20
demons 1, 6, 21, 23–26, 28, 53–54, 57, 63–64, 146, 148, 150–151, 158, 165, 177–178, 181, 183–184, 186–187–188, 191n42, 206
diasporic identity 17, 22–24, 27–28, 30
doppelgänger 136, 180

ecology 43, 143–145
emasculation 95, 99, 102–103
Enfield (London borough) 54
Enfield poltergeist case 2, 149
The Exorcist (film) 8, 53

Fast & Furious 7 (film) 6–7, 11–12, 84, 93–94, 98, 101–106
female gaze 131
female ghost 128, 132–133
female voice 11, 98, 128, 131–132, 135
femme fatale 135
flashback 105, 135, 161–162, 165, 188
Fourth Wave Feminism 95
Freud, Sigmund 2 2, 156–157

gaslight drama 131
gender 8–9, 11, 95–96, 98–99, 128, 133–134
ghosts 11, 54, 56, 58, 60, 63, 128, 130–134, 136, 157, 159, 163–164, 166–167, 182, 184, 187, 188, 190n30, 194, 196, 204–205; *see also* female ghost
global 6, 17, 21, 24, 31, 34–36, 38–39, 46, 48–49, 65, 73, 82
globalgothic 21
globalization 21
gore 4, 8, 101, 110, 121, 155, 173
Gothic film 11, 128
Gothic heroine 131, 175
Gothic melodrama 131
Gothic text 131, 137

211

212 Index

Guantánamo 113, 115
gun culture 93–94, 96–98, 101–103, 105–106

Hall, Stuart 74
hypermasculinity 94–103, 105–107

identity politics 10–11, 17–18, 20, 31
inanimate objects 98, 100, 105, 146, 148, 150
Insidious (film) 3, 6–8, 10, 12, 17–18, 20–21, 24, 26–28, 30–31, 84, 128, 143, 158, 164, 169, 171n8, 173–177, 179–183, 186–189–190n24, 190n34, 191n49, 194–195, 207n6–7
Insidious: Chapter 2 (film) 6, 8, 143, 169, 195
interracial 42
Iraq war 3
Islam 57, 78

Jigsaw *see* Kramer, John
jump scares 7, 12, 127, 194–195, 200, 206
Justice League (film) 71, 75

King in Yellow (character) 184
kinship 93, 96–99, 101
Kracauer, Sigfried 143–146, 150–152
Kramer, John 6, 109–110, 113–119, 122–123, 157, 160
Ku Klux Klan 76, 83, 85

Latour, Bruno 100
Lewton, Val 3, 12, 127, 194
LGBT 97
libertarianism 34–37, 45–46, 49
Ligotti, Thomas 8, 173, 179–181, 184, 186–188, 190n27, 191n41
Lovecraft, H.P. 12, 42–43, 82, 173, 180, 188, 189n3, 190n18

MacGyver (TV series) 2, 11, 94, 105–106
Malcolm X 83
Marvel Cinematic Universe 71
maternal 25, 128, 132–133, 158, 164–168, 171n28
McCarthyism 58–59
migration 21, 35, 47, 79
mise-en-scène 12, 21–23, 25, 28, 130, 143, 155, 157, 159, 164–166, 179, 182
monster 7, 45, 51n35, 83, 109, 116, 118, 132, 179, 187–188
monstrous 122, 132, 137, 168–169, 187
Muslims 57–59, 78

national identity 21, 57
Nazi regime 76, 83, 112
Nietzsche, Friedrich 56
A Nightmare on Elm Street (film) 8, 53
nonhuman 40, 42, 45, 100, 134, 143–144, 146, 149–152, 164, 171n24, 171n28

Nozick, Robert 11, 33–40, 42, 44–49
The Nun (film) 2, 6

Obama's regime 65
The Omen (film) 18
OOO (philosophy) 145, 153n14

paternalism 24, 102, 115, 117–118, 120–121, 133, 174–175
Perron family 2, 145–148, 164, 198, 200–201, 206
political instability 114
Poltergeist (film) 7–8, 173
possession 11, 24, 53–54, 57–59, 61–64, 66, 165–168, 182, 184

queer 96, 187

racism 57, 78, 85
Rand, Ayn 38
Reagan, Ronald 95
Reaganomics 95
recession 56

Salem witch trials 59
Saw (film) 1, 2–3–6, 8, 11, 84, 109–110, 112–113, 116–117, 119, 121, 123, 127, 157, 159–160, 169, 176, 187, 189n2
Schwarzenegger, Arnold 95–96, 101
September 11, 2001(terrorist attacks) 3–4, 78, 109
The Shadow Over Innsmouth (H. P. Lovecraft's novella) 42, 179
Sinister (film) 206
speciesism 46
Splat Pack 4
Stallone, Sylvester 95–96, 101
state of exception 11, 109, 110, 112–123
Stygian (film) 3
suburban 12, 174–175, 177, 188
Suspiria (film) 161

terrorism 109, 112, 120–122
torture 4, 11, 103, 109, 113–119, 121
torture porn 3, 121, 189n2
Tourneau, Jacques 4
Transnational film 17
Transnational identity 17
Trump, Donald 59, 65, 73, 79–80
The Twilight Zone (TV series) 186

uncanny 22, 30, 151, 156–158, 163, 174–175, 177, 180–182, 186, 188
U.S.-Mexico border 62
Universal Studios 6, 127
utopia 11, 33–40, 42–49, 145

Victorian era 26, 128, 181
vigilante films 118

Warren, Ed 1, 62–63, 128, 145, 148–149, 164–165, 169, 171n28, 202–206, 207n12
Warren, Lorraine 1, 62–63, 128, 145, 148–149, 164–165, 169, 171n28, 202–206, 207n12
Whannell, Leigh 3, 6, 10, 114, 173

white supremacy 11, 72, 76, 78, 83–85
winter of discontent 56
witch 164
Wonder Woman (film) 71

www.ingramcontent.com/pod-product-compliance
Ingram Content Group UK Ltd.
Pitfield, Milton Keynes, MK11 3LW, UK
UKHW041938210426
5322IPUK00016B/240